INSANE SISTERS

INSANE SISTERS

or, the Price Paid for Challenging a Company Town

GREGG ANDREWS

UNIVERSITY OF MISSOURI PRESS
Columbia

University of Missouri Press, Columbia, Missouri 65211
Printed and bound in the United States of America

First paperback printing, 2020.

Library of Congress Cataloging-in-Publication Data

Andrews, Gregg.
Insane sisters, or, The price paid for challenging a company town / Gregg Andrews.
p. cm.
Includes bibliographical references and index.
ISBN 978-0-8262-1240-5 (hardcover : alk. paper)
ISBN 978-0-8262-2226-8 (paperback : alk. paper)
1. Ilasco (Mo.)—History—20th century. 2. Real property—Missouri—Ilasco—History—20th century. 3. Insanity—Jurisprudence—Missouri—Ilasco—History—20th century. 4. Ilasco (Mo.) Biography. 5. Heinbach, Mary Alice. 6. Koller, Euphemia B. I. Title. II. Title: Insane sisters. III. Title: Price paid for challenging a company town.
F474.I23A54 1999
977.8'355—dc21 99-29913
CIP

⊗ This paper meets the requirements of the American National Standard for Permanence of Paper for Printed Library Materials, Z39.48, 1984.

Jacket designer: Kristie Lee
Text designer: Elizabeth K. Young
Typefaces: Trump Medieval, Helvetica 45 light

For Alexaundria and Zachary Andrews

Contents

Acknowledgments

When I set out in 1992 to write a community history of Ilasco, Missouri, little did I know that a second book would grow out of that research, or that a wild, controversial case such as the one examined in this study was buried in area courthouse records. I owe a particular debt of gratitude to area residents and former residents whose warm letters and supportive phone calls after the publication of *City of Dust* in 1996 gave me even greater encouragement to forge ahead with this spin-off study. I hope that this second installment of Ilasco's rich history in some way helps to compensate for their long, patient wait to have the story of their community told at last.

I owe special thanks to Fran and Jim Mitchell, owners of Big River Discount Books in Hannibal, for hosting a very successful book signing for *City of Dust* on November 2, 1996. Their interest in the area's history has had a contagious effect, and they have since helped to stimulate further excitement while waiting for this book to appear. In the process, they have become good friends and adopted citizens of Ilasco. To them, as well as to area residents who waited in long lines at the book signing, I am especially appreciative. Along with the Ilasco Association, the Ilasco-Saverton Methodist Church, Bev Darr of the *Hannibal Courier-Post,* Dave Lee of Hannibal's KHMO radio station, and Ed Husar of the *Quincy Herald-Whig,* they contributed much to the publicity of *City of Dust* in the area and cultivated further interest in my work.

In tracking the family roots of Mary Alice (Mollie) Heinbach and Euphemia B. (Feemy) Koller for this study, I was fortunate that one of their great-nieces—Jane Hemeyer, of Jefferson City, Missouri—responded to an advertisement that I put in a local newspaper several years ago. Through many letters, phone calls, and visits, Jane and I have become friends. The speed and intensity with which I researched this case grew in part out of her feverish excitement over a part of her family's history that was previously unknown to her. She generously shared photos, family memories, and observations in regard to family relationships, patterns, and conflicts. She also listened in a good-natured way to my observations and analyses in regard to the complex motivations and controversial role of her great-aunts in Ilasco's history.

I have also benefited from contacts with other members of the Sykes family, including Fay Scheiner of Hannibal, Maxine and Tip Harris of Center, and Don Sykes of Canton, Missouri, who shared memories and materials. Around fifteen years ago, I developed a friendship with Gene Sykes, son of Don and Katie, when he married Marcia Morgan Estes, a friend of mine since junior high school. At that time, of course, neither he nor I knew anything about this case. I only wish that Gene, who died unexpectedly a few years later, were alive to enjoy this slice of his family's history.

In the fall of 1998, I had the good fortune to meet Ray and Shirley Herren, of Pismo Beach, California, shortly after they had gone to Hannibal in a genealogical search for Samuel Heinbach, Ray's great-grandfather. I appreciate that after learning of my work in Hannibal, they then drove to San Marcos, Texas, to discuss with me Sam's role in this case. I especially thank them for photographs of Sam and his daughters.

Loretta Fields of Baltimore, Maryland, and I crossed paths in cyberspace as the result of our overlapping research interests in the Koller family's genealogy. Her generous sharing of materials made it easier for me to establish the parameters of the marriage and divorce of Euphemia Sykes and John A. J. Koller in Baltimore.

Many people in the Hannibal area helped me in a variety of ways, but I particularly want to thank Dorothy Eichenberger for sharing materials from her family files on the history of Saverton. Ruth Pickett allowed me to copy the deed to her Saverton area farm that once belonged to the Sykes family, and John Graves, of St. Louis, gave me materials on the history of the Glascock family in Ralls County. In addition, I wish to thank David and Sally Polc,

Jim and Dorothy Tatman, and Virginia Arthaud for making photos available to me.

I deeply appreciate the role of Virginia and Allan Sudholt—my mother and her husband—in this project. They at times provided a place to stay when I was in the area, and on several occasions made trips to the Hannibal Free Public Library and area courthouses at my request. More important, they eagerly discussed my findings along the way and looked forward to the publication of this study.

I could not have done the research for this book without the cheerful cooperation of area courthouse clerks in New London, Hannibal, Palmyra, Bowling Green, and Monticello. I especially thank Sandra Bangert, Ralls County Circuit Clerk and Recorder, who let me camp out in her office on many busy days. So did clerks Debby Rhodes of the Ralls Probate Court and Carolyn Conners of the Hannibal Court of Common Pleas. I also want to thank employees of the Court Clerk's Office in Shawnee, Oklahoma, for helping to locate, photocopy, and send copies of records to me.

The staff at the Missouri State Archives in Jefferson City facilitated access to county records on microfilm and to the Missouri Supreme Court Files, which contain nearly two thousand pages of trial transcript that I consulted for this study. Also helpful were employees of the Maryland State Archives, the State Historical Society of Missouri, and the Western Historical Manuscripts Collection at the University of Missouri in Columbia. I enjoyed productive visits to the Hannibal Free Public Library, where Anne Sundermeyer and her staff have worked hard to promote the study of local history in the Missouri Room.

I have benefited a great deal from the constructive criticisms and suggestions of several historians while this work was in progress, including LeeAnn Whites, Mary Frederickson, William G. Thomas III, and two anonymous readers for the University of Missouri Press. I also wish to thank students and colleagues at Southwest Texas State University who attended presentations of my work sponsored by officers of our local chapter of Phi Alpha Theta as part of its "Brown Bag" series. The following students in my graduate seminar in the spring of 1998 also discussed parts of my work: Amanda Brand, Christian Hack, Karen Holstead-Franzen, Patricia Jones, Carol Parsonage, Christopher Quinn, Meredith Summers, Beverly Tomek, Stephanie Ulrich, and Brian Walter.

Ever since I first discussed my idea for this book with Beverly Jarrett, director and editor-in-chief of the University of Missouri Press, she expressed strong encouragement and cheered me on at regular intervals. Thanks to her, Jane Lago, and the editorial staff, preparing this book for publication has been a smooth process. I particularly thank John Brenner for his customary editorial thoroughness during the final stages of production.

Vikki Bynum, my colleague and wife, read several drafts of this study and provided helpful, enthusiastic recommendations along the way. For several years now, sisters Mollie Heinbach and Feemy Koller have been a common topic of our household conversations, which often stimulated me to refine and clarify many of my arguments. Even more important, Vikki has shared and encouraged interest in the human elements that drew me to the sisters' story in the first place. Only she fully appreciates why it was important for me to locate Feemy's unmarked grave and to work to get a future tombstone erected at that site in New London's Barkley Cemetery.

INSANE SISTERS

Introduction

Pennsylvania Yankees in "Old Man Atlas's" Courts

> She [Mollie Heinbach] is neither insane nor crazy . . . the term crazy or insane was never applied to her so far as I can learn until she became possessed of valuable real estate.
>
> —*Euphemia B. Koller, 1911*

On January 23, 1928, seventy-three-year-old Mary Alice (Mollie) Heinbach, who in 1921 had been declared a "mental incompetent" by a local probate court, died as the result of burns suffered nearly two months earlier at her home in the Ralls County seat of New London, Missouri. As reported by a local newspaper, she had been "replenishing the fire in her heating stove and after she put some coke in the stove, the blaze flashed out and set her clothing on fire." She then ran out of the house, and James Parker, a neighbor who was passing by, threw his coat around her and put out the fire, but not before she sustained serious burns. After nearly two months of painful lingering, she died in a nearby hospital in Hannibal, Marion County.[1]

Two years later, a Hannibal newspaper reported the funeral of Euphemia B. Koller, Mollie's sixty-eight-year-old sister. "Feemy," as Mollie affectionately called her, died on February 24, 1930, from lobar pneumonia stemming from a broken hip she had suffered in a "fall" while confined in the State Hospital for the Insane in Fulton, Missouri. Harry G. Weaver, a Ralls County probate judge, had ordered her confinement as a private patient only a few months before her sister had caught on fire. To underscore the special tragedy of Feemy's confinement in the state hospital, a New London newspaper, the *Ralls County Record*, recalled that "many years ago she was a brilliant woman, being well-educated, refined, and a fluent talker."[2]

The circumstances surrounding the deaths of Feemy and Mollie were but the final bits of tragedy for two women who for their last two decades had shared more than just the common, loving bonds of sisterhood in their private lives. Between 1910 and 1927, they were embroiled in an extraordinarily bitter property dispute that pitted them against county officials as well as one of the nation's leading cement corporations and a host of its retainers in northeast Missouri. At stake was a lucrative twenty-six-acre tract of land that the sisters owned. The tract formed much of the Ralls County town site of Ilasco, an unincorporated industrial village three miles south of Hannibal, just across the Marion/Ralls County line. Ilasco, a largely Slavic immigrant community, lay on the perimeter of a large plant built by the Pennsylvania-based Atlas Portland Cement Company in 1901 next to the cave hollow popularized in Mark Twain's most famous novels. The new village's name—given it by a plant official—was appropriately derived from cement manufacturing ingredients (*I*ron, *L*ime, *A*luminum, *S*ilica, *C*alcium, *O*xygen).[3]

As a result of the most important property conflict in twentieth-century Ralls County, the sisters' tract ended up in the hands of Atlas, but not before the case generated considerable public controversy and took a devastating toll on Mollie and Feemy. The conflict cost Mollie her financial independence and legal identity, and it helped to destroy her tenacious sister's mental and physical vitality. In the end, the legal drama that absorbed so much of Feemy's energy and resources robbed her of even more. It led directly to her forced removal from the county and subsequent confinement in the state hosptial, where she spent the final two and one-half years of a once dynamic, vibrant life filled with incessant travel, intellectual passion, and expanded horizons.

During the seventeen-year furor over the tract, Mollie and Feemy became well known not only to area residents but also to Missouri Supreme Court justices and commissioners, many area judges, lawyers, and politicians, and many eastern cement industry executives. In fact, there was hardly a lawyer or judge in the northeast Missouri counties of Ralls, Marion, and Pike who at one time did not have a hand in the sisters' case, which went to the state supreme court four times in various forms. Area residents, Atlas representatives, and state and local officials clearly understood the important role that both sisters played in Ilasco's history.

Upon death, however, Mollie and Feemy descended into hushed obscurity, their role in history buried with them until now. When they vanished, they did so completely, almost shockingly so, for even family relatives had no idea as to their ultimate fate. In Feemy's case, burial in an unmarked grave in an area cemetery helped to conceal the tortuous path that took her to the mental hospital under questionable circumstances, and it made her vanishing all the more mysterious.

When Feemy died in 1930, her obituaries provided only tantalizing hints of the full sound and fury of the legal storm that this battle over property rights had kicked up in the courts of northeast Missouri. The *Hannibal Courier-Post* correctly noted that she and Mollie were former owners of the town site of Ilasco, but misrepresented the way that Atlas acquired the land from them. According to the newspaper, the company simply bought it from them "when it established its plant at that place about 25 years ago."[4]

The newspaper, although well aware of the connections between Feemy's fate and the bitter conflict over the tract, used her death to promote a boosterish version of Ilasco's history that concealed an important secret and glorified Atlas's paternalistic role in the community. In fact, the obituary was an important step toward erasing Mollie and Feemy from the community's rich history of conflict and resistance against Atlas's relentless efforts to control it. In this official, sanitized company version, there was no room for sisters who in many ways threatened conventional gender roles, or for the bitter conflicts that led to Atlas's acquisition of the Ilasco tract.

Why was this property so important to Atlas? From Ilasco's birth in 1903, it had posed serious problems for company officials, who at first denied even that they intended to create a company town in the area. In fact, the company assured local residents that it would not bring in workers from outside the Hannibal area. Citing Atlas sources, a Hannibal newspaper reported while the new plant was under construction in 1901 that most workers would live in Hannibal, not in housing around the rim of the plant.[5]

It quickly became apparent, however, that this would not be the case. To accommodate trainloads of Slavic immigrants who soon poured into the area to work at the plant, Atlas built barracks and houses on company property. In addition, individuals who owned land near the plant began to lease lots to workers, small businessmen, and others in what quickly became a congested community of mostly ramshackle houses. By 1910, Ilasco was home to approximately two thousand residents, about two-thirds of whom were Rumanian, Slovak, Italian, and Hungarian immigrants. Men outnumbered women in the crowded labor camp by approximately 4.4 to 1.[6]

At the time Mollie and Feemy became entangled in their legal case, Ilasco was the only major industrial town in an agricultural, formerly slaveholding county with strong Confederate sympathies, in which a handful of Democratic families (primarily southern in their origins) still held the keys to the courthouse. In Ralls County, where manufacturing and mechanical industries employed only 108 wage earners in 1900, Atlas offered the best and only way to bring the New South to that edge of Missouri's "Little Dixie." Taking advantage of the rich limestone and shale deposits in the northeastern part of the county, Atlas brought industrial jobs and thousands of southern and eastern European immigrants to the area, transforming Ralls County into the leading cement producer in the state.[7]

For the Yankee capitalists who came to convert the land of Twain's childhood romps, adventures, and secret hideaways into cement kilns, quarries, and smokestacks, managing this transformation posed numerous challenges. Ilasco stirred nativist hatreds in the area and aroused public fears of crime and alcohol abuse in the community. This created public relations problems for Atlas, even though the company, too, manipulated nativism and ethnic conflicts for its own purposes to divide its workers and keep out unions. To create a more efficient, disciplined labor force, company officials led a campaign to shut down Ilasco's saloons, but by 1910 that campaign had failed. When chronic labor unrest culminated in an explosive strike that brought the state militia to town in 1910, it underscored Atlas's inability to tame its workforce and control the town's institutions.[8]

The turbulence in Ilasco had much broader significance for Atlas, which had become the top cement producer in the nation. The Ilasco plant—Atlas's first west of the Mississippi River—was crucial to the company's campaign to challenge the Universal Portland Cement Company, its chief rival, in the markets of the Mississippi River valley. Financial problems in 1910, however, wreaked havoc on Atlas and caused a shakeup at the top. J. P. Morgan acquired a sizable stake in the company and put one of his representatives on the board of directors. Atlas's role in the Midwest was becoming increasingly important, but continued disruptions at the Ilasco plant threatened production and dramatized how important it was for the company to acquire greater control over the community.[9]

To understand the dynamics of the property dispute whose outcome gave Atlas complete control over Ilasco and consolidated its position in Midwest markets, we must take into account not only the class-based, corporate interests of Atlas that propelled the case, but also the gender-based assumptions that shaped it. In many ways at the time, Mollie and Feemy threatened conventional gender roles. When they took on powerful male elites—political, corporate, and legal—they did so as "eccentric" women whose aggressive public behavior particularly got under the skin of their enemies. In the end, this cost Mollie and Feemy much more than merely the Ilasco tract. Through the instruments of guardianship and insanity confinement, Ralls County authorities not only guided the transfer of property to Atlas but also punished and imposed control over the unconventional sisters.

As someone who grew up in the Ilasco area, I had heard of Mollie and Feemy long before I dipped into the court records, long before I became a historian. In fact, the colorful, eccentric sisters were household names to me, for since childhood I had listened to my mother routinely talk about them as if they were larger-than-life characters. At that time, however, I heard no mention of their role in the property dispute or of anything tangible in regard to why they should remain topics of conversation generations after their deaths. Since my mother passed on only fragmented images and pieces of disconnected stories about Mollie and Feemy, I dismissed them as nothing more than the manifestations of her attraction to colorful characters and community gossip.

It was not until I returned home in 1992 to begin research on a community study of Ilasco that I stumbled onto the sisters' case. Only then did I discover, much to my mother's delight, that there was hard evidence to support what she knew only intuitively: that Mollie and Feemy were important characters in the community's history. Never mind that she knew nothing about their battles in the courts or about their ultimate removal from the community. Never mind, in fact, that Mollie had died and that Feemy was committed to the state hospital even before my mother was born. The fragmented images of the sisters that my mother carried around—images passed on to her by parents, older siblings, and other members of the community—would now find fuller expression, shape, and vindication.

When I first came across the sisters' case, I intended only to incorporate it into my recent book, *City of Dust: A Cement Company Town in the Land of Tom Sawyer.* The more I dug into the matter, however, the more I realized that I had found a very important story that could not be adequately told and contained within the framework of *City of Dust*. It became clear to me that Mollie and Feemy richly deserved to be the subjects of a full-length study.

At first I toyed with the idea of trying my hand at a novel built around the sisters and other protagonists in this case, but as a historian I figured I should stick with what I do best. After all, I concluded, here was a story in which truth was even stranger than fiction. How could I create a more engaging novel with so many twists and turns, riveting plots and subplots, and rich characters? How could I write a fictional tale that more vividly portrayed the interwoven themes of political power and intrigue, deception, greed, and betrayal? That could make readers laugh one moment and cry the next?

To add to its appeal, here was a real-life story set within the cultural landscape that less than a half century earlier had inspired Mark Twain's fictional characters. One of the chief protagonists in this story, in fact, was the very cement company that had recently converted one of Tom Sawyer's caves into a shale mine. For Twain, this was "a painful subject," but for the company that grabbed the Ilasco tract, it was an opportunity to appropriate and shape Twain's legacy to justify Atlas's commercial transformation of his childhood playground.[10]

The property dispute would never have materialized had it not been for the behavior of Mollie, who stirred controversy from the time she first appeared in Ilasco as Mollie Scott. On December 18, 1908, when she married Ilasco's habitually intoxicated Samuel Heinbach, age sixty-nine, she broke a sacred commandment of True Womanhood: that marriage was the key to happiness, but only if women sought it for the noblest of reasons. At age fifty-four, she married Sam purely for money after carefully investigating his real estate assets and offering financial incentives to intermediaries who could facilitate a courtship. In doing so, she openly violated the stricture that "good" women must not pursue marriage actively, that they must instead wait for marriage to find them. In fact, she prided herself on acquiring land through marriage, which she had now come to view as a purely contractual business arrangement.[11]

For Mollie, who was nearly deaf at the time, the stakes were high in this, her fifth marriage, for Sam owned a lucrative twenty-six-acre tract in Ilasco. He had once barely eked out a living as a woodchopper and truck farmer, but when construction of the cement plant began in 1901, he discovered a much easier and more profitable way to use his land. He quit farming and suddenly derived a substantial income from leasing lots to workers who then rented cheap houses—mostly tar-papered shacks—hastily constructed by area businessmen on those lots next to the plant. Most Ilasco residents lived in company barracks or in rented houses on lots leased from either Sam or Theodore Johnson, his former partner. Johnson owned an adjoining twenty-six-acre tract.

Sam's land, worth between twelve thousand and fifteen thousand dollars at the time he married Mollie, produced a yearly "ground rent" income of about eleven hundred dollars.[12]

What particularly exposed Mollie to public criticism and gossip was the naked openness with which she pursued marriage for money, particularly in light of the vast class and cultural differences between her and Sam. Mollie, accustomed to middle-class associations, social amenities, artistic expression, and cultural pursuits, married a man who despite his recent good fortunes bore the scars of a life ravaged by poverty, family fragmentation, and alcoholism. Sam lived in a sparsely furnished log cabin, often went about Ilasco barefooted, and spent many of his days in an alcoholic stupor. Because of deteriorating health, he had also lost control over bowel functions. Given Mollie's class pretensions and self-cultivated image as a "lady," it was readily apparent to all observers why she had married Sam at a time when his health was in rapid decline.

At age fifty-four, however, Mollie faced numerous insecurities and limited job opportunities and marriage options, complicated by her near deafness. This had important implications for her future economic security, social autonomy, and the pinch of old age. By marrying Sam and taking care of him in the final days of his life, she could satisfy her own long-term needs and enjoy a steady, decent income from the lot rentals. She would be set for the rest of her life if she could only inherit his estate.

Mollie could do all of this, of course, by assuming a traditional role to which she and other women of that era had long been socialized—that of care-giver. In her case, however, she would shape this role to benefit herself rather than the traditional male-centered hierarchy that had characteristically defined the contours, significance, and meaning of women's role in society. At this point in Mollie's life, after numerous disappointments, setbacks, and struggles, she was ready more than ever to risk public gossip and manipulate the traditional care-giving role for financial gain. She would now use marriage on far more cynical terms to achieve financial and social independence during old age. Life with Sam Heinbach, whose mind and body were already ravaged by alcoholism, would certainly be no picnic, but if she could only endure the degrading conditions until his death, the financial payoff would be sweet, indeed.[13]

The American marketplace in the early twentieth century provided abundant rewards for similarly ambitious men on the make in the business world, but Mollie soon discovered that marrying Sam for money would bring her a peck of trouble. Her bold economic behavior brought rebuke when it collided with powerful political and economic interests in a county thoroughly dominated by the Atlas Portland Cement Company. Her aggressiveness did more than merely invite gossip, however, for the political stakes were high. Through marriage, Mollie stood to become a major landlord and power broker in a turbulent labor camp that owed its existence to the nearby plant. This upset powerful male entrepreneurs, lawyers, and politicians with private and public designs on the Heinbach tract. When Mollie tried to cash in on her marriage investment upon Sam's death, she clashed with those poised to challenge her right to inherit his estate. Local attorneys and county politicians with ties to the cement company instigated a dispute among Sam's heirs to smother the tract in litigation, force a sheriff's sale, and ensure that Atlas, not Mollie, would become Ilasco's sole landlord.

Three unrelated but significant developments in 1910 laid the foundation for a more aggressive but clever campaign by Atlas to strengthen its position in the area. First, endemic labor unrest at the cement plant led to a strike that year which ended in the military occupation of Ilasco by the Missouri National Guard. This prompted a shift toward a more paternalistic role for Atlas in the community to stabilize labor relations by promoting the growth of schools and churches. Second, the death of Mark Twain—which coincided with the strike—provided Atlas an opportunity to extend that paternalism by promoting the preservation of public landmarks to commemorate Hannibal's most famous citizen. This preservation campaign, led by George A. Mahan—Atlas's Hannibal attorney and future president of the State Historical Society of Misssouri—would repair Atlas's badly damaged image in the aftermath of the Ilasco strike. It would also shape the public's understanding of Twain's thought and writings to legitimize the "robber barons" who now walked the land of Twain's "robber caves" near Ilasco.

Finally, the death of Sam Heinbach in early 1910 offered an opportunity for local officials and entrepreneurial lawyers to tie up his estate in probate court. They did so by challenging the will that left the Ilasco tract to Mollie. Sam's death thus gave company officials and their junior partners in the area the opportunity to initiate a strategy to stabilize Ilasco by gaining complete control over the town.

Little did Mollie know at the time she married Sam that she was about to star in a long-running legal drama that would feature several scripts and subplots and costar her younger divorced sister. Feemy, who was forty-seven years old at the time of Mollie's marriage to Sam, had only recently returned to the Hannibal area after having left for education, marriage, and the Yankee urban world of Baltimore, New York, and Washington, D.C. A writer/businesswoman who also dabbled in spiritualism, hypnotism, horoscopes, and astrological forecasting, she was well educated, widely traveled, sophisticated, and financially independent after her divorce. Moreover, she was fiercely combative when it came to protecting Mollie and herself from men who, she suspected, were trying to take advantage of women.

Some, including Mollie, at times regarded Feemy as impetuous, even shrewish, quarrelsome, and unduly antagonistic, but the sense of power, self-confidence, and cockiness that Feemy exuded was a great asset to Mollie in the struggle over the Ilasco tract. Armed with a broader gender consciousness, impressive legal expertise, eloquent speaking skills, and an ability to entertain family and friends by putting subjects into trances, Feemy rolled into Ilasco on a train, ready to do battle with her sister's enemies.

Mollie, to enlist Feemy's aid, made her a joint owner of the property, thus further complicating what was already a very complex case. In a fierce struggle that consumed the rest of their lives, the sisters battled to hang onto their property and maintain a loving relationship with each other despite the grueling toll the case took on them. Differences between them deepened as the dispute dragged on, however, and thanks in part to the machinations of attorneys and intermediaries for the cement company, Mollie later tried to sell the entire tract and pocket all of the proceeds for herself. This, of course, required further litigation against Feemy, and Mollie's attorney, Charles E. Rendlen, Sr., a prominent Hannibal Republican, prosecuted a suit to break the sisters' joint deed on grounds that Feemy had forced Mollie to put her name on it. In the meantime, Mollie went into hiding out of state for more than two years, allegedly out of fear that Feemy would kill her if she knew her whereabouts.

Rendlen failed to break the joint deed, but Feemy along the way became the victim of a systematic campaign of harassment aimed at driving her out of Ilasco and breaking her down. After 1921, when the Ralls County probate court declared Mollie mentally incompetent and the circuit judge ordered a sheriff's sale of the Ilasco tract, an angry, defiant Feemy waged a lonely battle to protest the devious way in which Atlas had scooped up their property and converted Ilasco into a company town. With a deep-seated contempt for the male-dominated legal profession, she now acted as her own attorney and tried to oversee her own appeal of the sale to the state supreme court. She also sued Atlas and a handful of others in the case, including Rendlen, who was now an appointed member of the State Eleemosynary Board that governed Missouri's mental institutions.

Feemy refused to acknowledge defeat despite the strain on her health and financial resources. Finally, she, too, became the target of a campaign by authorities to place a guardianship over her. Leading this campaign was Ralls County Prosecuting Attorney Benton B. Megown, the former probate judge who had presided over Mollie's insanity hearing and who now was one of those charged with graft in Feemy's suit. He insisted that Feemy suffered from "monomania," a mental condition that allegedly left her with an obsessive compulsion to file lawsuits. Finally, in August 1927, just a few months before Mollie's tragic death, the Ralls County probate court ordered Feemy's confinement in the State Hospital for the Insane.

Unfortunately for Mollie and Feemy, their designs on Ilasco clashed with those of Atlas, which found a number of area Republican and Democratic lawyers and intermediaries eager to lend their services to the company's campaign to acquire the community. Because of Mollie's more materialistic tendencies, however, she ultimately became more vulnerable to the financial temptations to cooperate with the very forces against which she had long battled. In the end, these tendencies may have spared her a fate similar to that of her enraged sister. Feemy, facing an impressive array of lawyers and local officials bent on delivering Ilasco to Atlas one way or another, refused to concede defeat. Instead, she fought to the bitter end, until the doors of the Fulton mental hospital slammed shut behind her.

Feemy's fate raises several intriguing questions. First, when the county sheriff finally whisked her away to Fulton at her own expense in 1927, was it a clear matter of wrongful confinement and abuse of power by tightly interlocked elites eager to serve the long-range interests of Atlas? Or did the case itself break her down mentally? Feemy at times complained of nervous exhaustion and may have been manic depressive. If she did suffer from manic depression, were there other options for local authorities besides confinement? To what extent were perceptions of her alleged insanity merely a response to her eccentricities, unorthodox views, and combativeness? Would she have received the attention of authorities at all had she not locked horns with powerful area elites over the control of Ilasco? Would her fate have been different if she were a man?

The outcome for both sisters, in fact, raises questions about the use of guardianships and insanity as methods of social control against unconventional women who challenged the economic and political interests of a powerful corporation. Mollie and Feemy expanded the boundaries of women's sphere through manipulation of marriage and the law, but they probably would have suffered a different fate had they not antagonized powerful male corporate, legal, and political authorities by going after the Ilasco tract. Feemy's fate, in particular, illustrates just how dangerous it could be for a well-educated, angry woman with unorthodox views, deep convictions, and combative instincts to tangle with her community's most powerful men.[14]

The sisters' property dispute provides a fascinating look at how the intersection of gender, class, and law shaped the history of property and labor relations in Ilasco and helped to consolidate the power of the Atlas Portland Cement Company in the Midwest. This is important to understanding the wider consolidation of corporate capitalism in the early twentieth century. Their case also sheds light on the underside of Atlas's much-touted paternalism, which brought schools and churches to the community, but at an enormous price for Mollie and Feemy. It was the sisters' land, after all, that underwrote the company's paternalism. The case also contributes to our understanding of the interaction between law and society, and tells us much about the everyday world of marriage and strategies of economic survival for ordinary women around the turn of the century.

Fortunately, Mollie and Feemy left an extensive paper trail that made it possible for me to track them from courthouse to courthouse in northeast Missouri and to the state court in Jefferson City. Through these legal records, I have come to know the sisters as complex, even entertaining characters who had a great zest for life. Mollie and Feemy could hardly be criticized for passivity. After all, this was a daring game that they were playing in Ilasco. They did not simply sit back and resign themselves to the hand of cards that was dealt them in life. Not only did they play the cards skillfully, but they also often reshuffled the deck and raised the stakes in the battle for the Ilasco tract. In the process, they gave area lawyers, cement company officials, and politicians a run—a very long run—for their money.

It is largely through court records that I reconstruct the sisters' dynamic role in Ilasco's history and try to unlock the secrets surrounding the politics of Mollie's guardianship and Feemy's institutionalization in the Fulton state hospital. In my opinion, the sisters would not want to be seen as mere victims in this case, but rather as women who lived full lives and left their mark on Ilasco's history, despite the enormous price they paid in the end. I would like to think that Mark Twain, too, would especially appreciate their role in the rich history of the area that once produced his fictional characters. After all, Mollie and Feemy left behind a story filled with the best and the worst of the human condition. Their story combines triumph and tragedy, warmth and loneliness, hope and despair, loyalty and betrayal. It also features honesty and deception, as well as compassion and vindictiveness, greed and exploitation—elements that Twain both admired and eloquently criticized in "the damned human race."

One

Coming to Mark Twain's Salt River Country

Since the Ralls County context is crucial to understanding much of this case, I begin with a brief look at the family roots of Mollie and Feemy in Pennsylvania, followed by an overview of Ralls County politics at the time their family arrived there shortly after the Civil War. This will include a sketch of several leading families in county politics that produced men who later became principal figures in the dispute over the sisters' Ilasco tract. With the Democratic Party as their instrument, these interlocked families had monopolized control over the courthouse since before the Civil War. Only during Reconstruction did they face a major challenge to their power from Radical Unionists. The antagonisms produced by this conflict generated resentments that lingered for years, perhaps extending to the family of Mollie and Feemy at the very time of their arrival as Yankee Republican outsiders.

The long, winding journey to guardianships, mental competency hearings, and deliberations of insanity in the courts of Ralls County thus began for Mollie (Mary Alice) and Feemy (Euphemia Belle) Sykes on the rutted wagon tracks from Pennsylvania to Missouri after the Civil War. With them in the wagon were two other sisters, a brother, and their parents, Edwin Henry and Sarah Jane (Webb) Sykes, who had married on September 2, 1853. Mollie, born on June 9, 1854, was the oldest child, followed by Henry Thomas (September 14, 1856), Laura Jane (December 5, 1859), Feemy (April 23, 1861), and Emma Virginia (July 9, 1865).[1]

Mollie and Feemy were of English Quaker descent on both sides of their family. The Sykes and Webb families had manufacturing, milling, and farming roots in Delaware and southern York County, Pennsylvania, just across the Maryland line. Edwin

Sykes's older brother, Joseph B. Sykes, operated a mill in York County's Shrewsbury township before the Civil War, but by 1860 Edwin and Sarah had moved to Carlisle, Pennsylvania, where they owned and operated a restaurant. Edwin's paternal grandparents were Mary (Jones) and Joseph Sykes, Quakers from Fawn Grove in York County. Joseph once operated a woolen manufacturing business in the area.[2]

Sarah Sykes's paternal grandparents, James and Mary Ann (Miller) Webb, were prominent Quaker farmers in York County's Hopewell township, as were Sarah's mother and father, Mary Ann (Yost) and Henry M. Webb. By 1860, however, Sarah's parents had left York County and moved to Baltimore, where they owned and operated a hotel. Sarah's brother, Henry, still owned a farm near Stewartstown in York County that in 1860 was worth four thousand dollars.[3]

Shortly after the death of Sarah's father on January 16, 1868, she, Edwin, and their children became part of the post–Civil War migration to the trans-Mississippi West. It is unclear what led them to leave Pennsylvania, but it may have been related to disruptions caused in 1863 by Confederate General Robert E. Lee's invasion of the area around Gettysburg and Carlisle. The Sykes family was undoubtedly attracted to Ralls County, Missouri, by economic opportunities and perhaps by Sarah's family connections. A Virginia branch of the Webb family had already settled in Jasper township's small community of Madisonville in the southwestern part of the county, near the Pike County line. It was perhaps through them that Edwin and Sarah Sykes learned that the New London area needed a steam flouring mill, for in May 1866 the *Ralls County Record* highlighted the economic importance of such a mill and invited outsiders with capital to come to the area. By the fall of 1868, Edwin and Sarah had arrived in Madisonville, where they first obtained land along Spencer Creek. Their forty-acre tract was worth about four hundred dollars at the time, and their personal wealth was valued at three hundred dollars.[4]

Joseph, Edwin's much more well-to-do brother, along with his wife, Magdalene, and their six children, also came over the trail to Ralls County. Joseph and Magdalene also bought land along Spencer Creek in Jasper township, where Joseph opened a steam-powered sawmill. Ellen, an older daughter of Joseph and Magdalene, soon married William Johnson, of Lincoln County, Missouri, but her five brothers and sisters were still in their parents' household in early 1870. Eighteen-year-old Noah, the oldest son, was living at home, working as a farmhand.[5]

At the time of the Sykes's arrival, the area was torn apart by bitter conflicts that grew out of competing regional and cultural identities, the legacy of slavery, Civil War allegiances, and Reconstruction. This was Salt River country, an area that included Ralls, Pike, Lincoln, Marion, and Monroe Counties. It was once home to one-eighth of Missouri's slave population, and to a young Mark Twain. In 1860, 21 percent of the population of Ralls County consisted of slaves owned by tobacco planters and other smaller farmers. The size of landholdings in the county was not great, however, even when compared to those in neighboring Pike County to the south. Of Ralls's 1,248 farms in 1870, there were none that contained one thousand acres or more, and only seven that contained more than five hundred acres. In contrast, of Pike County's 1,850 farms in 1870, there were four that consisted of one thousand acres or more, and fourteen that had between five hundred and one thousand acres.[6]

In the antebellum period, most of Ralls County's economic and political power had resided with slaveholding families whose roots were in Virginia, Kentucky, and Tennessee. A good illustration is the family of James and Davilla Woodson Glascock, who in 1811 were born respectively in Culpepper and Fluvannah Counties, Virginia. James's father, Noah, bought land in Ralls County from the federal government and moved there along with his wife, Lucy, and several children in 1823, shortly after Missouri achieved statehood. Noah presided over the construction of a big house that became the center of a self-contained slave manor near Salt River, about five miles east of New London.

After Noah's death in 1836, James assumed control of the tobacco plantation and enlarged it further. In 1841, he married Davilla Woodson, a former teacher from Fluvannah County, who brought slaves with her to the marriage, thus helping to consolidate and extend the economic and political power of the Glascock family in Ralls County. To preserve their wealth, their children often married cousins or members of other prominent area families. In 1860, James owned twenty-six slaves, making him one of the few slaveholders in the county who could accurately be classified as a member of the powerful planter class. He owned at least nine hundred acres of land valued at $36,500 in 1870. Some of his Glascock relatives held positions as judges and clerks in the circuit, probate, and county courts of Ralls, and a couple of them served in the Missouri senate and house of representatives.[7]

Missouri did not join the Confederacy, but a raging guerrilla war set an acrimonious tone for the Reconstruction-era political climate that greeted the Sykes family. During the war, Ralls County Confederate Rangers and bushwhackers attacked Unionists and threatened to lynch slaves uprooted by the war, along with any antislavery Germans who harbored them. The county seat, New London, which was in Spencer township and had a population of 410 in 1870, was the postwar political center of Confederate sympathizers and of virulent racist opposition to extending civil rights to former slaves. It was here, in fact, that Mark Twain had earlier begun what turned out to be a very brief stint as a Confederate volunteer.[8]

Of Ralls County's seven townships—Center, Clay, Jasper, Saline, Salt River, Saverton, and Spencer—it was Jasper, the hotbed of Radical Unionism in the county, that became the new home of the Sykes family. Some county residents probably regarded the Sykeses as "carpetbaggers," since they were Pennsylvania Yankees, Unionists, and Republicans. When the newcomers arrived in Madisonville, they found a community that was in the middle of bitter, ongoing conflicts over Reconstruction. At that time Missouri's new constitution of 1865 was the instrument through which Radicals tried to curtail the political power of former Confederates and Confederate sympathizers. According to the new constitution, only those who would swear in a test oath that they had never been disloyal to the state of Missouri or to the Union would be allowed to vote, hold office, or serve as jurors, teachers, preachers, lawyers, or corporation officials. In addition, the new constitution called for a thorough cleansing of the state and local judiciary to get rid of judges and attorneys who were considered hostile to the Radical document. The governor would now have the power to replace such members of the judiciary until elections could fill the vacancies.[9]

In Ralls and other counties, the sweeping provisions of the new constitution, coupled with the abolition of slavery through the Thirteenth Amendment to the U.S. Constitution in December 1865, stirred hatreds and posed a fundamental threat to the structure of political power and wealth. More than in any other former slaveholding state, Missouri Radicals tried to weaken the political power of onetime Confederates and their sympathizers. At stake was control over the labor and lives of former slaves, race relations, and the levers of power inside local courthouses. If enforced, the new constitution amounted to a revolution. As a result, pro-Confederate elements and Conservative Unionists closed ranks to oppose the implementation of these provisions and to block the granting of black suffrage and citizenship rights.[10]

Thomas R. Dodge, coeditor of the New London–based *Ralls County Record,* was a Conservative Unionist who led the public campaign against Radicals in Ralls County. He and coeditor Clay Crittenden Menefee Mayhall, also a Conservative Unionist, regularly singled out Jasper township in their weekly attacks. In December 1865, for example, they attacked Radicals in Madisonville for the arrest of a Baptist preacher who had not sworn loyalty to the new constitution. The newspaper soon devoted space to an anonymous weekly series, "Chronicles of Jasper," in which the author used biblical language and imagery to blast Jasper Radicals.[11]

Several prominent "pioneer" families with whom Mollie and Feemy later tangled were threatened by Reconstruction. The test oath, if enforced strictly, had the potential to empower new forces in the county. Had the sisters been old enough and sufficiently conscious of politics at the time, they might have benefited from observing the way in which many local elites responded to the threat posed by Missouri Radicals. As Mollie and Feemy later discovered, Ralls's officials did not tolerate a threat from any quarter, not even if it came from a member of their own immediate family.

Perhaps no family illustrates this better than the Megowns, who later figured prominently in the outcome of the battle over the Ilasco tract. When Samuel Megown was appointed in 1866 to supervise the registration of qualified voters in accordance with a stricter registration law, the *Ralls County Record* at first praised the appointment. Megown, a former brick manufacturer who in 1836 had come to Ralls County from Pittsburgh, Pennsylvania, was a Democrat until the Civil War broke out. Then he converted to Republicanism and became a county judge and deputy assessor. Because of his wartime political conversion, he soon became a pariah in the family and the object of vitriolic attacks and death threats. As he disenfranchised many powerful residents in the county for their Confederate sympathies, newspaper editors Dodge and Mayhall regularly taunted him as the "High Priest" of Radicalism. This led to bitter divisions within the Megown family that lasted well into the twentieth century. For example, whereas Thomas S. ("Bud"), one of Samuel's sons, followed in the Republican path of his father, others remained loyal to the Democratic Party and thus ensured themselves access to the only vehicle to political power in the county for generations to come. John Megown, a Democratic critic of his father's registration activities, later became probate and county judge for many years. Two of his sons, Benton B. and John E. Megown, pursued careers in county Democratic politics and banking and played instrumental roles in the battle against Feemy and Mollie in Ilasco. For Benton, in particular, this battle would assume a raging intensity.[12]

As Samuel Megown's appointed registration officers did their work in Ralls County in preparation for the 1866 elections, the highly charged atmosphere mirrored the conflicts in national politics between President Andrew Johnson and Congressional Radicals. To resist Radicalism and protest Megown's role in disqualifying former Confederates and their sympathizers, Ralls Democrats formed Andrew Johnson clubs. As in many parts of Missouri where lawlessness and vigilante violence replaced political discourse, the partisan environment in Ralls County produced violence in the community. On July 28, 1866, both the Radicals and Conservative Unionists held meetings in Madisonville, and after they adjourned, a fight broke out in which John Dickerson (or Dickinson), a Conservative Unionist, and Milo E. Laylin, a Radical, were killed. In addition, six were wounded, including Thomas H. Webb. Webb and five other men were indicted on charges of murder, but the prosecution later dropped those charges when the accused agreed to plead guilty to a lesser charge of rioting and to pay a fine of five dollars each.[13]

In the election of 1866, the Conservative Union ticket included the names of several interlocked families whose economic and political connections would continue to shape county politics and family relationships during the litigation against Mollie and Feemy after 1910. For example, one of the county justices was William E. Harris, into whose family Thomas Sykes, the brother of Mollie and Feemy, would later marry. Harris had come to Ralls County from Madison County, Kentucky, long before the Civil War. He was married to Margaret Mayhall, whose family roots were in Franklin County, Kentucky. Her brother was coeditor of the *Ralls County Record* at that time. Another brother of hers, George E. Mayhall, was a Conservative candidate for county clerk in 1866. Finally, George C. Hays, Jr., elected as county treasurer in 1868, had kinship ties to Mark Twain. His Virginia-born father, who had owned eight slaves in 1860, was disqualified from voting by Samuel Megown because he had given provisions to rebel soldiers and sympathized with the Confederacy. George, Jr., had a son, Charles T. Hays, who later played a pivotal role as attorney and judge in the litigation that led to the Atlas Portland Cement Company's acquisition of the Ilasco tract owned by Mollie and Feemy.[14]

In addition to the politicians on the Conservative Union ticket, many members of Ralls County's prominent families were in the pro-Confederate ranks. Included were lawyers who would later help to instigate litigation against Mollie and Feemy. These names were synonymous with office-holding and political influence in the county. Several Briscoes were substantial slaveholders in 1860, including Phillip (nineteen slaves), Anderson (eleven), William T. (ten), and John (ten). Phillip was denied the right to vote in 1866 because of disloyalty to the Union, and so was William T., who reportedly growled that he would "fight in blood to his knees before he would be run over by the damn black republicans." In Madisonville, James W. Allison, one of the largest landowners in the county, was blocked from voting in the 1866 elections because of Confederate sympathies. His father, Alexander, owned five slaves in 1860. Two of James's sons—James O. and Thomas E. Allison—soon carved out careers in county and state Democratic politics that later put them on a collision course with Mollie and Feemy. It was James O. Allison, with the assistance of Jack Briscoe, Charles T. Hays, and his brother Thomas E., who later instigated the suit to deny Mollie's right to inherit the Ilasco tract.[15]

The 1866 voting returns in Ralls County ran counter to the prevailing trend around the state. Missouri Radicals strengthened their control of the state legislature with sizable majorities, but in Ralls County the entire Conservative Union slate of candidates won in spite of what the *Ralls County Record* described as the "mean tricks" of Samuel Megown (now a candidate for sheriff) and his fellow Radicals. After Radical candidates contested the election results, however, alleging fraud on the part of Conservative election judges in Saverton, Clay, and Spencer townships, the Radical-dominated state legislature nullified the election of representative Henry C. Wellman and instead seated Luzerne Bulkley, his Radical opponent.[16]

When Edwin and Sarah Sykes reached their new home in the Unionist community of Madisonville, their status as Yankee newcomers probably earned them antagonism from the county's pro-Confederate quarters. This antagonism probably increased when Edwin voted in the election of 1868 while the county's numerous Confederate sympathizers were banned from voting by Radical registration officials.[17]

The political atmosphere in Ralls County during the first couple of years of the Sykes family's stay in the area remained highly charged. Throughout this period, the Sykeses continued to live in Jasper township, where a sizable Radical population stymied efforts by Conservative Unionists to return power to the Democratic Party and block the extension of black voting and other citizenship rights. In the election of 1868, the Ralls County clerk threw out all of the votes from Jasper township because of alleged irregularities at the polls. Wilson B. Elliott, the Radical candidate for the state legislature, then lost the election to Henry C. Wellman by a margin of only two votes. In the rejected returns from

Jasper township, Elliott outpolled Wellman by an overwhelming margin of 82 to 17 votes. Once again, the state legislature intervened to deny Wellman his seat.[18]

Edwin Sykes apparently played no formal role in the politics of Jasper township, but by the summer of 1870, he and Sarah had left that part of the county—perhaps to escape the political tensions that wracked the township. If they had come to Missouri with an ideological commitment to building a more egalitarian society, they may have been like many other white Reconstruction Republicans whose earlier idealism and dream of racial justice began to wane. Maybe they simply found better money-making opportunities away from the swirling controversies in Jasper township. Perhaps, too, the appearance of J. W. Emison and Company's new incorporated steam flouring mill in New London in July 1869 made it harder for them to compete economically in that section of the county. Whatever the case, they moved to the small Mississippi River community of Saverton in southeastern Ralls County.[19]

The circumstances surrounding the Sykes family's acquisition of property in Saverton are not clear, but on September 24, 1870, Sarah acquired a small mill site of 1.6 acres along a creek that emptied into the river a few hundred yards away. Neil Cameron, a former steamboat captain and slave owner, along with James T. Matson, a Saverton physician from another prestigious family of prominent former slaveholders and millers, quitclaimed to the Sykes family their joint interest in the site. Edwin and Sarah then hired several workers to help run a steam-powered grain mill on the site. As we shall later see, Mollie had already left the household, but for Feemy and the other Sykes kids, a nice house on the north end of Saverton next to steep limestone bluffs overlooking the Mississippi River would become home.[20]

Feemy and Mollie grew up in a family with a tradition of strong, independent Quaker women accustomed to managing property, running households, and operating hotels and restaurants. In 1870, Mary Ann Webb, their recently widowed maternal grandmother, operated a household and substantial farm near Glen Rock in York County, Pennsylvania. This farm was reportedly worth three thousand dollars at that time. Their spinster aunt, Euphemia Webb, after whom Feemy was named, was an autonomous woman who also owned considerable personal wealth. Furthermore, thanks to Missouri's Married Women's Property Act, Sarah Sykes, their mother, also conducted property transactions in her own name in Ralls County.[21]

It was Sarah, in fact, who acquired the Saverton mill site. The decision to put the property in her name may have been the result of Edwin's failing health, or an attempt to protect the property from his business problems, some of which may have been related to antagonisms that grew out of Reconstruction. In a couple of unsuccessful collection suits in the Ralls County circuit court, for example, he had failed to recover sizable debts owed to him by customers. One of those customers had left the state owing him $740. To make matters worse, Edwin himself was the target of a suit by Edmund R. Bailey, who held a note on an overdue loan to him.[22]

Edwin died at the age of forty-three on January 29, 1874, during an outbreak of typhoid fever and pneumonia, but Sarah continued to operate the Saverton steam mill for the next few months amid growing financial problems. In May, a fire destroyed the uninsured mill while workers were taking a breakfast break. The entire building burned, leaving Sarah with a total loss of three thousand dollars. To make matters worse, Sheriff John H. Steers appeared in court on August 29 of that year with a deed that he had executed on March 31, 1871, conveying Edwin and Sarah's forty acres in Jasper township to Edwin's attorney, A. G. Lancaster. This conveyance grew out of an order from the circuit court in Shelby County, Missouri, to sell the property under three executions for the sum of six dollars.[23]

Now thirty-eight years old and widowed with four children at home, Sarah quickly remarried three months later. On September 1, 1874, she married Benjamin F. Eby, a Saverton farmer, cattle buyer, and merchant whose first wife, Emily, had died only five and one-half months earlier. This new marriage produced a son, Harry Eby, on December 5, 1876. Benjamin and Sarah, who continued to live on the Saverton mill site, headed a household in 1880 that included Harry, Emma Sykes, and eighteen-year-old Seth Eby, a son from Benjamin's first marriage.[24]

For political and cultural reasons, the bitter backdrop of Reconstruction may have shaped and limited the marital options of Sarah and her children in a county filled with Confederate supporters and shaped by southern cultural influences. This might partly explain their marriage patterns. After Sarah married Benjamin Eby, a Union Army veteran, two of her daughters married his sons from the previous marriage. On October 10, 1877, Laura married Charles Eby, and on September 22, 1878, she gave birth to Benjamin F. (Frank) Eby, Jr. Emma and Seth, after growing up in the same household as stepbrother and stepsister, married on April 2, 1889. Tom Sykes likewise married into a Unionist family. On January 24, 1881, he married Sarah F. Murphy, the daughter of Ignatius and Sarah Murphy, a Madisonville farming family.[25]

Like the Sykeses, the Eby family had roots in Pennsylvania. In fact, Benjamin F. Eby's family origins were in Lancaster County, which adjoins York County. He was from a prominent Mennonite family that included Peter Eby, a Mennonite bishop in Pennsylvania. Before coming to the Saverton area, Benjamin Eby had moved from Pennsylvania to New York, Canada, and Andalusia, Illinois.[26]

By marrying into the Eby family, the Sykeses strengthened their ties to middle-class society in the Saverton and Hannibal area. In 1880, Sarah E. Eby, now the stepsister of the Sykes children, married cousin David Henry Eby, a promising lawyer whose father, David S., a merchant and insurance agent, had moved to Hannibal in the early 1840s and acquired considerable property in Ralls County. David H., born on December 31, 1852, received a B.S. degree from Central College in Fayette, Missouri, and a law degree from the University of Missouri in 1874, before opening an office in Hannibal. He moved to Colorado Springs, Colorado, in 1877, but returned to Hannibal two years later and began to carve out a career in local Democratic Party politics. In Hannibal, he held the office of city recorder between 1881 and 1884, and then served as city attorney intermittently until 1898. In 1898, he was elected as judge of the Tenth Judicial Circuit, which included Ralls and Marion Counties; he was reelected in 1904.[27]

In many cases, such ties linked the Sykes family to others who had supported the Union. As charter members of the small Saverton Methodist Church when it was organized in 1885, Emma

Sykes, along with Sarah, Benjamin, and Laura Eby, developed religious and social contacts with Cassius M. Jeffers, a Union veteran. Jeffers, a Saverton township farmer and merchant, was one of the first Sunday school superintendents of the Saverton Methodist Church.[28]

Another prominent Unionist and founder of the Saverton Methodist Church with whom the Ebys and Sykeses associated was Richard Dalton, a commercial apple grower and leading political figure in the state. Dalton, an Irish immigrant, had located in the New London area after serving in the Missouri Cavalry during the Civil War. As a lawyer and prosecuting attorney, he played an important role as a peacemaker in Ralls County's turbulent Reconstruction politics, and he served as a Democrat in the Missouri legislature. Furthermore, he was only narrowly defeated in a bid for the Democratic Party's gubernatorial nomination in 1892. President Grover Cleveland appointed him surveyor of the port of St. Louis in 1893, and four years later Dalton returned to Saverton and soon became president of Missouri's Single Tax League.[29]

This, then, was the regional, cultural, and political context that reshaped the formative, childhood experiences of Mollie and Feemy. The way in which the sisters interacted with the forces around them, combined with their early Pennsylvania influences and, in Feemy's case, adult living experiences in New York, Baltimore, and Washington, D.C., would do much to determine their associations, values, goals, and ambitions. Both of them, but particularly Feemy, would come of age at a time when a growing number of educated women were using new forms of empowerment to demand greater opportunities in the public arena and to redefine women's role in marriage, the home, and society.

Two

Designing Women

The Lady and the Hypnotist

> It is not to be wondered at that even in this day and age Mrs. [Mollie] Heinbach and Mrs. [Euphemia] Koller do not entertain a high conception of the moral status of the legal fraternity. They are doubtless sincere in believing that moral delinquencies among lawyers are the rule instead of exceptions.
>
> —*Ralls County attorney Edmund L. Alford, 1920*

Since Mollie and Feemy were hardly youngsters at the time they tangled with area authorities in their legal case, it is important to take into account how their values, personalities, and life struggles prepared them for the protracted fight that ate up the final two decades of their lives. Only by tracing the different paths that took them to Ilasco can we more fully understand their willingness to tangle with county authorities, cement executives, and power brokers in the community. The following sketches of the sisters' adult experiences before Mollie's marriage to Sam Heinbach not only enable us to get to know them better, but also suggest the range of options available at that time to ordinary women struggling to cope with economic subordination and dependency on men. These brief sketches also reveal some of the sources of empowerment that later led Mollie and Feemy to risk such a bruising battle with area authorities.

Mollie, as the oldest of the Sykes sisters, followed a winding path through Salt River country that took her in a more traditional direction for women. She apparently did not become involved in church or civic organizations or other public forums.

This may have been related in part to her hearing impairment (apparently hereditary), although it is not clear at what age she became nearly deaf. Her relationships suggest that she was more attracted to southern influences and images of women in the area, where she spent nearly all of her adult life. In fact, the image of the lady had special appeal as she grafted her early Pennsylvania background onto the local landscape with its distinctly southern cultural cast.

Mollie's search for status got off to a rocky start, however, for a pregnancy drove her into a disastrous first marriage at the early age of fifteen. On March 29, 1870, she married John H. Kellogg, a nearly thirty-year-old itinerant painter from Tennessee, before Saverton Justice of the Peace Neil Cameron. Kellogg was a swarthy southerner whose scarred body bore the marks of a history of brawling, heavy drinking, and knife-fighting. He had scars on the right side of his forehead, on the left cheek near his nose, on his chin, left breast, and right shoulder, as well as a huge scar on the left side of his back under the shoulder blade. Whether he overpowered and preyed on Mollie or whether she believed she could reform him and get him to abandon his brawling ways is not clear. Upon marrying, they moved from farm to farm in Ralls County, boarding with families who hired him to paint and hang paper for them.[1]

John Kellogg's high-quality work as a painter earned him an endorsement by the *Ralls County Record,* but his criminal behavior quickly made an unstable married life even more shaky. If Mollie did believe that she could get him to behave respectably, she was sadly mistaken. Within three months, the combination of alcohol and violent behavior got him into trouble with the law in New London. In July 1870, when asked by saloon owner Isham O. Winn to pay a small whiskey bill, he burst into a rage, and "glass flew in every direction." Fortunately, nobody in this scrape was hurt, but Kellogg's behavior was symptomatic of deeper problems that soon disrupted Mollie's life even further.[2]

Kellogg refused to drop the matter with Winn, and again got into trouble on a visit to New London a few weeks later. After drinking a lot of "mean" whiskey, he beat up "an inoffensive old man" [Crow] without provocation, then he charged to a local barber shop where Winn was and verbally assaulted him. In response, Winn punched him, and both men were arrested. This time, however, John was arraigned and fined for assaulting Crow.[3]

Living with a man who could not control his drinking or his violent behavior in public must have been especially tough. John Kellogg was probably physically and verbally abusive of Mollie, too, particularly during heavy drinking binges. Yet John's criminal tendencies soon found even fuller expression, creating a nightmarish dilemma for Mollie and her newborn daughter, Bertha.

In March 1871, just a week before Mollie and John's first wedding anniversary, Ralls County Deputy Sheriff R. B. Caldwell, Jr., arrested John for stealing money and clothes from a Saverton township resident. This left Mollie with an infant to care for and a husband in the county jail awaiting a grand jury indictment on two counts of grand larceny. A month later, however, John, described now by the *Ralls County Record* as a "bad man," escaped from jail in New London. Deputy Caldwell caught him near Hannibal the following week, just as he was about to flee across the river to Illinois. In August 1871, after a trial in which Mollie's father appeared as a material witness for the prosecution of her husband, a jury in the Ralls County circuit court convicted John of grand larceny. On September 4, the judge sentenced him to two years on each of two counts in the state penitentiary.[4]

It is not clear with whom Mollie lived, or how she supported herself and Bertha, while John was in the penitentiary. Soon after the trial, someone to no apparent avail circulated a petition to the governor for executive clemency on John's behalf. What is clear, however, is that the stint in prison did not cure John's violent behavior. After serving a year of his sentence, he left the penitentiary when Governor Benjamin Gratz Brown pardoned him in October 1872, but he soon got into trouble again. In June 1874 he cut Tom Hewett, a New London resident, severely in the right leg in a knife fight in town. He also turned again to theft, making a lame attempt to use an alias when he was arrested. On August 27, 1881, the Ralls County circuit court sent him back to the penitentiary for three years.[5]

After Mollie's first marriage ended, either formally or informally, she turned to a safe relationship that brought stability. Having survived the sharp trauma of an early marriage that left her financially strapped with a baby and perhaps stripped of illusions about marriage and romance, she next married her first cousin, Noah Sykes, who worked as a sawyer in the area. This marriage offered safety with someone whom Mollie already knew well, but she and Noah had to struggle to achieve economic security. Shortly after her parents had moved to Saverton in 1870, they sold their forty acres along Spencer Creek to Noah, but he was unable to hang onto the property. During the Depression of 1873, he defaulted on the mortgage and lost the property at a courthouse sale before later regaining possession and selling it back to Mollie's mother.[6]

By 1880 Noah and Mollie, whose relationship no doubt relieved worried family members, had crossed the Ralls County line south to the town of Louisiana in northern Pike County, where they lived and raised Mollie's daughter for nearly a decade. At first they lived in a hotel while Noah worked at an area sawmill. After Noah became the head sawyer at the mill of O. J. Edmonds, however, they established a more permanent residence in Louisiana, buying a house and property in 1885.[7]

Now in her thirties, Mollie struggled to live up to the ideals of motherhood and domesticity. She and Noah must have had children who died during the 1880s, for according to information that Mollie provided to a census enumerator in 1900, she had given birth to five children in her life, none of whom were alive at that time. Bertha, her daughter from the previous marriage, lived at least until age eighteen, but by the late 1880s, Mollie perhaps could no longer give birth, and this may have strained her marriage. Whatever the case, she and Noah adopted a four-year-old child, Arthur Anderson, through the American Educational Aid Association of the State of Missouri in May 1887.[8]

Neither motherhood nor domesticity, however, satisfied Mollie's entrepreneurial instincts or provided outlets for her artistic and creative talents. Just a few months after she and Noah adopted Arthur, she put an advertisement in the *Louisiana Journal* to promote products that she was selling from her home. First, she urged the public to buy "Potato Cream Yeast." "It's like the sun in the east," she said, "[it] never fails to rise, and always takes the prize." She pointed out that many customers had formed groups to order two or three dozen packages by express mail. She may have been trying to recruit others to sell the product, for she took pains to emphasize that she had earned five hundred dollars in profits by selling ten thousand packages of yeast over the last five years.[9]

In the same advertisement, Mollie also touted her commercial painting and decorative skills. For example, she promoted "Cameo Photographs" that she had painted and put on display for sale at Pritchard's gallery in Louisiana. To attract customers, she stressed that she had painted for some of the most prominent families in town. In addition, she advertised low prices for her "Snow Drift Flowers," which she recommended for wedding presents and decorating churches and homes. "In the past year," she boasted, "I have sold $50 worth of 'Snow-Drift Flowers' and 'Leather Flowers,' oil painted."[10]

Mollie was one of nearly twenty-five thousand women in the United States at that time who were china painters. Victorian-era observers and critics generally accepted prevailing notions that women such as Mollie who painted china were "amateurs" whereas male artists were "professionals." Many believed that female china painters were especially suited to pursue artistic themes that showcased the beauty and cleanliness of the ideal Victorian home. Social conservatives endorsed women's pursuit of china painting on grounds that the use of leisure time for decorative arts would bolster the traditional women's sphere and discourage more ambitious efforts to encroach upon the male-dominated "professional" landscape. Even liberal advocates of female education who called for training women in the decorative arts argued that this would allow women to carve out new occupations that would not directly compete with men.[11]

In the eyes of those who championed the cult of domesticity, women who painted on china could also contribute to a nurturing, harmonious environment in which men could find comfort and relief from the highly competitive, exhausting world of the marketplace. Since china painting was often associated with aristocratic status in Europe, these women could also view their handiwork as an expression of their middle- or upper-class status and leisure.[12]

Mollie may have been motivated in part by such Victorian images and pretensions, but she also used the decorative arts to make money. Although "professional" artists often condemned the crass commercial motives of "amateur" china painters, rarely did the latter earn what could be classified as a middle-class income, despite instructional manuals and trade publications that stressed the economic potential of the decorative arts. Mollie turned to china painting and other activities to supplement the family's income. In doing so, she took advantage of one of the few occupations available to women from her background that also carried with it a reputation as a "genteel profession" suggesting refinement and culture.[13]

The adoption of a child by Mollie and Noah was perhaps a last-ditch effort to save their relationship, but it took place at a time of growing legal and medical opposition to consanguineous, or kinship, marriages. Opponents increasingly used biological arguments to warn that such marriages would contribute to an explosion of hereditary defects in the population. Following the lead of other states, Missouri adopted a ban on first-cousin marriages on November 1, 1889.[14]

This ban and the preoccupation with the transmission of hereditary defects stigmatized and put added pressure on Noah and Mollie's household. If by adopting a child they hoped to save their relationship, however, they failed. By 1890, their marriage had ended, and Noah had sold their house in Louisiana and moved to Kalkaska, Michigan. It is not clear whether he moved to Kalkaska after their divorce or whether Mollie had lived with him there awhile. They may have returned Arthur to the orphanage, or if the information in the 1900 census is correct, he had died by then.[15]

The divorce did little to diminish Mollie's bitterness about marriage, for Noah had kept her name off the general warranty deed to their house and property in Louisiana. Unless they had made other divorce arrangements in regard to the disposition of marital property, she received no share of the proceeds when Noah sold their Louisiana real estate on April 7, 1890.[16]

It is not clear where Mollie lived or how she earned a living during the next four years after her divorce from Noah, but sometime within that period she married Harry Broome, who died shortly thereafter. By 1894, after the death of her third husband, she was boarding with her now twice-widowed mother at 1350 Collier Street in Hannibal. Three years later, she was still living in Hannibal with her mother, but they had now moved to 338 Chestnut. The Hannibal City Directory listed her occupation as dressmaking.[17]

Mollie's fourth marriage soon helped her to get a foot higher up on the area social ladder. On August 12, 1903, she married John Mackey Scott, a former Pike County constable and recorder of deeds, in Bowling Green, about thirty-five miles southwest of Hannibal. They probably had known each other since around 1880, when they both lived in Louisiana, Missouri. At that time, John operated a grocery business. He had married Nannie Tinsley on October 10, 1880, but she died on September 9, 1897.[18]

Mollie's new marriage increased her economic security and social respectability in the area. For example, she now socialized with well-to-do families such as that of R. L. Falk, a well-known jeweler in Bowling Green. She also developed social and in-law contacts with the Tinsleys, a former slaveholding, tobacco planter class family that had come to Pike County from Bedford County, Virginia, around 1849. Her new husband's former wife was a Tinsley, and his sister was married to Perry Tinsley, whose father, James R., was a well-to-do farmer with a Continental Insurance business in Bowling Green. William N., Lafayette, and Addison Tinsley—brothers of James R.—operated a tobacco manufacturing plant in Louisiana, Missouri. The Tinsley family's post–Civil War households included African American domestic servants and field hands.[19]

Mollie's marriage to John Scott soon paid other economic dividends. After living for more than a year in Bowling Green, they bought Wildwood Farm from Mollie's mother on February 9, 1905. Sarah Eby had acquired this eighty-acre Ralls County farm near Saverton as the result of the deep depression of 1893. In 1895 she had loaned eight hundred dollars to George Creason, who mortgaged the farm to secure the loan. In 1898, after Creason failed to repay the loan, she acquired the property. The average value of Ralls County farmland at the time was sharply on the rise, increasing from $20.33 per acre in 1900 to $45.06 in 1910, but Mollie and John paid only $1,000, or $12.50 per acre, for Wildwood Farm. This transaction allowed Sarah Eby to enjoy money from the sale while ensuring that the property would stay in her family, specifically in Mollie's hands. Because of a survivorship clause in the deed, Mollie, assuming she would outlive John, would automatically retain sole ownership without tying up the land in probate upon his death.[20]

Mollie and John moved to Wildwood Farm and took up farming, but John's health steadily failed, soon confining him to bed. Two weeks before he died on January 15, 1907, at age fifty-eight, he drew up a will, leaving only one dollar to his son, Joseph Elisha Scott, and one dollar to his daughter, Pinkie Maude Ratcliffe. The rest of his personal property went to Mollie, and he left his real estate for her to own and use as long as she lived. After her death, this land was then to be distributed equally among his bodily heirs. He owned a one-third interest in a tract in Bowling Green and an additional strip of thirty acres in Pike County. Wildwood Farm, of course, would automatically pass into Mollie's hands.[21]

There was apparently some confusion about the cause of John Scott's death. Newspaper reports agreed that he had been sick for several months, but they gave conflicting explanations of the immediate cause of death. The *Bowling Green Times* reported that he died of dropsy of the heart, but the *Hannibal Courier-Post* claimed that his death was the result of a "sad accident," of injuries sustained when he fell from his bed at home. According to the *Ralls County Times*, "He had been sick for several months, was the morning of his death apparently no worse than usual, but when he attempted to walk across the room he dropped dead."[22]

This may have stirred gossip about whether Mollie had a role in hastening John Scott's death. He left a life insurance policy of two thousand dollars with the Illinois Life Association, but the company balked at paying the benefit. According to Perry Tinsley, executor of Scott's estate, Scott had paid all premiums at the time of his death, but the company claimed that the policy had lapsed on April 29, 1906, because of nonpayment of the semiannual premium.[23]

As executor of John Scott's estate, Tinsley hired Bowling Green attorney John S. Fitzgerrell, who filed a suit on May 10, 1907, to force the company to pay Mollie. The Illinois Life Association, represented by Hannibal attorney George A. Mahan and Bowling Green's Jefferson Davis Hostetter, resisted. In an amended answer to the plaintiff's suit, the company acknowledged that the insurance policy had a clause that provided for using part of the guaranty fund to purchase extended insurance, but argued that Scott had failed to give proper written notice that he intended to do so. Finally, on February 21, 1908, Tinsley withdrew the suit, paid court costs, and requested dismissal of the case, probably as the result of a settlement with the Illinois Life Association.[24]

This was the more well-trod traditional path that would soon lead Mollie to Ilasco, but her three younger sisters were more influenced by the growing public role of women in the late nineteenth century. In fact, Laura, Emma, and Feemy were partly representative of competing versions of the "New Woman" who was challenging barriers to women's full participation in American society at that time. For example, Laura stepped into the public arena through one of the most widely accepted and socially approved activities for women at that time—church involvement. As a charter member of the Saverton Methodist Church, she led a public campaign in the area to help organize the congregation and solicit subscriptions for a bell for the new church. Traveling from town to town in 1889, she raised money from sympathetic friends and institutions in a well-publicized campaign to promote the church. She continued to play an active role in the church until her early death at the age of thirty-five in 1895.[25]

Emma, besides helping Laura and others to organize the Saverton Methodist Church, had additional intellectual interests that she cultivated through public participation in civic literary groups. She played a leading role as an officer in the Saverton Literary Society alongside former state representative Richard Dalton and other civic-minded leaders. Members of this organization presented papers, recited poetry—including Abraham Lincoln's favorite poems—and debated important political, economic, philosophical, and social issues ranging from foreign policy to labor unions. This encouraged women such as Emma to formulate, clarify, and defend their intellectual positions on a range of issues in the public arena. A budding intellectual who helped to solidify the Sykes family's standing in the community, Emma participated in the Saverton Literary Society until she died at age twenty-four while giving birth on January 8, 1890, just nine months after marrying. Her newborn daughter died along with her.[26]

For Emma, death cut short a growing intellectual awakening, but according to the dominant gender strictures of the late nineteenth century, "natural" women did not seek intellectual stimulation or autonomy. As more and more college-educated women sought careers, personal autonomy, and productive outlets for their talents and creative energies, a confining Victorian ideology condemned them for channeling energies into higher education, social activism, or social independence instead of marriage and domestic pursuits. The New Woman, according to this view, was disruptive to harmonious social and gender relations. Countless male doctors, educators, politicians, psychiatrists, and asylum directors warned that chasing intellectual stimulation and independence would damage women's emotional and physical health and perhaps lead even to insanity.[27]

Of the Sykes daughters, however, it was Feemy who most resembled the New Woman. The evidence is sketchy on her adolescent and early adult years, but she was nine years old when her mother bought the mill site along the public road in Saverton, and not quite thirteen when her father died. As she grew into her early teens, the nearby sight of steamboat traffic on the Mississippi and the construction of railroad tracks near their house along the river perhaps stirred feelings of wanderlust and a desire to learn more about the world. In addition, the turmoil of Mollie's first marriage around that time helped to reinforce an awareness of predatory men and women's social vulnerability.

It is not clear how Feemy acquired her economic resources or where she received an education and met her husband, but she apparently returned to her Pennsylvania roots for the latter. Perhaps at the encouragement of her maternal aunt, Euphemia Webb, who lived in Baltimore, she left her mother's household and moved to that city. By 1880, she had married John A. J. Koller, a thirty-seven-year-old clerk who had grown up in Shrewsbury township in York County, Pennsylvania. John's family probably knew the Sykeses and Webbs, given their common roots in Shrewsbury township. Now nineteen years old, Feemy had married a man nearly twice her age with a seven-year-old daughter (Emma) from his previous marriage to Georgianna Medinger, now deceased. Their extended household also included John's fifty-six-year-old mother (Ellen), as well as his thirty-nine-year-old widowed sister (Mary Marsh) and her ten-year-old daughter (Minnie).[28]

For most, if not all, of the next thirteen years, John's relatives continued to live in the household. This put added strain on the marriage, and it increased the demands on Feemy as wife, step-mother, sister-in-law, daughter-in-law, and aunt-in-law. Whether she and John had children of their own is not entirely clear. The federal census enumerator in 1900 recorded that she had given birth to one child, and that this child was still alive at the time of the enumeration, but no child appears in any other records that I have used.[29]

After thirteen years of marriage, Feemy ended the relationship, perhaps in part because it stifled the expression of her intellectual interests and creativity as a writer. On August 5, 1893, she petitioned for a divorce, which the Baltimore circuit court soon granted, and this paved the way for a new life of independence, autonomy, travel, self-directed studies, and self-indulgence. She moved to Manhattan and worked as a writer, although it is not clear what kind of writing she did, or for whom. She returned to Hannibal on many occasions, but spent much of her time rotating between New York City, Baltimore, and Washington, D.C. At times over the next twelve or thirteen years, she also lived in St. Louis and Shawnee, Oklahoma. The freedom and autonomy of her new life thrilled her, for as she explained, she did not like to be tied down: "I am a writer, and I spend most of my time wherever I please. I don't spend any specified time in any place."[30]

Whatever the source of Feemy's income, she had enough economic security to underwrite a life of travel and several important property transactions. Due in part to the death of her sister Laura, she acquired two lots and a house at 338 Chestnut Street in Hannibal in 1900. At the time, she was temporarily staying in that house along with Mollie and their mother, whose husband, Benjamin F. Eby, had died on October 1, 1892, and whose house in Saverton had burned down in 1896. Also staying in Feemy's new house were Charles, Lewis, Seth, and Benjamin F. (Frank) Eby, Jr. Laura and Charles Eby had bought this property on March 5, 1895, but Laura died on May 29 of that same year. After her husband could not or would not pay the promissory note, the sheriff conducted a sale of the property at the front door of the Hannibal Court of Common Pleas. At the sale on November 19, 1900, Feemy picked up the property for $150. This provided a place where her family could continue to live for the time being, a source of rental income, and a base of operations for her in the area.[31]

Feemy, who was more critical-minded than Mollie, did not conform to traditional images and social expectations in regard to women. Her unrestricted freedom of mobility as a woman who chose divorce, along with her failure to live up to the caregiver responsibilities commonly assigned to women, drew resentment, particularly in a rural county such as Ralls. For example, when Sarah F. Murphy Sykes, the wife of Feemy's brother Tom, died as the result of a miscarriage in 1901 and left six children in the care of their father, the family expected Feemy to take care of them. She was divorced and had the wherewithal and the time. According to Jane Hemeyer, whose mother Ruby was the youngest of Tom Sykes's kids and a preschooler at the time, Feemy's refusal to do so strained family relations. In the view of family members, Feemy had selfishly neglected her motherless nieces and nephews.[32]

Feemy withstood social and family pressures to exchange a life of independence for a nurturing role as the surrogate mother of her brother's children. As a result, Tom Sykes, who at the time farmed outside New London, put Mabel, his unmarried teenage daughter, along with the younger children, in a hotel in town where they in effect raised themselves for awhile. Cora, the oldest daughter, was no longer in the household, having married Andrew J. Lusk on August 10, 1900. She now had a baby of her own to raise. The oldest boys—Roy A., Todd, and Harry—were apprenticed out to farm families in the area. Mabel, who would soon die from tuberculosis, supervised the younger ones—Zella Pearl, Van, and Ruby—in the hotel, where their father regularly looked in on them. This arrangement prevailed until Tom Sykes married Margaret Harris of New London on June 9, 1904. The children then rejoined the household of their father and his new wife.[33]

Partly as the result of occupational moves and geographical relocations on the part of Feemy's half brother, Harry Eby, who was now a bookkeeper, and stepbrothers Frank, Charles, and Seth Eby—all of whom were railroad contractors—she expanded her travels into the Oklahoma and New Mexico Territories. In March 1902, when the Santa Fe Railroad rolled into Shawnee (Pottawatomie County), Oklahoma, for the first time, so did she. On April 30, 1902, not long after Harry relocated to the nearby town of Tecumseh, she purchased a lot for twenty-one hundred dollars in an addition to the relatively new but growing town of Shawnee. A notarized mortgage that she signed to borrow one hundred dollars for the purchase indicated that she was a resident of Pottawatomie County. She may have been staying with her brother Harry at the time. In May 1907 she sold the Shawnee property while in New York City, only to buy it back again a few weeks later. Between 1910 and 1914, she invested in a rooming house on that property at 232 Union Avenue, which she owned for the rest of her life.[34]

Divorced at the age of thirty-two and excited by a new life after marriage, Feemy, like many cultured urban middle-class women in the Victorian era, shared a somewhat narcissistic preoccupation with cosmetic appearance.[35] In October 1902, at age forty-one, she entered a branch office of the John H. Woodbury Dermatological Institute in Washington, D.C., to discuss the removal of a "frown" wrinkle between her eyebrows and the removal of two "laughing" wrinkles on the sides of her nose. Upon the recommendation of the officer in charge, she went to New York City later that month to see Dr. Frederick S. Kolle, Woodbury's chief surgeon. She asked about the use of massage to remove the wrinkles, but Kolle explained that he could remove them through a much more effective technique that was both painless and scar-proof. According to Feemy, "He said he had a better way of treating it, which was to cut the scalp and draw the ligaments, I think he said, or the skin, which would give the face an upward look, take out all the wrinkles and brighten my face and make me look ten years younger and prettier."[36]

After examining Feemy on August 12, 1903, Kolle concluded that her scalp was too tight for such a facelift technique, and he instead opted for a different procedure. Unfortunately, he then botched it. To get rid of the wrinkles, he injected her with a compound of paraffin between the eyes and on each side of the nose. In addition, he removed a mole from her upper lip. Because he apparently injected too much paraffin or failed to massage the injected facial areas enough, the procedure left Feemy in pain with a swollen, lumpy jaw and a very inflamed nodule resembling a boil between her eyes. "I went home," she later recalled. "My face began to swell at once . . . it turned blue and green, and I though[t] I was getting lock jaw or blood poisoning. I suffered constant pain."[37]

On October 27, 1903, Feemy filed a suit against Kolle and the institute, but the case did not go to trial for more than three years. At the time of the trial on November 15, 1906, she still had residual swelling in her jaw and a painful red protuberance between her eyebrows that caused severe headaches if pressed on or rubbed. A jury found Kolle and the institute guilty of malpractice and awarded Feemy $1,200 in damages and $158.86 in court costs, far short of the $10,000 in damages that she had requested. Kolle and the Woodbury Dermatological Institute appealed to the appellate division of the New York State Supreme Court, but the high court upheld the award.[38]

The impact of this case on Feemy's countenance and emotional health is hard to ascertain from the evidence. The experience did cause her to seek medical help for her "nerves,"[39] but it is doubtful that this was the source of the nervous problems that plagued her for the remainder of her life. During the trial, a couple of doctors testified that medical procedures could remove the lump from her jaw and get rid of the redness between the eyes, but another doctor testified that the paraffin-related damage was permanent. It is not known whether Feemy sought further treatment or simply decided to live with the facial problems. If the latter is true, this must have had a quite traumatic effect on her, especially considering that before the medical procedure she was very conscious of her appearance and eager to get rid of facial signs of aging.

The case did little to enhance Feemy's respect for conventional authority—whether corporate, medical, or legal. Kolle, a salaried employee of the Woodbury Dermatological Institute, was deceptive on the witness stand in regard to his previous professional experience and in regard to the compound that he had injected into her skin. At first he led the jury to believe that he had not used paraffin, but under cross-examination he acknowledged that he in fact had used it in the compound. He also claimed initially that he was in private practice before joining Woodbury in 1900, but later admitted on the stand that he instead worked for an optical company, fitting customers for glasses.[40]

Feemy had good reason not only to see Kolle as an incompetent "company" doctor but also to be unhappy with her own lawyers, who despite the court victory had mishandled the case. Her financial award might have been even larger had the lawyers included a breach-of-contract allegation when they filed the suit against Kolle and the institute. During the trial, Feemy's attorneys tried to persuade the judge to allow them to amend the complaint, but he refused. This forced them to try the case solely on the complaint of malpractice, which limited the size of the court-ordered judgment on Feemy's behalf. Thus, after three years of delays, emotional frustration, continued facial inflammation and swelling, and numerous trips to other doctors, she had little to show for her efforts by the time attorneys took their cut from her award.[41]

Even before her experiences in this case, Feemy had been drawn to the mystical aspects of physical and emotional healing, including the power of hypnosis, magnetic healing, and clairvoyance. Her interests along these lines grew out of the spiritualist movement that had attracted many thinkers and reformers in the nineteenth century, particularly in the antebellum period. By the turn of the twentieth century, spiritualism as an organized movement was in sharp decline, but many individuals continued to be drawn to séances, astrology, mesmerism, hypnotism, and spirit phenomena.[42]

In 1902, around the time Feemy purchased property in Shawnee, Oklahoma, her attraction to the unconventional teachings of Sidney Weltmer prompted her to enroll in a course on the power of hypnotic suggestion and clairvoyance at his popular American School of Magnetic Healing in Nevada, Missouri. Weltmer, a licensed Southern Baptist preacher with well-educated parents, had established the institute in 1897 after leaving the pulpit in Sedalia to pursue healing. Influenced by his own recovery from tuberculosis, by self-directed study of mesmerism, and by his teaching experience in a Sedalia business college, he and a business partner created a boardinghouse structure in Nevada where patients could stay, and where disciples could study thought transference and "the science of healing" by attending three lectures per day for ten days at the cost of one hundred dollars.[43]

Weltmer's renowned healing powers attracted thousands of curious onlookers and desperate cure-seekers looking for relief from a variety of afflictions ranging from asthma to tobacco addiction to insanity. To cultivate business, he and his associates provided hypnotic entertainment to public audiences in a densely packed auditorium that held several hundred people. Because of Weltmer's growing popularity, money poured into Nevada, especially into the bank account of the institute, which handled hundreds of patients daily. This in turn drew countless practitioners of psychotherapy to Nevada. As a result, the town was transformed into a wellness center teeming with an eclectic assortment of magnetic healers, clairvoyants, and others promising miracle cures. Widely advertised and controversial, Weltmer's institute even featured correspondence courses in magnetic healing, and it later became the site of annual conventions of the American Association of Suggestive Therapeutics.[44]

Unfortunately for Weltmer, he also attracted the attention of conventional physicians in the area, who convinced postal authorities to pull the plug on mail services to the institute. On May 15, 1900, the postmaster general authorized Nevada's postmaster to stop delivering all mail to the school on grounds that

Weltmer was engaged in illegal use of the postal system to defraud customers. This was intended, of course, to cripple the institute financially, for Weltmer took in thousands of dollars from customers and clients through the mail. In response, the American School of Magnetic Healing filed a suit against the postmaster general, lost the case in the U.S. Circuit Court for the Western District of Missouri, and then on January 29, 1902, took an appeal to the U.S. Supreme Court. On November 17, 1902, the institute triumphed when the Supreme Court reversed the judgment.[45]

It was during this period of legal harassment that Feemy developed an interest in the institute. In early 1902, the very year that she enrolled, Weltmer and one of his disciples, J. O. Crone, had gone to Washington, D.C., to deliver a series of lectures, treat numerous clients, including several U.S. senators and their wives, and no doubt to look after the suit pending in the Supreme Court. It was perhaps one of these lectures that inspired Feemy to attend the institute in Nevada. She may have gone there simply to gather writing material, but she probably arrived with some background and previously cultivated interests in magnetic healing, clairvoyance, and hypnosis.[46]

Feemy learned the art of hypnotism, one of the chief components of the institute's healing strategies. According to family memory, she both claimed and demonstrated upon request the power to induce willing participants into trances. Maxine Harris recalled hearing her mother-in-law, Pearl Sykes Harris, relate a story of how Feemy on a visit to Tom Sykes's house entertained with her hypnotic powers. According to the story, family members were seated around the dining table when teenagers Pearl and her friend, Carrie Scott, urged "Aunt Feem" to put them in a trance. Feemy at first refused, but after considerable coaxing from them, she relented. Carrie reportedly entered a trance, alarming friends and family when she did not come out of it until the next day.[47]

Feemy's search for wellness also took her into the Great Southwest, where a variety of flamboyant magnetic healers, folk doctors, herbalists, snake-oil salesmen, and other itinerant lecturers and healers offered their services to frontier customers. Some, like brothers Roscoe G. and George R. Milling, drew on their Native American heritage and the basic components of Weltmerism to sell a package of healing services that blended the use of hypnotism, massage, magical water, and magnetism. They opened sanitariums in a number of west Texas towns, including Putnam, Glen Rose, and Mineral Springs, where patients came to enjoy special baths and treatments, drink from artesian wells, and relax to the music of orchestras employed by the proprietors.[48]

When Feemy's niece, Mabel, contracted tuberculosis, Feemy took her to the Southwest for such alternative health treatments. They may have stopped first at Weltmer's Institute in Nevada, or at mineralized water resorts in west Texas, but they apparently also made their way to hot springs resorts in New Mexico Territory, long known as a haven for consumptives and other health-seekers. At a time when state officials and owners of many health resorts in Texas and the Southwest had begun to discourage and turn away tuberculars, the territory of New Mexico still welcomed all health-seekers.[49]

Although the popularity of such spas and mineral springs retreats had contributed to the demise of cold-water cures that had been popular earlier in the nineteenth century, the two approaches still retained certain common features. Those in charge of water-cure establishments stressed not only the magical curative powers of water but also the importance of fresh air, relaxation, exercise, and dietary and other lifestyle changes. In some cases, such retreats also offered a female-centered culture and community that helped to nurture gender consciousness. Particularly for young women such as Mabel, who spent her youth caring for younger brothers and sisters after their mother's death, these centers offered an attractive social atmosphere and escape from a tedious, daily routine of unremitting work. Without Feemy's help and encouragement, Mabel probably would have never sought such treatments, for it was primarily middle- and upper-class clients who could afford to stay for extended periods at these establishments.[50]

Feemy sought similar treatments for herself, as well as for Mabel, sometimes staying for months at a time. A bundle of energy on certain occasions while prone to excessive fatigue and exhaustion on others, she periodically traveled on the Santa Fe

Railroad to New Mexico (probably Las Vegas) for prolonged treatments to recover from nervous and physical exhaustion. Like many middle-class women at the turn of the century, she at times displayed symptoms of irritability, physical weakness, nervous ailments, and other debilitating "fashionable diseases." Like many others, too, she tried magnetic healing, homeopathic, and water-cure remedies out of frustration with more conventional medical practices and orthodox physicians. If she did indeed suffer from manic depression, she was probably aware that in the early 1900s some hospitals for the insane were touting continuous hot-water therapy to calm highly nervous, excitable patients afflicted with mental disorders.[51]

For many orthodox (predominantly male) doctors disturbed by the popularity of magnetic healing and alternative health remedies at the time, the underlying cause of nervous ailments and spiritualism's popularity among restless women such as Feemy was rooted in a rejection of the traditional women's sphere. In other words, critical thinking would purportedly lead women astray and inflict untold psychological and physical damage, particularly to reproductive organs. In the end, according to the prevailing wisdom, this would bring on hysteria and insanity.[52]

In keeping with popular cultural attitudes, however, some doctors inverted the alleged interrelationship of women's reproductive diseases, nervous ailments, hysteria, insanity, and rebelliousness. They argued that the uterus held the key that unlocked the secrets as to why some women felt compelled to challenge their subordination to male authority. According to one well-known physician, R. Frederic Marvin, reproductive diseases were not the result, but rather the cause, of some women's rebelliousness and attraction to more radical doctrines. "The angle at which the womb is suspended in the pelvis frequently settles the whole question of sanity or insanity," he explained. "Tilt the organ a little forward—introvert it, and immediately the patient forsakes her home, embraces some strong ultraism—Mormonism, Mesmerism, Fourierism, Socialism, oftener Spiritualism." In his view, a woman suffering from "utromania" was convinced "that she has some startling mission in the world. She forsakes her home, her children, her duty, to mount the rostrum and proclaim the peculiar virtues of free-love, elective affinity, or the reincarnation of souls."[53]

For some trained physicians, then, a heavy dose of submissiveness, domesticity, and male authority would provide the perfect antidote for what ailed women such as Feemy. What ailed was a selfish devotion to education, social autonomy, engagement in public issues, ambition, and intellectual and business pursuits. Such pursuits, according to the prevailing medical and cultural wisdom, would upset women's physiological equilibrium. In the view of Dr. George Beard, a preeminent medical authority on "neurasthenia," these pursuits exhausted a woman's supply of "nerve force." For him, whereas urban middle-class white women were the ones most likely to suffer from this, "The Indian squaw, sitting in front of her wigwam, keeps almost all of her force in reserve." In an analysis filled with racist cultural assumptions, he attributed this to what he regarded as "the slow and easy drudgery of the savage domestic life in the open air—unblessed and uncursed by the exhausting sentiment of love; without reading or writing or calculating; without past or future, and only a dull present."[54]

One remedy for nervous women that had become popular among conventional male medical authorities by the 1870s and 1880s was the "rest cure" developed by a prominent Philadelphia doctor, S. Weir Mitchell. To restore patients' "femininity," Mitchell took them from their homes and made them stay in bed for about six weeks in an isolated environment, allowing them to see or discuss their ailments with no one other than him and an employed nurse. He also denied them access to reading materials, forcing them to become ever dependent and submissive to his authority. Patients, while bedfast, gorged themselves on food to gain weight, and they received a daily treatment of massage and electricity to keep the muscles firmed up. By the time their stay ended, they were often overweight, infantilized, and submissive—at times even addicted—to his all-encompassing authority.[55]

Little wonder, then, that Feemy and many of her contemporaries rejected such remedies and became increasingly angry and insistent that less, not more, dependency on men was the answer to their problems. Feemy chose not to remarry, preferring to be unencumbered by marital obligations. With her own economic resources and a large trunk filled with personal belongings, she was constantly in and out of train stations, crisscrossing the nation at what was often a frenetic pace to visit relatives, vacation, study alternative theories of healing, and gather material for her writings. Her sister Mollie regularly gave her advice on how to "catch" a rich husband, but the peripatetic Feemy did not jeopardize an active, independent lifestyle by reentering marriage.

As the years ahead would reveal, the law was another source of empowerment for Feemy, who by the early 1900s had acquired considerable legal expertise, apparently through self-study. Former neighbors in Ilasco later recalled her powerful intellect and knowledge of the law, as well as her personal eccentricities. In fact, she became known as the community's resident legal expert. Many asked her for legal advice when they ran into her in the stores of Ilasco, and she shared with them her critical analysis of the shortcomings of the legal process and of the lawyers who manipulated it for their own material ends. On one occasion, as Ilasco resident Angelo Venditti later recalled, she responded to a male questioner after an exchange by pointing a finger and lecturing, "Young man, you've got a lot to learn."[56]

Although the law represented an important outlet for some of Feemy's intellectual passion, this was an area that provided few professional opportunities for women at the time, despite important breakthroughs. Although most law schools accepted female students, and most states admitted women to the bar by the early twentieth century, the law remained a thoroughly male-dominated profession with formidable structural barriers for women. By 1910, the year in which litigation began over Sam Heinbach's will in Ilasco, there were only fifteen hundred female lawyers in the entire nation. Most wound up working in some other capacity for women's organizations, government agencies, journals, and colleges.[57]

Institutionalized masculinity, a central feature of the nineteenth-century legal system, still cast a long shadow over the legal profession at the time Feemy entered Ralls County courtrooms to do battle over the Ilasco tract. The county probate court, soon to become a quagmire for her and Mollie, was an institution that had long reflected male prerogatives and attitudes and women's special vulnerability in regard to property.[58] Moreover, bar association meetings, judges' chambers, courtrooms, and informal and formal professional codes were filled with masculine discourse, rituals, and assumptions. In St. Louis, for example, the exclusion of women from the area bar association prompted Victoria Conkling-Whitney to found the Women's Bar Association of St. Louis in 1912. When feminists mounted a challenge to the barriers against women's participation in the legal profession, many male lawyers in the late nineteenth century resisted, insisting that women inherently lacked the intellectual and physical attributes necessary for the tough business of lawyering.[59]

Despite such attitudes, it is clear that on the eve of the property dispute in Ilasco, Feemy was not one to leave legal matters entirely to lawyers. We can only imagine the resentments that she provoked when she stepped into the courts of Ralls County as an ad hoc attorney, or even when she played a role outside the courthouse in taking depositions, lining up witnesses, and devising strategy on her sister's behalf. As we shall see, she took a hands-on approach despite the protestations of Mollie's lawyers as well as the frustrations of her own counsel. In particular, Feemy enjoyed personally confronting those in authority who had offended her or Mollie. During the suit against the Woodbury Dermatological Institute in 1903, for example, she insisted on serving the subpoena in person to the doctor who had bungled the cosmetic procedure on her face.[60]

By 1910, Feemy had become an increasingly angry woman who was anything but deferential to men whom she suspected of taking advantage of women. In a capitalist society whose legal superstructure and commercial relationships rested on the sanctity of contract, she was especially combative when men failed to live up to their contractual obligations. Whether a contract of marriage or a commercial contract for goods and services, she aggressively took men to task for their failure to fulfill the terms of their contractual relationships. This disturbed some who regarded her confrontational behavior as a violation of proper conduct for women.

A good example is Hannibal's Josh Brashears, who faced her

wrath on May 5, 1909, when he went to her house to collect a bill for carpentry work that he had done for her. Either because she disputed the bill or because of the poor quality of his work, she gave him a sharp tongue-lashing at the door. He was so outraged by the "unladylike" boldness with which she attacked him that he filed a complaint against her for allegedly disturbing his peace. The police arrested her, but in a trial before Judge Thomas Anderson, she was acquitted and released. As a local newspaper observed, "Brashears evidently doesn't like to have women talk to him in anything but a moderate feminine tone."[61]

Three months before this confrontation, Feemy's anger at scheming lawyers had deepened as the result of her direct role in defending Mollie's interests in a battle over the estate of John M. Scott (Mollie's deceased husband) in Bowling Green. John's will left Mollie a one-third life-interest in his real estate, stipulating that upon her death this would then pass to his son and daughter, but there was an important complication. John legally owned only a one-third interest in the real estate because his two adult children each held a one-third interest as stipulated in the will of their deceased mother, Nanny Tinsley Scott.

This meant that the estate had no real immediate value to Mollie or John's children—Joseph Scott and Maude Ratcliffe—unless they could reach an agreement on how to divide it, but if they did attempt such an agreement, the effort failed. Mollie was perhaps unwilling to give up the security guaranteed in her life-interest in the estate, even though she remarried in December 1908 and no longer lived in Bowling Green. After all, as we shall soon see, the new marriage to Ilasco's Sam Heinbach was a high-risk gamble, and the prospects of life in Sam's log cabin at that time hardly afforded security and stability.

On January 12, 1909, just weeks after Mollie remarried, the Scott children filed a partition suit against her. With Bowling Green attorney Jefferson Davis Hostetter representing them, Joseph Scott, who lived in North Carolina, and Maude Ratcliffe, of Jacksonville, Illinois, requested sale of the land with proceeds to be distributed among the parties to the suit after the payment of delinquent taxes. In a move that caught Mollie off guard, they named as codefendant John S. Fitzgerrell, her lawyer in the earlier suit to force the Illinois Life Association to release payment of John Scott's death benefit to her. The children alleged that Mollie may have conveyed her life-interest in the estate to Fitzgerrell in payment of attorney fees.[62]

The suggestion that Fitzgerrell had somehow obtained a claim to the property as Mollie's lawyer brought Feemy hurriedly to Bowling Green to defend her sister's interests against the Scott children and, if necessary, against her former lawyer, too. On February 5, 1909, armed with the power of attorney to act on Mollie's behalf, Feemy went to the circuit clerk's office in Bowling Green and filed a petition denying that Mollie had conveyed her life-interest in the property to Fitzgerrell or anyone else. Requesting that the real estate in question be partitioned in accordance with John Scott's will to protect Mollie's life-interest, she protested that if Fitzgerrell, in fact, had maneuvered to get his name on the deed, then he had done so "by misrepresentation and fraud."[63]

In the meantime, Fitzgerrell was playing a double game. He had worked to get his name on the deed, but not through Mollie, as the Scott children alleged. He did so through the children themselves. On February 4, the day before Feemy filed her petition, Ratcliffe and Scott concluded an arrangement with Fitzgerrell. What they received off the record in return is not clear, but for one dollar they quitclaimed to him their interests in the estate. When Perry Tinsley, the executor of John Scott's estate, conducted a private sale of the property two days later as ordered by the Ralls County probate court, it was Fitzgerrell who bought the thirty-acre strip for only $100, and the tract in Bowling Green for $150. The role of Hostetter, the Scott children's lawyer, in the arrangements is unclear, but on February 16, 1909, he appeared in court, paid the costs, and requested dismissal of the case.[64]

The dispute over John Scott's estate is significant for three important reasons. First, it revealed an important dimension of the relationship between Mollie and Feemy. It illustrated a pattern in which Feemy would help to clean up behind Mollie in legal entanglements with adult children of a dead husband. Second, by playing the Scott children against Mollie to his own advantage, perhaps with the cooperation of Hostetter, Fitzgerrell deepened the contempt of both sisters for lawyers. Despite recent efforts by the state legislature and Missouri Bar Association to standardize and professionalize admission requirements to practice law, Mollie and Feemy shared what was a common public perception of lawyering as a money-grubbing business rather than as an honorable, dignified profession.[65] Their experiences in this case did nothing to dispel the view that courthouses were playgrounds for crafty lawyers who manipulated law to further their own economic self-interests.

Finally, in the earlier suit to force the Illinois Life Association to pay John Scott's death benefit, Mollie had bumped up against George A. Mahan, counsel for the life insurance company. Mahan was a powerful corporate attorney from Hannibal who represented many banks and companies in northeast Missouri. A former Democratic state representative, he was a member of the board of directors of the Hannibal Mutual Building and Loan Association, the Hannibal National Bank, and the Mississippi Valley Trust Company in St. Louis. Most significantly, he was the chief area attorney for the Atlas Portland Cement Company, which had recently built its Ilasco plant just outside Hannibal.[66]

The conflict over John Scott's estate thus involved several figures who would become even more closely acquainted in the years ahead. Mollie and her urbane sister had taken very different roads in life, but by 1910 they would link up in Ilasco. Until now, Feemy had been the bold, adventurous one with an exciting life of intellectual stimulation and travel, but Mollie was about to initiate a drama that would put both of them at the center of a political firestorm in Ilasco. It was there in the "city of dust" that their paths, along with those of several ambitious lawyers, politicians, and cement company officials, would cross again. Designing women were about to confront designing men in a furious battle over the future of Atlas's "foreign colony" in Tom Sawyer's backyard.

Three

Marrying "Down" for Money

Mollie and Samuel Heinbach

> Even when he [Samuel Heinbach] was sober he wouldn't dress very much, [he would] go barefooted and never dressed very much.
>
> —*H. F. Fleurdelys, Sam Heinbach's agent, 1911*

Given Feemy's spiritualist background, critical outlook, and divorce, she likely shared the view of nineteenth-century spiritualists and other reformers who complained that marriage was often the source of women's degradation and subservience to men. Perhaps none expressed this view more clearly than Marietta Stow, who complained in 1876 that a woman's "individuality is confiscated upon the rose-wreathed altar of Hymen. She may have sold herself for a home, or she may have married for love; it is all the same: her place and her duties are made very plain by inexorable laws. She is a most silent partner."[1]

Lizzie Doten, a spiritualist writer and trance speaker, also expressed this in an 1870 essay, "Marrying for Money," in which she emphasized that economic necessity often drove women into degrading marriages devoid of any spiritual quality. Other spiritualists shared this critique of marriage and sympathized with women condemned to endure such empty relationships. For Feemy, now freed by divorce with an independent source of income to support an autonomous lifestyle of travel and adventure, this critique was about to assume a special relevance that extended to her sister's plight after the death of John M. Scott, Mollie's fourth husband.[2]

After John's death, Mollie quickly searched for a new husband to provide economic security in her old age. Her life experiences had progressively deepened her cynicism toward marriage, and if any romantic notions lingered, they were swept away by the economic realities that faced her. She certainly did not worship the socially constructed mystique that surrounded marriage, but unlike Feemy she needed and pursued marriage for financial security and status. At a time when Feemy was spending a lot of money on train tickets to pursue writing, intellectual, and health-related interests, Mollie chased money for more traditional goals and purposes. For Mollie, as we shall see, finding a prospective husband with money had become a game that she had come to relish. In her view, a prospective husband should be scouted much like a real estate deal.

Mollie rejected prevailing cultural assumptions that the pursuit of wealth and materialistic designs were to be expected and encouraged among men, but not among women. Such "grasping" behavior among women was regarded as unnatural and destructive. "Ideal" women were to focus instead on their nurturing duties as mothers and wives and leave the nasty, competitive world of the marketplace to their husbands, sons, and fathers. Despite the economic realities of marriage for women, they were not to tarnish the image of marriage by viewing it in pragmatic, economic terms. Marriage would bring women happiness and blessed fulfillment, but they were certainly not supposed to set out to "catch" a man. Instead, courtship was to be initiated only by men.[3]

Before John Scott's estate was even settled, however, Mollie was developing bold plans to acquire even greater matrimonial property. Like area lawyers and politicians, she had kept a watchful eye on developments and possibilities in the Atlas Portland Cement Company's new labor camp of Ilasco. After John's death she leased Wildwood Farm, moved to New London, and set her sights on Sam Heinbach, who owned nearly half of the land on which Ilasco was located. Sam, an alcoholic in broken health, was under normal circumstances an unlikely marriage partner for a woman with Mollie's class pretensions, background, and sensibilities, but he did own an increasingly lucrative piece of real estate. Never mind that he had revolting personal habits, lived in a tiny shack, and suffered from delirious tremors and hallucinations that marked the advanced stages of alcoholism. He had the good sense to hire an agent to run his business affairs, and because of the strategic importance of his tract, he was a prominent force to be reckoned with in Ilasco. Besides, he might not live long.[4]

There was nothing in Sam's past to predict that he would ever enjoy financial success and power in his old age. In fact, for many Americans at the time who were preoccupied with the genetic assumptions of the growing field of eugenic studies, his life, habits, and behavior, particularly in his final years, reinforced popular images of "poor white trash." According to such prevailing stereotypes and public fears of depraved country folk, Sam's degeneracy was rooted in his genetic makeup and had nothing to do with environmental factors.[5]

It was mainly a stroke of luck that brought Sam good fortune in Ilasco, for his newfound landlord status had simply fallen into his lap after about fifteen years in the area. A native of Indiana and a veteran of the Union Army, he moved, along with his wife, Sarah, and their three children, from Cambridge, Indiana, to Watseka, Illinois, around 1880. He and Sarah had married in Richmond, Indiana, on December 24, 1872. In what would become characteristically erratic behavior, however, he and a male friend one day without warning left Watseka in a wagon. Sarah and the kids, stranded without financial resources, had no idea where he had gone. After Sarah's mother wired her money with which to come home, she and the kids returned to Cambridge.[6]

While Sarah and the children lived with her mother, Sam carved out an existence as a woodchopper in Pike County, Illinois, in an area known as the Sny along the Mississippi River across from Hannibal. He later sent money to Sarah, who at his request then brought the kids and again lived with him for awhile. After their log cabin was flooded, however, Sarah apparently had had her fill of their rough existence in the river bottoms and asked Sam to take them back to Cambridge. He complied with her request, but soon left them again without warning or resources. Sarah had expected Sam home for dinner one evening, but he did not show up. This forced Sarah, ten-year-old Jesse, six-year-old Edith, and one-year-old Naomi onto a nearby poor farm, while Sam once again returned to the tall cottonwood trees along the Illinois shore of the Mississippi River. The shock of abandonment left his oldest daughter with a vivid memory of his departure. "Well when he left he just went down the street," she later recalled, "just bare-footed, without hat or anything."[7]

Sam would never see his children again. In 1885 or 1886, he did return to Cambridge one last time to try to see his family, only to find when he reached the home of Sarah's mother that they were not there. By now they had left the poor farm, but Sarah still could not find a way to support and keep the family together. Either unable or unwilling to care for the children alone, she moved away by herself to Roseland, Indiana, leaving Jesse, Naomi, and Edith behind with her widowed mother. In the end, however, the children's grandmother took them to an orphans' home in nearby Richmond, and later they lived with an aunt before being apprenticed out to local farmers.

Sam apparently did not try to see his kids after discovering this, and Sarah remarried in 1896 without formally divorcing him. He returned to Pike County and resumed woodchopping with his partner, Theodore Johnson, until a flood in 1888 drove both of them across the river to Saverton township, about three miles south of Hannibal. There, Theodore married Eliza Jane Smashey, and on December 1, 1890, he and Sam bought as tenants in common about fifty-two acres of land on which they grew vegetables and produce for sale.[8]

It was the coming of the Atlas Portland Cement Company in 1901 that boosted the value of nearby land in northeastern Saverton township. When Sam and Theodore began leasing lots, charging ground rent of about one dollar per month, the thriving community of Ilasco suddenly sprang up on their property next to the plant. In March 1903, Ilasco workers produced the first cement at the plant, and later that year the post office opened. Until Sam and Theodore officially divided their tract in June 1906, a verbal agreement governed their collection of rents, recognizing the public road as the boundary between their holdings. They then legalized this arrangement through deeds. In March 1906, Sam also legalized his divorce from Sarah in order to eliminate a potential claim against his holdings. Rents from his 106 lots yielded a gross income of approximately eleven hundred dollars per year, which, as the Missouri Supreme Court later pointed out, amounted to "a princely income for him."[9]

Although the rentals from Sam's lots provided him with a nice income, the convenience of Ilasco's numerous saloons contributed to his ever-deepening alcohol problems. No longer pressed to devote most of his time to truck farming, he now found the saloons an easy outlet for leisure and entertainment. He continued to raise apples and cherries and to sell garden vegetables a bit, giving them away at times when he was drunk and selling them when he was sober. More and more, however, he whiled away his time in Ilasco's saloons.

Like corporations and other entrepreneurs of that era, Mollie used agents, or intermediaries, to make a marriage investment in Sam. She first inquired about the value of his property and went to Ilasco to investigate with someone who showed her the boundaries of the Heinbach tract. According to William Cutsinger, a neighboring Saverton farmer who at Mollie's request had witnessed the drawing up of John Scott's will, she offered him one hundred dollars if he could persuade Sam to marry her. With a clear sense of purpose, she set in motion forces designed to get Sam to marry her. As she later boasted to Feemy, she first wrote a letter to Sam, and "then things went."[10]

It was apparently through John Hinkson, formerly of Bowling Green, that Mollie established a relationship with Sam, but only after a shaky start. She wrote her first letter to Sam, who in turn took it to Hinkson, an Ilasco saloon owner and lessee of Sam's, to have him read it to him. Sam was not illiterate, but perhaps because of failing eyesight or frequent intoxication, he asked Hinkson to read the letter for him. Upon hearing the contents, however, Sam was unimpressed. He allegedly gestured and replied, "To hell with her."[11]

Sam did not even answer the first letter, but Mollie persisted. She soon sent another letter, and Sam again took it to Hinkson. This time, Sam asked him to answer on his behalf. Hinkson composed a letter, read it to Sam for his approval, and then sent it to Mollie, who set out to arrange a "chance" meeting. With Hinkson's help in making the arrangements, she deliberately showed up at the train depot in Ilasco at a designated time when Sam would be there. At the depot she and Sam met for the first time, and afterward she further tried to enlist the matchmaking services of J. T. Fisher, a Saverton resident and acquaintance with business interests in the Ilasco Supply Company.[12]

The road to marriage nevertheless was a bit bumpy. According to Hinkson, Sam told him one day thereafter that he was on his way to New London to marry Mollie. Something apparently went wrong, however, and when Hinkson asked Sam the next time he saw him if he had gotten married, Sam confirmed that he had gone with Mollie to New London, but pointed out emphatically that the ceremony did not take place. "No . . . God damn her—I wouldn't marry her," Sam angrily snapped. "I wouldn't marry no woman."[13]

It is not clear what sabotaged the ceremony, but Mollie refused to accept defeat. She continued to work on him through Hinkson. She quickly sent several additional letters until Sam underwent a change of heart. J. W. Tanquary, a local Methodist minister, married him and Mollie at the home of Tom Sykes, her brother, in New London on December 18, 1908.[14]

Mollie must have created quite a commotion when she moved to Ilasco with Sam. The class differences between them, as well as those between Mollie and most of Ilasco's residents, became quickly apparent when they merged their belongings and set up a household in the community. They at first lived briefly in Sam's log cabin with a box kitchen attached to it, in which his previous furnishings were valued at less than fifty dollars. The cabin was clearly inadequate, however, to accommodate Mollie's household furniture and belongings, which were insured at her insistence in the amount of eleven hundred dollars. She and Sam soon moved after he bought what was undoubtedly the nicest house in Ilasco from Dr. L. H. Tutt for six hundred dollars. They moved into their new home on a hill overlooking the town that lay between them and the cement plant. The house, situated on five or six acres of their twenty-six-acre tract that included an orchard, was more befitting their status as two of Ilasco's most prominent landlords.[15]

As the newlyweds prepared to carve out a life together in Ilasco and supervise their property, gossip ran wild in the community. The marriage touched off a lot of laughs and teasing. Dora Doyle, who lived just behind Sam's log cabin, could not resist teasing him the first time she ran into him after his marriage: "Uncle Sam, I heard you were married . . . How in the wide world did you stay sober long enough to marry?" He playfully replied, "Damn it, I wasn't sober . . . I was drunk and had a pint bottle of whisky in my pocket when I got married." Then, according to Doyle, he "put his fingers up like he had it [whiskey] in his pocket."[16]

For Mollie, however, the marriage brought rebuke from some observers. Apparently, Sam had shown up drunk for the wedding ceremony in the home of Mollie's brother and his second wife, Maggie Harris. According to Ilasco's Mary Fell, Maggie disapproved. On one occasion, when Mollie returned from visiting Maggie and Tom in New London, she told Fell that Maggie complained that she "did wrong in marrying the old man when he was drunk and [that she] only married him for his money." Mollie dismissed Maggie's criticism and reportedly replied that "she didn't care if he did drink, just so he was good to her."[17]

By all accounts, Mollie treated Sam well and met all the contractual obligations of her new marriage under trying circumstances. As the Missouri Supreme Court later noted, she was "uniformly kind and attentive" to him, "omitting for his care and comfort no wifely duty, though his filthy drunken condition often rendered the performance of these duties peculiarly onerous and revolting."[18] Ilasco's Mamie Smart recalled that Mollie "treated him with kindness as far as I could see." William H. Fisher, a Hannibal lawyer who operated an area insurance business, also observed that Mollie was "properly attentive" to Sam. Fisher insisted that Sam thought highly of her, too. Certainly Sam often expressed his high regard for Mollie to others. "I believe I have got a good woman," he bragged to Volney West, an Ilasco carpenter. He proudly invited Petru Sirbu, a Rumanian immigrant, businessman, and Atlas labor agent, to their house one Sunday to meet her and listen to her playing the piano. Sam was so impressed that he emphasized to Ola Gregory, a neighbor, that in fact Mollie "couldn't be a better wife."[19]

Mollie paid a terrible price, however, in terms of the quality of daily life with Sam. She certainly earned whatever profits she hoped to make on her marriage investment. In order to position herself to acquire his property when he died, she routinely endured and cleaned up awful messes that were the result of his drunkenness and failing health. Sam, who had lost control of his rectum muscles, often had bowel movements in his pants, and Ilasco residents at times saw him in town with flies swarming around him. On one occasion when Thomas Shannon, an Atlas worker, brought him home drunk after a Rumanian wedding celebration, Sam vomited all over the floor. Mollie quickly cleaned it up and then sat down and calmly began to play the piano while they sat there. According to Shannon, the piano playing had a soothing effect on Sam and helped him to sober up.[20]

Playing the piano was perhaps a way, too, for Mollie to tune out much of the chaos around her and bring a dignified calm to what was otherwise an undignified environment. At her behest, Sam had bought the player piano in May or June of 1909. It cost five hundred dollars, nearly as much as what they had paid for their house.[21]

The piano undoubtedly helped her to cope with many of the degrading features of her new life, and so, too, did her determination to maintain middle-class associations and appropriate social amenities in the midst of domestic chaos. She hosted small dinner parties attended by William H. Fisher and Sam's physician, Dr. R. Marvin Winn. Sam was hardly a skilled dinner conversationalist, and so the burden of conversation fell largely on her. Visits by the likes of Elizabeth Falk and her mother, friends from Bowling Green, provided Mollie ongoing contacts with a prominent, wealthy area family in the jewelry business. Such visits reminded Mollie of the world that she had left behind and that perhaps she would be able to return to in the future. They no doubt made it a bit easier to get through the days until her husband died.[22]

Differences in class, culture, and social aspirations set Mollie apart from the vast majority of Ilasco's poor residents. For many hardscrabble immigrant and native-born women in Ilasco who were forced by economic necessity into a daily grind of washing grimy cement- and coal-soiled clothing of Atlas workers, she became an object of curiosity as she played the piano, displayed her jewelry, and painted self-portraits and other designs on fine china. Her piano playing attracted curious onlookers and those looking for entertainment and social interaction. Among them was Ola Gregory, who recalled that on many evenings "there would be a crowd go up there."[23]

Mollie, who was viewed by some as "prissy," and who may have been an object of resentment as well as gossip, took her new status seriously but endured humiliating teasing as she tried to achieve status and respectability in the community. Even children's teasing often followed her as she walked to the post office with a parasol, wearing elbow-length gloves with the fingers cut out and fashionably tight clothes that suggested she was wearing a corset. Angelo Venditti later recalled how his sister Stella and other kids at times used to rush out to greet Mollie as she passed by the homes of her tenants. Venditti smiled as he described how Stella typically curtsied, bowed, and said "Good morning" to Mollie with exaggerated deference. Mollie enjoyed the attention, he said, and at times his sister would trail along behind her through town to the post office.[24]

The sight of Mollie and Sam walking together in town must have amused onlookers. Their modes of dress presented striking contrasts. The ladylike image that Mollie projected must have seemed especially comical to those accustomed to seeing Sam barefooted in the summertime with soiled pants. H. F. Fleurdelys, a French immigrant and Atlas worker whom Sam once employed as an agent to collect the Ilasco rents, pointed out that "even when he [Sam] was sober he would not dress very much, [he would] go barefooted and never dressed very much."[25]

Despite Sam's pathetic condition, he had a reputation in Ilasco as a kind, sympathetic man with a heart of gold. According to him, he could have made more money by growing produce on his Ilasco tract, but he would rather lease lots because cement plant workers needed a cheap place to live, and he "preferred to give them a show." Furthermore, many Ilasco residents borrowed money and extracted favors from "Uncle Sam," as he was affectionately known in the community. For example, Marion T. Rodgers, a teenager, borrowed money from him and repaid it by working off the debt in Sam's orchard and garden. In some cases, Sam did not charge widows any ground rent at all. In fact, he finally hired an agent to collect his rents each month rather than risk allowing his sympathies for the poor to sink him completely.[26]

Although Sam had abandoned his wife and children, he told Fred Jeffers, an Ilasco merchant, a different version of how the final separation from them occurred. He blamed it on Sarah's infidelity in Indiana. According to Sam, he came home from fishing one day, found her with another man, and simply "left it with them."[27]

Sam ducked out of parental responsibilities, but he was generous to the children of Ilasco. Thomas Hedges, an Atlas worker, remembered that Sam played Santa Claus every Christmas by giving each child a sack of candy and an orange. This generosity was not confined to Christmas. "He never saw my five-year-old child without picking her up and calling her his little sweetheart," recalled Lula Brown, who once prepared meals for cement plant workers and bought vegetables and produce from Sam. "He thought a lot of her . . . The last time I think that he saw her he took her in the drugstore and set her on the stool and paid for ice cream for her. He did this lots of times."[28]

Such generosity and kindness made life with Sam a bit easier for Mollie, and unlike her first husband, John Kellogg, Sam was not mean or rude when he was drinking. "If you would meet him with your wife," noted Mitchell Thomas Smashey, who once operated a candy store and grocery business in Ilasco, "if he was intoxicated—he would always step out to the side of the walk and wait until we passed, but he always tipped his hat, no matter where you met the man with your wife, whether in his cups or not he was always polite." Fred Jeffers further described Sam as a "sympathetic" churchgoing man: "Yes, sir, I have seen him come in church and sit in the church when the preacher was preaching, and I have seen him shed tears in church."[29]

Sam's ownership of the Ilasco tract also gave him considerable influence beyond that associated with his landlord status. Since he knew many people in the area, newcomers to the community often sought him out for important introductions. For example, when Robert Hammer moved to Ilasco from Monroe City in April of 1909, he went into the butcher business. Soon upon arriving, he went to Sam, who took him around the countryside to introduce him to farmers who could supply beef to him.[30]

From Sam's perspective, Mollie also provided important care-giving services to him. She cooked and cleaned for him, brought him considerable flattering attention, and generally took care of him during what was no doubt physically the toughest year of his life. Perhaps even more important, she brought dignity, companionship, and stability to a lonely if pathetic man whose life had become increasingly unstable and degraded.

Leaving nothing to chance in regard to the future disposition of Sam's property, Mollie soon went to work trying to convince him to devise a will. Having learned about his children, she purportedly urged John Hinkson to use his influence with Sam to persuade him to draw up a will deeding all of his property to her. In an era in which it was common for businessmen to hire agents and intermediaries to conduct business transactions, she offered to pay Hinkson for his service. He claimed that she promised that "if the will was made that I should not be forgotten . . . if the will was not broken, she would deed me a lot or two . . . as good as she had."[31]

In the meantime, Sam, too, discussed plans for a will with some of his friends in Ilasco. Volney West, a carpenter, stopped by one day to pay for some apples that his wife, Alice, had gotten from Sam. After Sam refused to accept payment, he gave West a mellow apple to eat and gestured for him to sit down. Sam then told him that he wanted to discuss making out a will. He said that he planned to leave all of his property to Mollie, who, he pointed out, "had taken him, picked him up out of the ditch, [and] kindly cared for him." In contrast, his children, who had never even bothered to contact him over the last twenty-five years, would get only one dollar each. "They deserted me when I was a poor man," Sam stressed, "and now [I've] got a little bit to keep me on and [a] little bit to leave my wife and [I'm] just going to leave them a dollar a piece and let them go."[32]

By late September 1909, Sam's sharply deteriorating health lent a sense of urgency to Mollie's efforts to convince him to draw up a will. Shortly after Dr. L. H. Tutt, a Hannibal physician and businessman with financial interests in the Ilasco Supply Company, treated him for pleurisy pain on September 22, 23, and 24, Mollie persuaded Sam that it was time at last to fix out a will. She was careful of legal considerations as she prepared for the will to be drawn up. On the evening of September 26, when she ran into constable T. B. Wilson on the public road in Ilasco, she asked him to come to the house early the next morning to witness Sam's will. She also asked him to bring Charles Perkins, an Ilasco businessman, with him to verify the will's authenticity.[33]

Shortly after eight o'clock the next morning, Mollie walked downtown to the office of John Northcutt, an Ilasco justice of the peace, and asked him to come up to the house to write a will for Sam. Judge Northcutt, constable Wilson, and Perkins arrived at the Heinbach home shortly thereafter, but found Sam sitting with a half-empty bottle of whiskey on the table in front of him. Northcutt then told Wilson and Perkins that the will would not be ready for signing for about an hour. Sam offered them a drink and told Northcutt that "he wanted to give his property to his wife" and asked him "to fix up legal papers." In keeping with Sam's wishes, Northcutt wrote a will that left all of Sam's property to Mollie. Sam left only one dollar to each of his children.[34]

Through Mollie's aggressive economic behavior, however, she had made enemies in Ilasco, among them Theodore Johnson, Sam's former partner. Shortly after she married Sam, she had examined the deed to his twenty-six-acre tract and determined that when Johnson and Sam had divided their fifty-two acres in 1906, Johnson had wrongfully claimed a strip of 2.23 acres where most of Ilasco's lucrative business section was located. To no avail, she complained to Johnson that this strip belonged to Sam and insisted that he owed them for the "ground rent" that he had collected on these lots to date.[35]

Such aggressiveness, coupled with Sam's failing health and perhaps persistent rumors about how her last husband had died, fueled community gossip that Mollie was trying to poison her ailing husband. This explains why she invited two prominent guests from Hannibal to the Heinbach home for a dinner party shortly after the will was drawn up. Since she had been forced to sue the life insurance company after John Scott's death, and since the gossip about alleged poisoning was sweeping Ilasco, she invited Sam's insurance agent, William H. Fisher, and his regular physician, Dr. R. Marvin Winn, for dinner to allay suspicions that there was anything wrong in their home.[36]

Theodore Johnson, who remained convinced that Mollie was poisoning Sam, went to their home to investigate on December 15, 1909. He first stopped at Sid Smart's saloon and convinced Smart to go with him. They then went up to the Heinbachs' house to check on Sam. When they arrived, they found a scene that disturbed them. Mollie was playing the piano and Sam was lying on a cot, very sick. Johnson and Smart then went over to Sam's cot and asked him about his relationship and life with Mollie. According to Smart, Sam assured them that "him and his wife was living happy, [that] he had a good home." Johnson, nevertheless suspicious and worried since Mollie had not called a doctor, left to summon a physician without telling her what he intended to do. He contacted Dr. Andrew J. Detweiler's office in Hannibal and left word for him to hurry to his house in Ilasco as quickly as possible.[37]

When Detweiler went to Johnson's house, he found him drunk and was surprised to learn that neither he nor his wife, Eliza Jane, required medical attention. Only then did he learn that Theodore had summoned him in fact to examine Sam Heinbach, who was not a patient of his and whom he had never even met. Detweiler was upset that Theodore had brought him to Ilasco under false pretenses, but he relented and agreed to examine Sam after Theodore convinced him that time was of the essence. "I rather protested," Detweiler later recalled, "[but] he insisted there were a great many reasons why I should go there."[38]

The intoxicated Johnson took Detweiler up the hill to the Heinbachs, but "there was quite a row" when they arrived. Mollie, furious with Johnson, at first threatened to throw him out of the house. Apparently, Sam opposed his meddling, too. "He [Johnson] never came up here for a long time before," Sam complained to Robert Hammer and Sam Smashey, neighbors and friends who were also in the house that night. "I don't want him up here." According to Hammer, Sam wanted Dr. Tutt, not Detweiler, to examine him, but he finally relented after he learned of allegations that he was being poisoned. As Detweiler later remembered, "Various things were said and done there that disturbed me some what, but I was allowed to make an examination." With no knowledge of Sam's medical history, he determined at that time that Sam, who in the meantime had fallen into a comatose stupor, was suffering from a partially diseased lung, senile dementia, and possibly tuberculosis. By this time, Sam weighed less than ninety pounds.[39]

Johnson tried to pay Detweiler's fee, but an enraged Mollie intervened and insisted that she would pay it. She then told Detweiler that neighbors were spreading rumors that she was poisoning her husband. Johnson told him that he, too, suspected her. Detweiler obtained Mollie's permission to return to examine Sam again in a few days. In his view, she at the time seemed eager to cooperate in order to clear her name in the community.[40]

Detweiler, sensing that he might be in the middle of an unfolding murder mystery, took extra precautions. When he returned on the eighteenth to examine Sam again, he conducted further tests that revealed a tiny, shriveled-up liver. Having since learned of Sam's alcoholism, he diagnosed the case as alcoholic dementia, but he was alarmed by the allegations of poisoning. After discovering that Sam's regular physician, Dr. Winn, had also examined him during the last week, Detweiler told Mollie that he would not return again unless Winn came with him. Two days before Christmas, he and Winn examined Sam for the final time. After discussing the case, the doctors agreed not to have anything more to do with the matter except in consultation with each other. As Detweiler explained, "There was considerable talk of poisoning and that sort of thing, and [it was] rather a grave matter for me to take the responsibility of that kind; if there was any possibility of poisoning, why it would necessitate careful examination and possibly an autopsy."[41]

With Sam on his Christmas deathbed and with gossip about his alleged poisoning sweeping the community, Mollie surely had mixed emotions as she contemplated what the coming new year might usher in. On the one hand, she had endured a year of marriage under what at best were trying circumstances, and she had upheld her end of the marital contract. That she treated Sam well and provided important caregiving services in their home was beyond dispute, and Sam had rewarded her appropriately in his will. On the other hand, Theodore Johnson's role in bringing Dr. Detweiler to their house was a disturbing indication that she had enemies in Ilasco and elsewhere. Johnson had his own reasons for trying to stop Mollie from inheriting Sam's estate, but time was about to reveal that he was a mere tool in the hands of others with enormous influence in county politics. Behind the scenes were powerful political figures determined to control the fate of Sam's Ilasco tract. Pending Sam's death, they were ready to manipulate Mollie's aggressive pursuit of marriage to him, and they were prepared to capitalize on his alcoholism and earlier unstable family history to force a legal showdown over the validity of his will in the courts of Ralls County.

Four

Samuel Heinbach's White Horse

> Well Sam had a very funny way of talking when he was drinking, [he'd] say little things, did not seem like much sense to, he would tell us down there [Ilasco], "when he was gone we would see nothing but [a] white horse without saddle and bridle, he would pass round," [it] seemed as though something haunted him, after he was gone that was.
>
> —*Ilasco constable T. B. (Barney) Wilson, 1911*

Sam Heinbach's death at the age of seventy on January 3, 1910, set the stage for the first of two circuit court trials over his testamentary capacity to make a will, for a prominent Democratic attorney/politician/businessman with designs on the Ilasco tract at once challenged Mollie's rights to the estate. Although the lawyers opposing Mollie in the case did not pursue the poisoning issue, a subtext throughout both trials was her use of marriage to acquire property and money. In effect, she was put on trial for having laid bare the economic realities of marriage for women in the early twentieth century.

In what became a highly celebrated case in the area, attorneys and others who opposed Mollie took advantage of her well-known entrepreneurial approach to marriage in an attempt to discredit her before local juries. Because of her actions in Ilasco, she became the object of a campaign of vilification that included attacks on her very sanity. For Mollie and Feemy, who soon stepped into the fray at Mollie's request, this would exact an enormous price. The sisters' relationship would never be the same again. Neither would property relations in Ilasco.

In the months before Sam died, Ilasco residents often heard

him predict that a white horse would mysteriously appear in the village after his death. To anyone who would listen, he rambled on about how an unbridled, unsaddled white horse would roam freely across his Ilasco tract. "You'll see," he confidently predicted with a firmness that did not match his shaky physical and mental state. As he moved from saloon to saloon, filling up before staggering back up the hill to Mollie and his house overlooking the village, he often greeted friends and neighbors by conjuring up this vision of a white horse whose symbolic significance was apparently known only to him. "After I am gone, though," he told Max Lomax, who years earlier had farmed with him on shares, "there will be a white horse pass over here without bridle or saddle, and no telling what will take place. You know what I mean by that."[1]

For some residents, Sam's strange predictions were merely the hallucinations of an old man whose mind had gone bad, ravaged by senility and a lifetime of hard drinking. Others discovered, however, that the vision of a white horse had important symbolic connections to reality. Specifically, it had to do with the future of his Ilasco tract, for in Sam's mind the white horse conjured up images of a no-holds-barred property dispute in which lawyers and those whose interests they served would ride roughshod over his estate. "When I am dead and gone," he predicted to James T. Mooter, Ilasco resident and millwright at the cement plant, "I mean [there's] going to be a lawyer or somebody else eat up this property . . . This lawyer—white horse—would have no bridle or saddle on it."[2]

Before peering through the hovering mists of alcohol surrounding Sam's mind to get a closer look at his white horse, it is important first to consider why the Ilasco tract was so important to area officials and the Atlas Portland Cement Company. And why did the company not simply buy it from Mollie after Sam's death? It is possible that Mollie at first intended to sell the tract to Atlas, perhaps through an understanding with businessmen who had close ties to the cement plant. If that was the case, something obviously went wrong when unexpected conflict unleashed forces that she could not control. The ensuing conflict may have been the product of competition between local elites—particularly between Democrats in New London and Republicans in Hannibal—to determine who could deliver the tract to Atlas and gain greater influence and political power in the process. As we shall later see, however, there is evidence to suggest that Mollie did want the property for more than purely financial reasons. She intended to make Ilasco her home and to enjoy the prestige and status that came with ownership of the tract.

From the time that Atlas first purchased options on the land for its plant outside Hannibal, it had used prominent Hannibal and New London attorneys as intermediaries to acquire land for its operations. In fact, when Hannibal attorneys George A. Mahan and George Clayton secretly negotiated the land deals for the plant site in 1901, Atlas officials at first tried unsuccessfully to buy a strip of land that soon became part of the town site of Ilasco. The company refused at that time to pay the asking price of nearly one hundred dollars per acre.[3]

By the time of Sam Heinbach's death, however, the value and importance of land in Ilasco had shot up even higher, largely as the result of the town's unanticipated, mushroomlike growth on the edge of the plant. Ilasco posed a threat to Atlas's long-range plans for land use and contributed to the company's inability to control alcohol use by workers or to improve job efficiency and productivity. From the outset, in fact, the community's saloons and proximity to the plant had frustrated plant officials, who on the eve of Sam's death had stepped up efforts to tighten control over Ilasco's institutions and regulate the lives of workers. These efforts included the formation of a company-affiliated store—the Ilasco Supply Company—in 1907 and an unsuccessful campaign in 1906 to deny saloon licenses in Ilasco. They also included construction of new company housing to relieve overcrowding and move some of Ilasco's residents further from the saloons on the perimeter of the plant.[4]

Despite these company initiatives, a bitter strike in the summer of 1909, just a few months before Sam Heinbach's death, further dramatized Atlas's failure to create a more disciplined labor force and exert control over the community. Immigrant strikers captured the company's powder magazine and dynamite and used it to blow up one of its small buildings. Nativist hatreds poured forth from local newspapers in response to the growing militancy of Ilasco's Slavic workers: newspapers typically blasted the "foreign mobs," "hunks," and "garlic-smelling" workers who protested dangerous working conditions, wages, and Atlas's anti-union policies.[5]

To make matters worse for Atlas, an even more explosive strike led by native-born machinists and Italian production workers in the late spring of 1910—less than four months after Sam Heinbach's death—put the company's failures in Ilasco in the national spotlight. This strike could not have come at a worse time for Atlas, which had recently signed a contract to provide cement for a new power station and dam at Keokuk, Iowa. Construction on this project began a week after Sam's death. By the time the costly strike's reverberations stopped, there was a shakeup at the top of Atlas's corporate command and at the Ilasco plant, and New York financier J. P. Morgan had acquired considerable control over the company. Even more important in the Hannibal area, Missouri Governor Herbert Hadley had sent the state militia into Ilasco to break the strike.[6]

Sam Heinbach's death thus coincided with Atlas's search for new strategies to stabilize Ilasco after nearly a decade of deepening public concern and warfare over saloons, "new immigrants," labor unrest, and crime in the community. Under harsh conditions, Ilasco residents did the best they could to create a stable community, but many native-born residents in the New London and Hannibal area expressed open hostility toward the "chunks of heathenism" in Atlas's camp.[7] In their view, Ilasco represented the worst of what industrialization had to offer: social volatility, class conflict, and cultural tensions created by the influx of Slavic immigrants. Perhaps the most vivid reminder of this was the occupation of the village by the militia to quell the 1910 strike.

Since Atlas was by far the largest single employer in Ralls County, many local attorneys recognized how politically advantageous it was to become disciples of the Yankee capitalists who had come to develop the area's resources. After all, there was a lot of money to be made by lawyers who as intermediaries could help Atlas to get what it wanted, particularly if what the company wanted was Ilasco land next to the plant.

The coming of Atlas afforded area attorneys an excellent opportunity to serve public as well as private interests. Of course, attorneys could pad their own pocketbooks and build greater political connections, but some could also represent injured workers in job-related damages suits and contribute to the broader stability and economic development of the area. Company-sponsored schools and churches were to play a vital role in consolidating Atlas's power in Ilasco and the Midwest. After a turbulent decade of labor unrest, local policymakers were more inclined to seek company paternalism as a replacement for the failed policy of naked repression. A lack of adequate educational facilities to accommodate the children of Ilasco's exploding population in 1910 made the need for such solutions even more pressing.[8]

For several years before his death, Sam Heinbach had watched the value of his Ilasco real estate rise sharply. When he and Theodore Johnson bought their tract about twenty years earlier, they paid only around ten dollars per acre for it. At the time of Sam's death, however, his twenty-six acres were worth between twelve thousand and fifteen thousand dollars. Throughout the years, he had refused to incorporate his tract or to sell portions of it, preferring instead to continue leasing lots at very cheap rates to cement plant workers, small businessmen, and other residents. He had left the estate to Mollie in his will, but he sensed correctly that others with entrepreneurial appetites were waiting in the wings to do battle over his estate when he died.[9]

Immediately after Sam's death, his celebrated apparition of a white horse appeared in the form of James O. Allison, a wealthy New London attorney and landowner with powerful Democratic Party connections in the state. Allison may have harbored longstanding resentments against Mollie's family, since he lived in Madisonville at the time the Sykeses arrived there in 1868. In fact, since he and Mollie were the same age, they probably attended the same school in Madisonville at a turbulent time when their families were on different sides of the Reconstruction political fence. Whatever the case, it quickly became apparent that when Mollie had burst on the Ilasco scene and married Sam, she upset Allison and others with designs on the Heinbach estate. To block her, Allison fomented a dispute over Sam's will, beginning the first leg of what would become a lengthy, wild, and spirited ride through the courts of northeast Missouri.

Allison, whose father was one of the largest landowning farmers in Ralls County, had graduated from the State Normal School in Kirksville in 1882. He then returned to Ralls County, where he became a teacher and superintendent of public schools in New London for the next two years. Between 1884 and 1890, he served in the Missouri legislature and chaired several legislative committees, including the important Committee on Corporations.[10]

By the time of Sam Heinbach's death, Allison had further enhanced his reputation and connections in state and local Democratic Party politics. After studying law at home, Allison was elected as Ralls County prosecuting attorney in 1890, and in 1896 he became a member of the Democratic Party's state committee. Governor Alexander M. Dockery appointed him as a commissioner to the Louisiana Purchase Exposition at the 1904 World's Fair in St. Louis, and Allison was chosen as a presidential elector in the national election of 1908. As the result of his extensive business interests and political contacts, the Ralls County court appointed him as a delegate to the Northeast Missouri Commercial Association Convention in Hannibal on February 3, 1910. In addition, he had a close friendship with former Missouri Governor David R. Francis, of St. Louis.[11]

Allison enjoyed considerable political popularity in Ilasco, where he had worked hard to drum up legal business and cultivate a network of political associations. From atop a bar stool in Sid Smart's saloon, where he was a "good patron," he listened to gossip, socialized, observed and encouraged divisions and squabbles in the community, cultivated clients, and learned much about the personal affairs of Ilasco residents. He had close ties to Theodore Johnson in particular, and in 1906 he had played a major role in defeating a local option campaign to outlaw saloons in the county, which undoubtedly enhanced his popularity among Atlas's hard-drinking workers. In many ways, Ilasco was his town, and he helped to ensure that its new native-born and immigrant population would seek a relationship with the Democratic Party and thus not upset the party's long-standing viselike grip on county politics. The Republican *Hannibal Courier-Post* described

Allison as the "political boss" of Ilasco with a "certain pledbian [*sic*] following."[12]

Perhaps even more important in terms of Mollie Heinbach's case, Allison's brother and law partner, Thomas E. Allison, was the probate judge of Ralls County at the time of Sam Heinbach's death. Thomas had received a law degree from the University of Missouri and served as city attorney in Hannibal between 1880 and 1890. In 1906 he was elected as judge of the Ralls County probate court. He and James established a practice together, and it was they who had handled Sam's divorce from Sarah in 1906. This put the Allison brothers in an even better position to become intimately acquainted with Sam's fragmented family history. Thomas also had real estate interests in Ilasco, where he owned houses on lots leased from both Sam Heinbach and Theodore Johnson.[13]

As soon as Mollie Heinbach filed Sam's will in the Ralls County probate court on January 8, 1910, James Allison set out to locate Sam's adult children to contest the will. Accompanied by Ilasco constable T. B. Wilson, he took a trip to Indiana in search of them. It is not clear exactly what arrangements Allison had made with Theodore Johnson, or what understanding Allison had reached with county authorities or company officials beforehand, but for legal purposes at least, it was Johnson who allegedly paid Wilson's expenses for the trip. Wilson, one of the witnesses to Sam's will, was a public officer, of course, but he later made a second trip alone on Johnson's (or Allison's) behalf to contact Sam's children. After locating Sam's only surviving children—Edith Britton in Momence (Lake County), Illinois, and Naomi Summers in Greenview (Menard County), Illinois—Allison persuaded them to sign contracts on January 17–18, 1910, conveying to him six-tenths of their interest in their father's estate if he could break the will.[14]

This enabled Allison to challenge Sam's will when it was presented for probate before his brother, the judge. Appearing in chambers with Judge Thomas Allison on February 12, 1910, were Dr. L. H. Tutt and William F. True to sign an affidavit that Sam was of sound mind at the time of his will, but James Allison produced others who disagreed. Meeting with the judge at James's behest on that same day were Ilasco residents C. F. Hoover, Mark K. Kinder, Harrison F. Decker, and George Douglas, who provided a sworn statement that Sam was *not* of sound mind at the time. Although T. B. Wilson and Charles E. Perkins, who was True's brother-in-law, had signed the will as witnesses, they, too, now told the judge that in their view Sam was of unsound mind.[15]

Judge Allison rejected the will and on February 18, 1910, appointed True, an Ilasco businessman and former justice of the peace, as administrator of Sam Heinbach's estate. This appointment assured the Atlas Portland Cement Company that it had nothing to fear from the litigation, for True had close ties to Atlas. He was an incorporator and president of the Ilasco Supply Company, which at the time operated two general stores, two butcher shops, and a drugstore in the community. This company, an Atlas subsidiary since its incorporation in 1907, had driven some of its chief business competitors out of Ilasco.[16]

After True's appointment, Mollie initiated a suit against Sam's children, who filed their response through James Allison on October 24, 1910. Britton and Summers, who had not seen their father in about twenty-five years, alleged that he was of unsound mind at the time his will was made. His condition, they argued, was the product of physical impairment due to old age and abuse of strong drugs and intoxicating liquors. This allegedly had allowed Mollie to exert undue influence over him through "coercion, threats, duress, fraud, and over persuasion."[17]

The stage was now set for the first trial in a case that featured some of the most prominent attorneys in northeast Missouri, many of whom had ties to both New London and Hannibal. To a large extent, the case pitted New London Democrats from prominent former slaveholding families against Hannibal Republicans. Joining James Allison on the defense team were Jack Briscoe, Charles T. Hays, and Hays's partner, H. Clay Heather. Hays, who later became chief justice of the Missouri Supreme Court, had important connections in both New London and Hannibal. He was born in New London in 1869 to parents with southern slaveholding roots and distant kinship ties to Mark Twain. He was the son of George C. Hays, Jr., a wealthy New London merchant and county Democratic official whose family had followed a line of migration from Virginia to Tennessee to Missouri at a time when tobacco production was booming in Missouri. In 1860, George C. Hays, Sr., and his wife, Mary J., had owned eight slaves, and after the Civil War, county registration officials disqualified him from voting because of his support for Confederate rebels.[18]

Charles T. Hays received a B.A. degree from Bethany College in West Virginia. He then studied law at the University of Missouri and in the office of New London's Reuben F. Roy, his brother-in-law. Hays was admitted to the bar, became Judge Roy's partner, and then worked as a tax attorney for Ralls County. After serving as mayor of New London, he moved to Hannibal in 1907 and became a law partner of J. Will Hays and later of Heather, a former Democratic state senator from Marion County. Charles T. Hays, who became the mayor of Hannibal in 1911, was also the next-door neighbor of W. H. Baker, new superintendent of the Ilasco cement plant at the time of the Heinbach trial.[19]

When Jack Briscoe joined the legal team headed by James Allison and Hays against Mollie Heinbach, he, too, was well familiar with Ilasco, Mollie, and Sam Heinbach, in particular. In addition, his family had deep roots in Ralls County. Born west of the town of Center, he grew up in New London and became a school commissioner and public administrator. After marrying and gaining admission to the bar in 1901, he went to work for Atlas when the cement plant opened in March 1903. At that time, he was living in Saverton on property formerly owned by Mollie's mother. He resigned at the cement plant on September 8, 1905, to open a private law office in Ilasco. Sam Heinbach hired him to collect rents on his leases, an arrangement that began in October 1905 and lasted until Briscoe, a Democrat, was elected to the office of Ralls County prosecuting attorney in 1906. According to this arrangement with Sam, Briscoe deducted a commission of 10 percent from the rentals before turning the money over to him each month. As a strong opponent of saloons in a recent local option campaign, he had often pointed to Ilasco as an example of alcohol's destructive impact.[20]

Whereas the main lawyers arrayed against Mollie represented New London's powerful Democratic families, Mollie turned to Charles E. Rendlen, Sr., one of Hannibal's finest up-and-coming

Republican attorneys, to represent her in the case. Rendlen was in the early stages of a promising career in Missouri Republican politics that later included an unsuccessful bid for the U.S. Senate in 1944. Born on May 4, 1878, to William C. and Albertina Ziegler Rendlen, he began his law practice at the age of twenty-three immediately after graduating from William Jewell College with a Bachelor of Laws degree in 1901. He served as Hannibal's city attorney from 1902 to 1904 and began to work for the Republican Party. He had extensive business contacts, and his brother Theodore was a well-known Hannibal lawyer and merchant in the liquor industry.[21]

Playing a supporting role as Rendlen's assistant in the case was Frederick W. Neeper, who in 1892 had moved to Hannibal from Clark County, Missouri, shortly after being admitted to the bar. Neeper served as Hannibal's city attorney and referee in bankruptcy for the Northern Division of the Eastern District of Missouri. Business law was his specialty, and he represented several eastern corporations in the area.[22]

As lawyers prepared for the case, Mollie, with the advice and help of her sister Feemy, did not simply sit back and defer to them. The sisters thoroughly immersed themselves in the case, taking an active role in lining up friendly witnesses in the community. The uncertainty of what would happen to the Heinbach tract unsettled Ilasco residents whose future living arrangements hinged on the outcome of the dispute. Forty friends and acquaintances of Sam Heinbach signed a statement circulated by Mollie on June 9, 1910, expressing their view that he was sane and thus mentally capable of transacting business when his will was drawn up on September 27, 1909.[23]

Although Feemy rented out her house in Hannibal and came to live with Mollie in Ilasco, it was still not clear what role, if any, she would play in the upcoming trial set for April 1911. In fact, it was still not clear whether she would even attend. Feemy had already helped to secure witnesses and plan strategy, but the work had left her thoroughly exhausted. As a result, she left the state a couple of months before the trial to undergo alternative health treatments somewhere in New Mexico. This left Mollie alone to cope with loneliness and anxieties about the legal battle that lay ahead. Mollie, who had apparently seen Feemy off at the train station when she left, wrote her a letter on January 20, 1911, expressing loneliness and concern for her health: "I got home all right. When I came in it was lonesome and so still because you were gone. I hope you will get better taking your treatment. If you find you are not getting better come right back to Hannibal."[24]

For the next two months, the sisters exchanged letters discussing the will suit, gossip, domestic matters, and Feemy's health, but Mollie grew increasingly anxious about the upcoming trial, particularly after her lawyers insisted that Feemy not attend. Rendlen and Neeper had apparently already clashed with Feemy over how to handle the case. Nevertheless, it is clear that Mollie wanted her there against the advice of her lawyers. "I wish you had the means to come," she wrote on March 16. "How much does it cost for you to come and go? Are you better? Well if you want to see Ellen [cousin Sarah Ellen Londenberg, formerly Johnson] you had better come. Hope you are better little sister."[25]

By the following week, Feemy was back in Ilasco. Her swift return was no doubt motivated in part by the news from Mollie that Rendlen and Neeper did not want her in the courtroom. Neither sister trusted lawyers, and Feemy perhaps suspected that Rendlen and Neeper were about to take advantage of Mollie. Whatever the case, Feemy rushed home for the trial at the urging of her sister.

On April 3, 1911, Judge William T. Ragland presided over the trial's opening before a packed crowd in the circuit court in New London. For four days, spectators were treated to what seemed like endless details of Sam Heinbach's most routine transactions, personal habits, conversations, and intoxicated mutterings. Courtroom observers learned everything about him, ranging from his bathroom habits to favorite church songs to the name of his dog, "Old Joe." The *Ralls County Record* called the case "one of the most interesting suits ever brought in Ralls County."[26]

As the plaintiff, Mollie's attorneys began by presenting evidence of the authenticity of Sam Heinbach's will. They faced a big problem, however, for justice of the peace John Northcutt, constable T. B. Wilson, and businessman Charles Perkins—all of whom had observed the drawing up of the will—now opposed

Mollie's claims to the estate. Although Mollie's attorneys had subpoenaed Northcutt, who had written the will, they did not put him on the stand for fear that he might present damaging testimony. Instead, Rendlen first put Perkins and Wilson on the stand to describe their role as witnesses, as well as Northcutt's role as scrivener, when the will was drawn up on September 27, 1909. Then Rendlen turned on his own witnesses, attacking Wilson and Perkins for testifying in Judge Allison's probate court in February 1910 that the will was not authentic. Suggesting that they were engaged in deception, Rendlen elicited testimony from Wilson to reveal that at the behest of and allegedly in the pay of Theodore Johnson, he had accompanied James Allison as a public officer to search for Sam Heinbach's children to persuade them to contest the will.[27]

To establish further that Sam knew what he was doing at the time of his will, Mamie Smart, a witness for the plaintiff, testified that she had seen Sam that morning near the bridge across Marble Creek and asked if she could talk to him. Sam, who, she observed, was sober at that time, told her that he did not have time to talk to her because he was on his way to sign his will.[28]

It was crucial, of course, for Mollie's attorneys to convince jurors that Sam was of sound mind and to show that many people had routinely conducted business transactions with him. Under direct examination by Rendlen, Dr. L. H. Tutt, a partner in the Ilasco Supply Company and Hannibal physician who had examined Sam on September 22, 23, and 24, 1909, offered that Sam was sane. To reinforce that Sam was capable of transacting business, Tutt testified that Sam had bought the house and orchard tract from him through Tutt's agent shortly after Sam married Mollie.[29]

Mollie's attorneys particularly sought to show that several Ilasco saloon owners and other businessmen had in fact regularly entered into contracts with Sam Heinbach. Following Tutt to the witness stand was William F. True, the court-appointed administrator of Sam's estate, to confirm that he had acted as Tutt's agent when Sam bought the house and tract from him. True, who was also Tutt's former partner in the Ilasco Supply Company, had disposed of his interests in the company just before the trial, perhaps to avoid a conflict of interests. He also acknowledged that he had signed "ground rent" leases with Sam on behalf of the Ilasco Supply Company. Rendlen and Neeper entered into evidence copies of numerous other leases with Sam Heinbach, including one signed by T. E. Allison, the probate judge himself. In addition, they offered copies of fire insurance policies that Sam had taken out on the house and household furniture that belonged to him and Mollie. Finally, they even put J. W. Conn, a New London merchant, on the stand to testify that Sam had signed an installment contract with him to purchase Mollie's Baldwin piano.[30]

When it was time for the defense to present its case, James Allison immediately set out to establish that Sam Heinbach was under the undue influence of Mollie when he made his will. Allison conjured up images of Mollie as a scheming, conniving woman who desecrated the sacred institution of marriage by using it solely for calculated financial gain. Such images were designed to disturb the all-male jury,[31] for they contradicted the prevailing assumptions that underlay traditional attitudes toward marriage.

Defense attorneys tried to show through several witnesses that Mollie had first schemed through intermediaries to meet Sam, even while the body of her previous deceased husband was still warm in the grave, and then again to arrange marriage and a will. In the case of their first witness, however, Judge Ragland refused to allow Allison to question William Cutsinger about his role as an intermediary until defense attorneys had made a showing in regard to "actual undue influence" upon the making of the will. Allison had asked Cutsinger, a neighboring farmer who knew Mollie and her previous husband, John Scott, if she had offered him one hundred dollars two or three months after Scott's death to persuade Sam to marry her.[32]

Allison then put John Hinkson, an Ilasco saloon owner from Bowling Green, on the stand to establish the connection between the will and undue influence. Hinkson testified that when he talked to Sam about making a will at Mollie's behest, "Well he told me she talked to him a great deal about making a will and asked him to make a will, and tried to persuade him to make a will willing his property to her, that she thought he ought to will what he had to her." According to Hinkson, Mollie promised not to forget him if Sam indeed made such a will. Hinkson also claimed that after the will was made, she promised to reward him with two choice Ilasco lots if the will was not broken.[33]

Allison hit a roadblock, however, when he again tried to pursue the role of matchmakers in the marriage of Sam and Mollie. When he asked Hinkson if Sam had asked him to read and answer Mollie's courtship letters for him, Judge Ragland sustained the objection of Mollie's attorneys that this line of questioning was leading and suggestive. The court blocked similar efforts to elicit testimony that Mollie had also offered money to Ilasco saloon owner John Moore and to J. T. Fisher, a Saverton businessman and another partner in the Ilasco Supply Company, for help in arranging the marriage.[34]

Since the court refused to admit this line of questioning for lack of evidence, the defense spent much of its time challenging Sam's testamentary capacity at the time of his will. Allison, Briscoe, Hays, and Heather tried to establish that Sam's alleged mental incompetence was the product of old age and alcoholism. Generally, witnesses did not dispute that Sam was a hard drinker. They only disagreed about whether he was always drunk or whether there were times that they saw him sober. For example, Mamie Smart noted that Sam was sober when she saw him just before he signed the will, but constable Wilson observed that Sam was "pretty well jagged" when he saw him on the street in Ilasco shortly afterward. "Well," noted James T. Mooter, "I never seen him over twice when he was down and could not go, [but] he was pretty full about every time that I did see him. What I call pretty full, he had sense enough to talk to you, in going home. I seen him twice when he could not go." Volney West, who had customarily seen Sam at least once or twice a week, testified that he had not seen Sam drunk for the last two years of his life. On the other hand, Harrison Decker observed that "I don't believe I ever saw the man sober in my life, if I ever did I never knew it, he was always down in town there at the saloon." Dr. R. M. Winn, Sam's physician, described him as "the worst alcoholic I ever knew, one of the worst regular drunkards."[35]

For the defense, Sam's delusions or hallucinations were an indication of his mental unsoundness. Several witnesses related things that he had said to them at one time or another that did not make sense. For example, Wilson remembered an occasion on which he and Northcutt had gone up to see Sam during a period when illness had confined him to bed. After carrying on a normal conversation for awhile, Sam suddenly interjected that he had been in town that morning and insisted that "if he had his gun though he would kill Tom Ryan [a neighboring farmer] that morning." Northcutt and Wilson knew that Sam had not even left the house that morning, but to humor him they asked what the trouble was between him and Ryan. According to Wilson, Sam replied that Ryan "had it in for me quite a while . . . I met him this morning . . . he just beat me to it, he had his gun and I didn't, you see."[36]

The defense hammered away at Sam's inability to sustain a coherent conversation, which they attributed to mental unsoundness derived from alcoholism and senility. When Allison asked Dr. Winn if Sam "could hold a connected conversation," Winn, whom Mollie had also invited to their home as a dinner guest, replied, "I never was able to get a conversation with uncle Sam in my life. I don't think he ever had an idea, if he did he never expressed it." As Harrison Decker explained, Sam "talked kindy at random, [he would] commence one conversation and then go through some kind of maneuvers, talk about affairs at home, [the] way [he was] going to [be] buried and all of this and that; he would cry, he would pull out money and show money and tell you he had money to bury him."[37]

It was Sam's vision of a white horse, however, that defense attorneys particularly focused on. "Why he talked queer about people going in and out of the windows of the house and then about a white horse he said was in and about the house," observed Eliza Jane Johnson, Theodore's wife, in a deposition. As Wilson further explained, "Well Sam had a very funny way of talking when he was drinking, [he'd] say little things, did not seem like much sense to, he would tell us down there, 'when he was gone we would see nothing but white horse without saddle and bridle, he would pass round,' [it] seemed as though something haunted him, after he was gone that was."[38]

Defense attorneys also paraded Sam's filthy habits before the jurors. They elicited testimony from Wilson, H. F. Fleurdelys, Russell Smashey, and others who had seen him in town so drunk on numerous occasions that they had to help him back up the hill to his house. In particular, the defense team manipulated vivid, pathetic images of Sam's unbuttoned, feces-filled pants and of flies swarming around him as he walked through town. How could any woman, they suggested, marry someone with such disgusting habits, except for the basest of economic reasons? There must have been a few chuckles among courtroom spectators when attorney Heather asked Ilasco merchant Fred Jeffers during cross-examination if he had known of any other woman whom Sam had ever paid attention to or gone with prior to Mollie. "Why I don't know of him paying any attention to any woman," Jeffers remarked. "He was not regarded as a lady's man."[39]

Defense attorneys tried to convince jurors that at times Sam did not even know he had married Mollie. Ilasco's C. F. Hoover testified that Mollie had once confided to him that on occasions in the evening Sam forgot that she was his wife. According to Hoover, when she urged Sam to "come let's go to bed," Sam sometimes insisted that "no I would not think of going to bed with you without being married to you."[40]

There was no evidence introduced in the trial to suggest that Mollie did not hold up her end of the bargain in the marriage. She regularly took care of Sam, cleaned up behind him, and did far more than what was expected of a dutiful wife. According to Volney West, the marriage had been good for Sam, who "seemed to enjoy life better than [he] did since I knew him."[41] From the standpoint of Allison and all others who had an interest in the future of the land next to the Atlas cement plant, however, the problem was that she now expected a return on her marriage investment. From her viewpoint, to get at Sam Heinbach through intermediaries and agents was no different from the way so many business deals were regularly negotiated. Certainly, Atlas officials had used intermediaries to acquire land. Why couldn't she?[42]

If Mollie was not a True Woman because of her calculated financial use of marriage, neither was Sam Heinbach a True Man, for he allegedly lacked the hard-driving lust for money that she did possess. Whereas Allison used Mollie's acquisitive manipulation of marriage to discredit her, he exploited the absence of an aggressive entrepreneurial spirit in Sam to suggest that he was not competent to make judgments about the disposition of property. For example, he called attention to a lease that Sam had signed on July 1, 1905, with Herman Lefkovitz and Herman Schwartz, business partners who at that time operated a saloon and mercantile business in Ilasco. The lease stipulated that Sam would not rent the rest of his land to anyone else involved in the saloon or mercantile business. According to Allison, Sam believed that he was to receive twenty-five hundred dollars for granting this monopolistic privilege, but Lefkovitz and Schwartz paid Sam only twenty-five dollars instead. In Allison's view, how could any man in his right mind consent to such a lease?[43]

More important, for Allison the entire "ground rent" arrangement was insane, since it hindered the maximization of profit from the buying and selling of land, thus impairing the capitalist vision of land as a mere commodity. This put limits on investors—among them, his brother, the probate judge—who wanted to buy and sell homes on land that belonged to Sam Heinbach. For example, when James McCann tried to sell a house to James Bolomey in early October 1909, Bolomey agreed to buy it, provided he could persuade Sam to grant a ten-year extension on the lease. The deal went through, but the very fact that the sale required Sam's approval of the lease extension impeded the marketplace transaction between buyer and seller.[44]

Allison suggested that such arrangements were a sign that Sam was feebleminded with no business sense. During cross-examination of Hannibal lawyer and businessman William H. Fisher, for example, Allison delved into Fisher's financial interests in Ilasco, where he had a twenty-year lease on a lot from Sam. Fisher paid one dollar per month for the lot, put a building on it for five hundred dollars, and rented it for fifteen dollars per month to Herman Schwartz for a saloon. "Now don't you know, Mr. Fisher," Allison asked, "that a long lease like this one or longer . . . on a piece of property would injure the sale of it, if it was put up and sold, injure the market value of the property very materially?" Fisher replied that it might in some cases, but that it would make good business sense for Sam if he could derive more income from ground rent than he could from farming.[45]

As illustrated in the cross-examination of Volney West, a witness for Mollie, Sam was not the only Ilasco resident whose economic behavior did not always conform to the so-called natural laws of the marketplace. At times, the defense lawyers showed exasperation over this. West, who made his living doing a little gardening around home, carpentry work, "and such like, whatever comes up," particularly bewildered attorney Clay Heather. When Heather asked if he honestly believed that Fisher's abovementioned lot was worth only one dollar per month, West affirmed after a testy exchange, "I expect it is, I would not give fifty cents for it . . . I have no use for it."[46]

The frustration that the opposing attorneys expressed was rooted in elite attitudes at the time that condemned the absence of capitalist values among poor "white trash." For many welfare workers, asylum superintendents, eugenics field workers, and other social control professionals who worked to instill capitalist values in the poor, Sam's lack of interest in maximizing profit on his land, coupled with his general disregard for material possessions, was a sure sign of feeblemindedness. When Sam's filthy habits, fragmented family history, alcoholism, and otherwise erratic behavior were thrown into the mix, there was nothing left for Allison to conclude but that Sam had no right to preside over the supervision of property.[47]

For Allison, further proof of Sam's mental incapacity was that he failed to oversee the agents he hired to collect rents from his lessees. H. F. Fleurdelys, one of those agents, testified that Sam signed his own receipts and examined the receipt book with him each month before they settled accounts, but Fleurdelys admitted under cross-examination that Sam never questioned any of his transactions or settlements. He acknowledged that he knew Sam's business better than Sam did, and that Sam's alcohol problem rendered him incapable of preparing his own leases, collecting rents, or handling any business transactions.[48]

During redirect examination by Neeper, however, Fleurdelys acknowledged that William F. True, as administrator of Sam's estate, continued to rely on him to handle the collection of rents, just as Sam had done. In fact, True had authorized Fleurdelys to sign his name on his behalf, whereas Sam had signed his own name to the leases and receipts. Fleurdelys further testified that True, during a recent extended absence from the state, in fact had left him in sole charge of collecting rents for the Heinbach estate.[49]

Jack Briscoe, a member of the defense team and former rent collector of Sam's, also took the stand to offer direct testimony that Sam was not competent to transact his own business, that he was not of sound mind. According to Briscoe, during the period in which he worked for Sam, he often had to wait several days for Sam to sober up before asking him to sign leases. He emphasized that Sam merely took his word when he turned the rent money over to him after deducting his fee of 10 percent.[50]

Rendlen conducted a particularly aggressive cross-examination to challenge Briscoe's contention that Sam was mentally incompetent to conduct business transactions. He called into question whether Briscoe would have contracted services, notarized leases, and taken money as Sam's agent if indeed he truly believed that Sam was mentally unsound at the time. Rendlen called attention to the fact that Briscoe, in his capacity as county prosecuting attorney, had checked off Sam's name as a legal, qualified signer on numerous petitions for dram shop licenses in Ilasco.[51]

Rendlen used the rapidly escalating value of Sam's estate to illustrate that Sam had made a wise financial calculation by refusing many offers to buy parts of it from him. Under questioning by Rendlen, Briscoe estimated that Sam's estate was worth between twelve thousand and fifteen thousand dollars at the time of his death, compared to only about five thousand or six thousand dollars when he and Theodore Johnson had formally divided their tract in the summer of 1906. Rendlen asked rhetorically if the fact that Sam held onto the property while it more than doubled in value during the last four years was a manifestation of insanity, or of an unsound mind. Briscoe responded that the only reason Sam ever had for not selling the land was "that he would drink it [money] all up if he got it." After Rendlen followed by suggesting that Sam's refusal to sell land was "an act of prudence" in that "he recognized his weakness of drink," Briscoe grudgingly conceded, "Might so construe it, [he] realized probably his condition as a drunkard."[52]

What made Briscoe's testimony especially controversial was his intriguing role as attorney for the defendants. When Rendlen asked who had hired him to join the defense team, Briscoe responded that Theodore Johnson was the first to speak to him about it, but he conceded that Johnson was not his client. Briscoe, evasive about who employed him for the defense or about whether he expected to be paid for his services, denied that he had a contingent contract with any client in the case. Rendlen pressed harder in an effort to show that Briscoe had a financial stake in the suit's outcome: "Who are you definitely employed by now in this controversy?" Briscoe, again evasive, responded, "Well, I don't know whether J. O. Allison, he afterwards said, He wanted me to assist in the matter." Determined, Rendlen pressed forward: "Mr. Allison when he told you definitely he wanted you to help in the case, you undertook it?" Briscoe's final response in this exchange obfuscated more than it clarified. "Yes sir," he replied, "I undertook it from the time Mr. Johnson spoke to me." When Rendlen tried to link Briscoe's financial interest in the case to James Allison's six-tenths contracts with the Heinbach children, however, Judge Ragland sustained the defense's objection that these contracts had no bearing on the case.[53]

The defense team produced several witnesses, including Briscoe himself, who testified that Sam was unhappy with his will. Ilasco's William Burns emphasized that Sam once told him that he intended for his son, Jesse, to take his place in the community after he died. Eliza Jane Johnson gave a deposition in which she claimed that Sam had complained that he should have left some of his property to his children. According to her, Sam told her that he had once seen his son in Chicago. Harrison Decker testified that Sam told him three or four years earlier that he and Theodore Johnson had once visited his children on a trip to Niagara Falls. By this account, Sam's two daughters, Edith and Naomi, were working in a millinery shop, and his son Jesse was running a dry-goods store in Chicago at that time. A different version related by George Douglas held that Jesse had become a lawyer in Chicago.[54]

To win the sympathy of jurors, Allison put Edith Britton, Sam Heinbach's eldest surviving daughter, on the stand as the final witness in the presentation of the defense's case. Jurors listened as she told how poverty had torn apart their family after their father abandoned them. She explained that she and her sister Naomi, along with their brother Jesse, ended up on an orphans' farm for awhile. Britton, who was living in Liberal, Kansas, at the time of the trial, testified that her sister, Naomi Summers, who was also in the courtroom, was now living in eastern (Checotah) Oklahoma. Neither of them, she said, had any idea as to whether Jesse was still alive.[55]

Somewhat surprisingly, the defense wrapped up its case without directly asking one of its witnesses, Dr. Andrew J. Detweiler, about Mollie's alleged poisoning of Sam Heinbach. The court may have previously instructed the defense that this line of inquiry was off-limits. Nevertheless, the topic did surface during Detweiler's response to a question about his diagnosis of Sam's alcoholic dementia during medical examinations of him in December 1909. Although defense attorney Hays did not pursue it further, it was Mollie's attorney who seemed eager to address the issue in the courtroom in order to minimize the sting of pretrial gossip upon jurors. Rendlen quickly asked on cross-examination: "Now, what about this poisoning business, let's know about that?"[56]

Detweiler's response suggests that there may have been some confusion and disagreement among authorities in regard to Mollie's alleged poisoning of her husband. It is unclear whether in fact an autopsy was performed, since the Missouri Bureau of Vital Statistics does not have a record of Sam's death certificate. Local newspapers did not mention an autopsy at the time, and there was no reference to an autopsy during the trial. If an autopsy was not performed, this is rather surprising considering the suspicions at the time. In response to Rendlen's questioning, however, Detweiler said that after he made an investigation, he concluded that poisoning was not involved in Sam's death. However, part of his response indicated that there may have been some lingering questions about it, even fifteen months after Sam's death. "I did not believe it," responded Detweiler, "and don't believe it now."[57]

As attorney Neeper prepared to guide Mollie's suit through the rebuttal stage, one of the most important issues to clarify was that of Sam Heinbach's white horse. Witnesses for the plaintiff suggested that Sam's alleged hallucinations about a white horse in fact had a rational basis. Fred Jeffers testified that Sam talked to him about the white horse when they bumped into each other in town on the morning after Sam had made his will. According to Jeffers, when he asked Sam what he meant by the white horse, Sam replied that "I have some heirs . . . when I am gone there will be a squabble over this property, that is what I mean by the white horse . . . be a big time in Ilasco."[58]

Jeffers also offered an explanation for Sam's alleged hallucination about people's going in and out of windows at his log cabin. Jeffers, who along with Albert Lester and Mary Baker at one time boarded in Sam's cabin, linked this remark to the tumultuous domestic relationship of Baker and Lester. Jeffers pointed out that there was a period during which Lester had either run away from or was chased off by Baker after a quarrel. Baker, "quite a drinking woman," would come home late at night, discover that Sam had locked her out, and then break into the house. "I often be waken up in the night by her racket and noise," Jeffers remembered, "and I would hear Uncle Sam talking and hear her talking and cursing and trying to get in, and finally I would hear the door burst open or window be broke open."[59]

To shore up the case during rebuttal, Neeper also tried to challenge the image of Sam as a complete degenerate who could not carry on a conversation, and to counter claims by defense witnesses that Sam had wanted his children to inherit his property. John Moore, an Ilasco saloon owner, testified that Sam "was a great hand to read the paper, he read the paper nearly every day . . . Yes sir, greatest man down there [Ilasco] to read the paper." In regard to allegations that Sam in truth intended to leave his property to his children, James T. Mooter insisted that Sam clearly aimed to leave all of his possessions to Mollie. As Amanda Douglas recalled, Sam appreciated what Mollie had done to improve his life: "He was very well pleased, he had a home and [was] living a different way to what he did . . . Cleaner way and had a nicer home than when he was batching."[60]

All in all, however, Neeper did not present strong rebuttal evidence, an obvious indication that he did not prepare well for this phase of the trial. He used a few witnesses who contributed little or nothing to strengthen Mollie's case. For example, Marshall Combs took the stand only to say that he had never conducted a single business transaction or conversation with Sam Heinbach. Neeper, in a very brief examination of Lizzie Janney, who operated a boardinghouse on Theodore Johnson's tract in Ilasco, elicited so little information that it must have been embarrassing. Under questioning, Janney noted that although she had seen Sam several times when he came in her place to eat, they had never even had a conversation, not in regard to his children, to Mollie, or to his property.[61]

As we shall see, Mollie and Feemy fumed over Neeper's lackluster performance as he put on the stand rebuttal witness after rebuttal witness who had so little to contribute. An intoxicated Mart Wood testified during rebuttal that Sam Heinbach told him that he intended to leave his property to Mollie, but Wood admitted under cross-examination that he was drunk on the stand. Neeper put Alice West on the stand only to elicit testimony that she had once sent her husband, Volney, to buy some apples from Sam. Neeper was trying to use this as evidence that Sam conducted business transactions, but Volney had already testified that Sam had refused to let him pay for the apples. The only contribution that witness William Youell, a butcher for the Ilasco Supply Company, made in regard to Sam's capacity to transact business was to affirm that Sam used to come into the store to buy a loaf of bread. This made it easy for attorney Heather to ask during cross-examination of Youell: "[Don't] Children five or six years old come in to buy bread?"[62]

To make matters worse, Neeper failed to persuade the judge to allow him to enter two depositions into the record from witnesses whom he regarded as valuable. Neeper had lost the original copy of a deposition by Mary Smashey, who had become very sick in the courtroom and left unable to testify. He offered to read a carbon copy of the deposition, instead, but he could not explain whether interlineations on it had been made by Smashey or before she signed the copy. As a result, the judge refused to allow the introduction of the carbon copy into evidence. Likewise, the court refused to allow Neeper to introduce the deposition of Ola Gregory. Since Gregory lived in Ilasco, it was up to Neeper to make a showing as to why she could not appear in court.[63]

As the end of the trial neared, it became apparent that two of the main figures in the case would not testify. Mollie's lawyers apparently considered it too risky to put her on the stand. Not only was she nearly deaf, but she undoubtedly would have invited some tough, sticky questions about her past use of marriage as a vehicle for accumulating property and perhaps about the circumstances surrounding the deaths of her last two husbands. Likewise, defense attorneys chose not to use Theodore Johnson as a witness. To have done so would have exposed him to tough questions about his financial relationship with James Allison and his role in allegedly subsidizing trips to search for the Heinbach children. In addition, he was vulnerable because of his own heavy use of alcohol, and if the ground-rent arrangements on Sam's tract were a sign of mental incompetence, what did that say about Johnson, who used similar arrangements on his tract?

It also became apparent what public price some of the women who testified on Mollie's behalf would pay for supporting her. The defense's strategy for discrediting witnesses sent a clear message that poor women like those in Ilasco could expect little mercy as aggressive male lawyers raised questions about their moral behavior. For example, at the end of cross-examination of Alice West, a defense attorney suggested that she and her husband, Volney, in fact might not have been legally married. When she insisted that they were married, the attorney responded, "You are certain about that now are you?"[64]

A few other women who testified endured a similar line of attack. Before attorney Heather concluded his cross-examination of Anna Rupert, he asked her abruptly, "How many times have you been arrested or fined?" Under further questioning, she admitted that she had been arrested and fined for disturbing the peace. She told the court that she had once verbally assaulted a woman who had gossiped about her, and that this woman pressed charges against her. She also acknowledged under questioning that she was not living with her husband at the time of the trial.[65]

During the defense's cross-examination of Ola Gregory during her deposition, attorney Hays further pursued this strategy. He first asked if she was living with her husband, and in response she noted that she and her husband had been separated for eight years. Under direct examination, Gregory had testified that Sam Heinbach employed her to wash his laundry and clean his log cabin before he married Mollie, and to wallpaper his new house shortly after their marriage. She had also noted how good Sam was to her, explaining that he often gave her apples and did not charge her ground rent because he knew how hard she had to struggle to raise three children by herself. Hays, in response, hinted that there may have been something untoward about their relationship. He invoked an image of Gregory as a woman who may have sexually manipulated Sam's paternalism for economic favors.[66]

Mollie's attorneys did not hesitate to employ a similar strategy to discredit female witnesses for the defense, but Eliza Jane Johnson was the only Ilasco woman who testified for the Heinbach children. Johnson did not attend the trial, but in a deposition she gave damning testimony about Sam Heinbach's drinking, hallucinations, and alleged unhappiness over his will. During cross-examination Rendlen hammered away at her public behavior, too. He asked if it was not a fact that she had drunk with Sam and Theodore, her husband. After she denied that she had ever been drunk, she admitted to having an occasional drink but emphasized that she did not drink in public: "No sir, I have drunk beer with my husband but not with other people."[67]

To conjure up images of grasping women, defense attorneys raised questions about the way Mollie and Feemy played an aggressive role in securing witnesses and affidavits for the suit. Attorney Allison insinuated that Mollie had offered to deed Mamie Smart two lots if she testified on her behalf. Attorney Hays tried to make Feemy an issue in the cross-examination of Lula Brown and Ola Gregory. Hays suggested that it was Feemy, in fact, who was "prompting" Mollie. Asking Gregory how long Feemy had been living with Mollie in Ilasco, he seemed to impute mercenary motives to Feemy's activities in Ilasco on behalf of her sister's suit. Furthermore, he emphasized that it was not the plaintiff's attorneys, but the plaintiff herself, coached by her sister, who had lined Gregory up to testify.[68]

In effect, Hays was calling attention to the fact that the practice of law was a male domain upon which Mollie and Feemy had come dangerously close to trespassing. Such women who manipulated the process of law for personal gain, even if informally outside the courtroom, not only encroached on male professional turf but also stripped away the mystique surrounding the intersection of law and society. They had antagonized their own lawyers, as well as the defense team. To that extent, Mollie and Feemy were interlopers who posed a threat to the masculine assumptions that underlay the legal process.[69]

Before the case went to the jury, Judge Ragland sustained a motion by Mollie's attorneys to strike from the transcript that portion of John Hinkson's testimony which claimed that she had offered him a couple of Ilasco lots if the will was not broken. In the judge's instructions to the jury, he also emphasized that no evidence had been presented to show that Mollie had exerted undue influence in the making of Sam's will.

In most other respects, however, Mollie's attorneys objected to Ragland's instructions to the jury. Particularly objectionable was an instruction that although Sam may have been able to perform certain business transactions such as signing leases, receipts, and checks, this did not mean that he had sufficient capacity to make a will. Ragland told jurors that they should reject the will unless they found that Sam "possessed a mind and memory sufficiently clear and unimpaired to take into consideration all his property, and the persons who had a natural and reasonable claim on his bounty, if any, and the disposition he desired to make of his property."[70]

Although the court threw out the issue of undue influence because of a lack of proof, the images of Mollie's climbing up the economic ladder on the backs of unsuspecting men through marriage were too overwhelming for uneasy jurors. When testimony ended on April 6, 1911, the all-male jury conducted only brief deliberations before returning a verdict against Mollie that same day. The *Ralls County Record* described the trial as a "royal battle," and pointed out that although Rendlen lost the case, "there remained a halo around his effort." On May 13, the court overruled Mollie's motion for a new trial but granted an appeal to the Missouri Supreme Court and fixed her bond at one thousand dollars.[71]

The finger-pointing quickly began. Mollie and Feemy blamed their lawyers for not calling some of the witnesses whom they had suggested. They were especially disgusted by what they regarded as Neeper's pitiful, anemic role in the case. Neither was Mollie happy with Feemy. Mollie had wanted to move the case out of Ralls County, and she blamed Feemy for failing to persuade their lawyers to do so. "It would have been won," complained Mollie, "if you had made them take a change of venue."[72]

With the reading of the verdict, the first phase of the case thus came to an end. As Mollie and Feemy made their way through the crowded courtroom, they no doubt heard a lot of gossip and casual remarks aimed at them. Feemy perhaps engaged in verbal sparring with some of the bystanders, and she no doubt had a few choice words for Mollie's lawyers, especially Neeper, whose performance at times bordered on incompetence. At least Mollie and Feemy saw it that way. They had suggested other witnesses, but he had ignored their advice and lined up witnesses of his own for the rebuttal phase of the trial.

It would soon become apparent, however, that this was going to be a war of attrition over "Uncle Sam's" estate. The sisters would no longer wait for the lawyers to tell them what to do next. As time was about to reveal, in fact, Mollie and Feemy had already slipped a surprise legal card up their sleeve without telling Rendlen and Neeper. To play that card would sharply raise the stakes of the game and intensify the fury of the battle that lay ahead.

Mary Alice (Mollie) Sykes, c. 1880. Courtesy Jane Hemeyer.

Samuel Heinbach, c. 1905. This is probably the log cabin in which he and Mollie Sykes lived briefly after they were married. Courtesy Ray and Shirley Herren.

Business section of Ilasco on the perimeter of the cement plant, c. 1910. This tract, acquired by the Atlas Portland Cement Company at a sheriff's sale in 1916, belonged to Theodore Johnson, but Mollie Heinbach claimed that it legally belonged to her and Sam Heinbach. Courtesy David and Sally Polc.

Ilasco, created in 1903, obtained a depot and freight agent in 1909. Courtesy David and Sally Polc.

Part of the Heinbach tract in Ilasco, c. 1910. Courtesy Jim and Dorothy Tatman.

H.T. (Tom) Sykes, brother of Mollie and Euphemia, c. 1900. Tom owned and operated a sawmill in New London, where he also served as a Republican postmaster. Courtesy Jane Hemeyer.

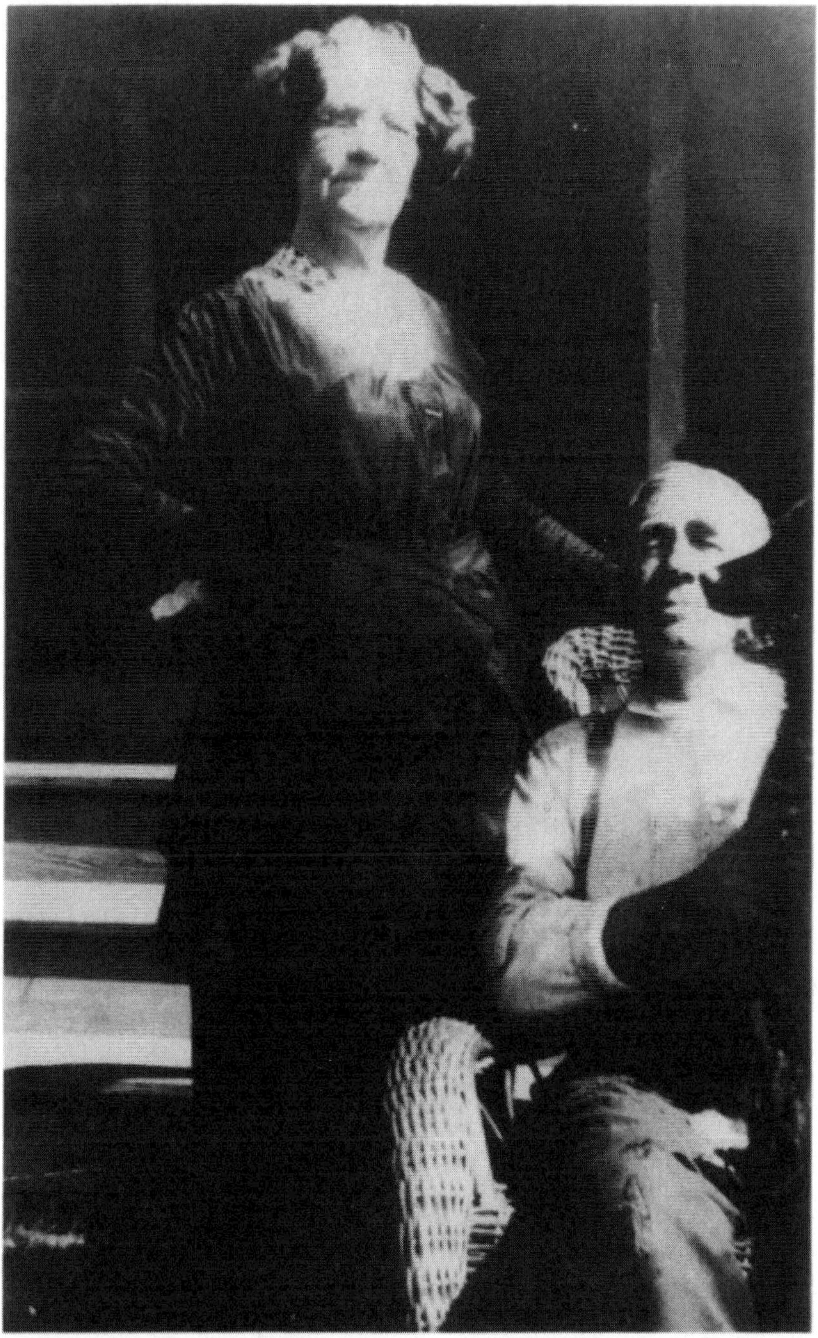

Mollie Heinbach and brother Tom Sykes, c. 1910–1920. Tom, at someone else's urging, initiated a mental incompetence suit to impose a guardianship on Mollie in 1921. Courtesy Jane Hemeyer.

Euphemia (Feemy) Koller and the children of her brother, Tom Sykes, c. 1905. Seated in front, L–R: Ruby Sykes, Zella Pearl Sykes, Standing in back, L–R: Van Murphy Sykes, Mabel Sykes. Feemy took Mabel, soon to die of tuberculosis, to New Mexico for treatments at hot water spas. Courtesy Jane Hemeyer.

Feemy and her niece, Ruby Sykes, c. 1905. Jane Hemeyer, Ruby's daughter, recalled that her mother was in "awe" of "Aunt Feem." Courtesy Jane Hemeyer.

Edith Heinbach Britton and Naomi Ruth Heinbach Summers, daughters of Samuel Heinbach, c. 1940. In January 1910, Ralls County attorney James O. Allison located Edith and Naomi, who had been abandoned as children by their father more than twenty-five years earlier, and encouraged them to challenge the validity of Sam's will. This sparked the initial round of litigation to prevent Sam's entire Ilasco estate from passing into the hands of his new wife, Mollie. Courtesy Ray and Shirley Herren.

Dora Doyle, Ilasco resident, c. 1915. Doyle, a neighbor, testified against Mollie Heinbach in the second trial of Sam Heinbach's will in 1916. Courtesy Virginia Sudholt.

Teachers and students at Ilasco's elementary school, c. 1924. Ralls County officials condemned and appropriated land from the Heinbach tract for construction of this school, but later transferred ownership to the Atlas Portland Cement Company in exchange for permission to use it for educational purposes. Courtesy Virginia Arthaud.

Ilasco High School, c. 1929. The school was built on land donated for educational purposes by the Atlas Portland Cement Company. This land, too, once belonged to the Heinbach tract. Courtesy Charles Glascock.

Company banquet in New York City attended by officials of the Atlas Portland Cement Company, January 9, 1918. Courtesy USX Corporation.

Sons of Thomas Sykes. Kneeling in front, L–R: Todd, Roy. Standing in back, L–R: Harry, Van. Courtesy Jane Hemeyer.

Site of the public road in Ilasco that marked one of the boundaries of the Heinbach tract, 1992. Courtesy author.

The Universal Atlas Cement Company's new automated plant, June 6, 1967. Courtesy Fred's Photos.

Jane Hemeyer, grandchild of Thomas Sykes and great-niece of Feemy and Mollie. Courtesy Jane Hemeyer.

Five

The "Whole Crowd of the Gang"

> If I die you will never get this place [Ilasco]. I believe the whole crowd of the gang will jump onto you . . . I tell you they will do everything in their power now [so] that [neither] I, nor you either one, will get this.
>
> —*Mary Alice Heinbach to Euphemia B. Koller, 1911*

As Mollie and Feemy left the Ralls County courthouse upset with their attorneys and with each other, they, along with their cousin, Sarah Ellen Londenberg, shared an important secret that soon further complicated and forever widened the scope of the case. Just a few days before the trial, the three had held a closed strategy session to which neither Mollie's attorneys nor any other men were invited. In particular, they discussed what to do next if Mollie lost the suit in the circuit court. They decided on a course of action that they hid from their brother, Tom, as well as from Rendlen, Neeper, and everyone else at the time. If the jury's verdict went against Mollie, her next move would be to bring Feemy more directly into the case to ensure a more vigorous gathering and presentation of evidence if the state supreme court upheld their appeal for a new trial. Mollie would not only benefit from Feemy's analytical skills, knowledge of the law, and boundless energy, but also gain access to her financial resources, which she needed to continue prosecuting the suit.

Of course, Feemy required compensation, so with that in mind, she and Mollie worked out an agreement that bound them closely together in a successful struggle to win a new trial and establish the validity of Sam Heinbach's will. Mollie made her a joint owner of the Ilasco tract, and in return Feemy agreed to devote more of her life and resources to the case. As we shall see, however, there were tensions in this new partnership and an important catch: Feemy could not profit from the joint tenancy until Mollie's death. Feemy renounced her rights to any of the rental income from the Ilasco tract, and in return Mollie gave her a long-term stake in the tract: economic security in old age. Mollie first transferred the land in litigation to Ellen via a warranty deed, and Ellen then made out a new deed transferring ownership back to her and Feemy as joint tenants. The new deed contained an important survivorship clause providing that upon the death of either sister, the survivor would assume full title to the land.[1]

This surprising transaction, soon to be made public, injected a new legal wrinkle into the case, pulling Feemy into the thick of the fighting and in the process sowing new political conflicts in Ilasco. Although the sisters' partnership was shaky at times, they stood together for the next seven years as the case dragged on through the first appeal to the state supreme court, a new trial and verdict, and another trip to the high court in Jefferson City. During the new trial in particular, Feemy demonstrated how useful she could be to the new partnership. The state supreme court upheld the sisters' sweet victory, but winning the suit did not come without a price. Fighting intensified in Ilasco during the seven-year period, a clear indication that some of the area's power brokers, including Mollie's chief attorney, resented the joint deed as well as Feemy's interference in company town politics.

By creating a joint tenancy instead of a tenancy in common, the new deed not only made Feemy a formal party to the appeal to the Missouri Supreme Court but also made it harder for the tract to be split up by crafty lawyers and others bent on denying the sisters' ownership. By the early 1900s, joint tenancies had become much less common than tenancies in common. The latter, which created separate, distinct, undivided shares, allowed parties to dispose of their respective interests however they saw fit. This made it much easier for landowners to operate in a capitalist legal climate that recognized land as a commodity to be bought and sold. In contrast, a joint tenancy indicated that Mollie and Feemy intended to preserve Sam Heinbach's entire Ilasco tract. They did not view it as a mere commodity to be carved up and sold for profits that they could then easily divide with each other.[2]

The only basis on which the tract could be divided was if the sisters had a spat and initiated partition suits against each other, but they took steps to ensure that this did not happen. In a separate transaction witnessed by Ellen, they signed a notarized statement agreeing never to enforce a partition suit without the other's full consent. Significantly, however, they did not yet file this statement or the deeds in the county recorder's office before or during the trial. Perhaps they did not intend to file the deed at all if Mollie won the suit, or perhaps the delay was purely strategic. Whatever the case, they chose to keep these transactions concealed until the time was right to reveal them.[3]

It is not clear who came up with the idea to create a joint deed, but both sisters had considerable experience with property transactions. Since Feemy at this time forfeited the right to claim a share of the rental income from the tract, she had little to gain from the joint tenancy unless, of course, Mollie as the older sister died first. Mollie, on the other hand, had nothing to lose in the arrangement unless she later tried to partition the tract without Feemy's permission or to change her beneficiary to the property. In the short term, Mollie stood to benefit by encouraging her sister to unleash her defiant personality, sharp intellect, and spiritualist powers on opposing lawyers if the dispute over Sam's will did not end in the Ralls circuit court.

Discussions between Mollie and Feemy over creating the joint tenancy did reveal important tensions within the family, however. According to Ellen, Mollie at first wanted to grant a one-third interest in the deed to Tom Sykes, her brother. Tom, formerly a Republican postmaster in New London between 1902 and 1904, now owned and operated a sawmill there. Feemy objected to giving him an interest in the deed, insisting that "no my brother is not going to have anything to do with it." It is unclear whether this reflected long-standing tensions over Feemy's earlier refusal to raise Tom's kids after his first wife died, or whether Feemy simply wanted to keep male influences out of this deal. Maybe she did not trust the fact that Roy Sykes, one of Tom's sons, was dependent on Atlas for a living at the Ilasco cement plant. Maybe she was suspicious of the timing of Roy's recent promotion from system oil tender to first engineer just as the trial ended.[4]

Feemy might have opposed putting Tom on the deed also because she did not trust his wife, who had criticized Mollie for marrying Sam Heinbach merely to acquire his money. Tom's granddaughter, Jane Hemeyer, remembered that her mother, Ruby, regarded Maggie as an "operator" who was cold and much stronger-willed than Tom. According to Hemeyer, her grandfather was not very forceful, avoided conflict if at all possible, and was easily manipulated by Maggie.[5]

The issue went beyond mere personality, however, for Feemy and Mollie were well aware that Maggie had important family connections in state and local politics, and that these connections had elevated Tom's status in New London politics and society. Maggie was the daughter of William E. and Margaret Mayhall Harris, both of whose families had migrated from Kentucky long before the Civil War. Her mother had died in 1892, and her father in 1906. William Harris had been a justice of the peace and county court judge for many years. One of Maggie's brothers, Guilford, was senior editor and co-owner of the *Ralls County Times* (and later the *Ralls County Record*), and another—Frank—was a state representative from Boone County at the time. In addition, Zella Pearl Sykes, one of Tom's daughters, had married Clifford C. Harris just three months before the trial over Sam Heinbach's will opened in the circuit court in 1911. The Harris family, and now that of Tom Sykes, were also thoroughly linked to other prominent families through county politics and New London organizations such as the Knights of Pythias. In short, nothing happened around the New London courthouse without the Harris's knowing about it.[6]

As Mollie and Feemy geared up for the appeal process to the state court, they deliberated over strategy. In particular, they had to decide what to do about the new deeds that they had kept concealed. The opposing lawyers had raised questions about Feemy's motives in the case, and Mollie now became wary of the fact that the deed was in the possession of her impetuous sister. Two weeks after the trial, Mollie warned Feemy not to alter the deed, and she made clear that she did not want to make the property transactions public yet: "Now be careful of those deeds and you can't put them on record until I wish, and don't you change the deeds. Let them be a joint deed. Don't deed it all to yourself. You can't put [them] on record without me being there."[7]

Headstrong, combative Feemy was now calling the shots, however. She was ready to come out after the trial with both legal barrels blazing, eager to let the lawyers and others know that they now had a bigger fight on their hands. After a quick trip to Oklahoma and New Mexico to get rejuvenated for the battle that lay ahead, she returned to Ilasco ready for combat. Without consulting Mollie or her attorneys, she slipped over to the New London courthouse on May 23, 1911, filed the deeds in the recorder's office, returned home, and waited for the fallout.[8]

Three days later, it came. Guilford Harris, in the *Ralls County Times*, reported the filing of the deeds, noting that this would "further entangle the situation in the Heinbach case." As gossip swept like wildfire around the courthouse, Maggie Sykes quickly whipped off a letter to Mollie and enclosed a clipping of the newspaper report. With a sense of drama and urgency, she urged Mollie to hop a train and hurry to New London "as fast as the cars could bring her." She claimed that Feemy had filed a deed that put all of the property in her name alone.[9]

Maggie was disturbed by the sudden turn of events, but from the newspaper article's description of the deed and accompanying transaction, Mollie saw that there was no cause for alarm. The documents were the same ones that she, Feemy, and Ellen had fixed out. Mollie disapproved of the timing of the filing of the property transactions, but at that time did not even complain about it, although she must have been more than a bit exasperated with Feemy. Nor did Mollie charge that Feemy had coerced her into creating the joint deed.[10]

Tensions and bitterness increased over the summer, however, as Mollie now had to explain the joint deed to her infuriated lawyers, witnesses, and supporters. Rendlen's unhappiness over the surprise transaction put added pressures on Mollie, who worried that her lawyers would no longer work as hard for her since the joint deed had reduced the value of her security for legal fees.

As the deadline of August 30 approached for filing a bill of exceptions in her appeal, she expressed growing anger at Feemy for rushing prematurely to the courthouse to file the deed. On August 6, 1911, she reminded her that "I wanted you to put it on record immediately after the case was won . . . [otherwise] that Lawyer Neeper and Charlie Rendlen would not work for me." A few days later, apparently amid growing pressures from her lawyers, witnesses, and others whom she perceived as enemies in the case, Mollie blamed Feemy for losing the case, and she again scolded her for headstrong behavior: "It [the will suit] would have been won if you had made them take a change of venue. Now because you put that deed on record the whole gang are making it worse than ever. I told you to wait until the last minute. No nothing would do you but to put it on record."[11]

Mollie worried that her attorneys would "lay down" on her now, but her letters to Feemy in the summer and fall of 1911 continued to show sisterly love and affection. In those letters, the sisters even discussed how to make out wills in each other's favor since neither had surviving children. Furthermore, Mollie continued to give Feemy tips on how to "catch a rich husband." More importantly, she reaffirmed that she wanted Feemy to get the land in the event of her death. Nevertheless, Mollie expressed a sense of foreboding as she thought about the powerful political forces aligned against them in the suit. She doubted that "the gang," which in her mind included her brother's in-laws, would ever allow Feemy to have the property. "You bet if I die first the Harris and all will fight you to the last minute," she warned, "but I suppose [neither] you nor I will never live to see this settled." She also sounded an ominous, chilling warning about what Feemy's hasty filing of the deed had unleashed. "If I die you will never get this place. I believe the whole crowd of the gang will jump onto you. If you had only waited until we were starting to Jefferson City and let them found it out when they came back. You would not listen to me. I tell you they will do everything in their power now [so] that [neither] I, nor you either one, will get this."[12]

Despite Mollie's frustration with Feemy, she needed her help in the suit. Feemy was tenacious, smart, and a loyal sister, if too compulsive, combative, and exhausting to suit Mollie. They had different styles. The cockier Feemy preferred the method of frontal assault, whereas Mollie enjoyed subterfuge, intrigue, and manipulation to get what she wanted. Feemy apparently turned a deaf ear to Mollie's husband-hunting advice, preferring instead to assert herself vigorously in defense of principles and convictions against men in positions of power and authority who tried to ride roughshod over women.[13]

Feemy was disturbed by the accusations, innuendoes, and gossip that had swirled around the New London courthouse during and after the trial. She resented the images of Mollie that were portrayed inside and outside the courtroom, particularly those suggesting that her sister was crazy. In an affidavit that Feemy drew up a week after the trial, she attributed such images to the ongoing attempt to dispossess Mollie of the Ilasco tract. Feemy, emphasizing the material motives of those responsible for the gossip campaign to raise questions about Mollie's sanity, insisted that "she is neither insane nor crazy, nor unnatural in an act nor deed in which she is concerned, the term crazy or insane was never applied to her so far as I can learn until she became possessed of valuable real estate."[14]

Feemy also pointed out that Mollie had fulfilled her end of the marriage contract and thus lived up to the social expectations placed on married women. Mollie "was all that could be required of any good wife . . . affectionate, dutiful, hardworking and kind," Feemy insisted. "Her home was clean and attractive. She was considerate for the well being of . . . her husbands in her home and abroad." Feemy emphasized that both John M. Scott and Sam Heinbach loved and trusted Mollie, and that "she is true and truthful and just to those who are true and truthful and just to her."[15]

Equally upsetting to Feemy were accusations that she had her own sinister motives in the case. Even Mollie, perhaps projecting her own acquisitive tendencies onto Feemy or reflecting her lawyers' concerns, expressed suspicions of her sister's intentions. She requested that Feemy draw up an affidavit swearing that she would never try to place a guardianship over her, drive her from her house, or interfere in any way with how she disposed of her rental income should she win the case on appeal. Feemy complied with this request, affirming that her support for Mollie's right to handle her own business affairs was but part of a broader gender consciousness. "I shall never seek to make myself her guardian, nor aid any one who so seeks to be such," she pledged. "My belief is that if justly and fairly treated by men [with] whom it becomes necessary for her to transact business in the course of life, that she is competent to do so—and that this condition applies to mostly all women alone in the world unprotected by father or husband or brother."[16]

At her own expense, Feemy traveled to Oklahoma, where one of Sam Heinbach's daughters now lived, in an unsuccessful effort to arrange a compromise settlement on Mollie's behalf. Before doing so, however, she complied with a request from an ever-mistrustful Mollie to draw up another affidavit. In this one, Feemy swore that in the event of such a settlement, she would surrender all claims to this money as long as Mollie was alive, but affirmed that she intended to claim it in the event of Mollie's death.[17]

In part, Mollie's insistence on these affidavits may have grown out of pressures applied by—and fears encouraged by—her witnesses and lawyers, who expressed anger over Feemy's growing involvement in the case. The attempt at a compromise settlement with Sam Heinbach's children came without Rendlen's knowledge. He undoubtedly questioned Feemy's motives and pressed Mollie to keep her off the case. From his perspective, how could he map out a strategy with Feemy running around Oklahoma trying to make compromise settlements with defendants in the suit? To add to Mollie's frustration, she was under financial pressure from Neeper to pay a fee for the services of his assistant during the trial. On November 1, 1911, she put up her eighty-acre Wildwood Farm as security in a trust deed to pay $125 to him within six months.[18]

By early 1912, anxieties over raising money to prosecute the appeal to the state supreme court contributed to rumors that Mollie intended to repudiate the joint deed. She denied these rumors, however, insisting to Feemy that she was still committed to the joint tenancy. "I did not tell Mr. [John T., or William H.]

Fisher I had taken the joint deed from you," Mollie assured her. "Nor I haven't."[19]

The financial squeeze pinched both sisters, in fact. On October 3, 1912, Feemy mortgaged her Hannibal property to secure a loan of five hundred dollars, which she repaid in full three years later. In Mollie's case, the squeeze may have jeopardized Wildwood Farm. The note that she took out to pay Neeper was due on May 1, 1912, but it was not produced and canceled until July 3. This perhaps left the mortgaged farm temporarily in danger. To help pay Neeper and to finance the ongoing suit, or perhaps simply to protect Wildwood Farm by transferring ownership out of her name, Mollie sold the farm to her brother Tom and his wife Maggie on May 29, 1912, for twenty-six hundred dollars. Tom and Maggie set up a trust deed through John E. Megown, cashier at the Ralls County Bank in New London. The deed named Mollie as the beneficiary. The note was due in eighteen months at 6 percent interest. Eighteen months later, Tom and Maggie quitclaimed back to Mollie their interest in the farm to release the trust deed to Megown. The note was never canceled or produced, but the parties swore that the note had been either lost or destroyed.[20]

On October 13, 1914, three and one-half years after the trial in New London, the Missouri Supreme Court made public its ruling on Mollie's appeal. On all but one of thirteen arguments laid out by Rendlen as the basis of appeal, the high court upheld the trial judge's actions. For example, the justices refused to criticize the decision to allow the jury to consider testimony from witnesses who offered lay opinions about Sam Heinbach's testamentary capacity. The court ruled that although the evidence on this point was by no means conclusive, in the end it should be up to the trial judge to determine what testimony should go to the jury.[21]

The high court also upheld the trial judge's refusal to let the jury consider as evidence the contracts of retainer between James Allison and Sam Heinbach's children. In the court's opinion, such contracts had no bearing on the testator's mental capacity. The court determined that to have allowed these contracts into evidence would have been prejudicial to the defendants. Furthermore, Jack Briscoe's role on behalf of Naomi Summers and Edith

Britton was irrelevant, since he had no formal contract for remuneration as an attorney in the case. [22]

Also rejected by the state supreme court was Rendlen's argument that Judge Ragland had improperly kept out evidence offered by the plaintiff. Ragland had refused to allow the plaintiff to admit in evidence a carbon copy of a deposition taken from Mary Smashey, who was unable to attend the circuit trial for medical reasons. At the time of the trial, Rendlen could not find the original deposition. He offered a carbon copy instead. In addition, Ragland had rejected the deposition of Ola Gregory on grounds that Mollie's attorneys had not demonstrated why she could not attend the trial.[23]

On one key issue, however, the high court agreed with Rendlen—that Judge Ragland's instructions to the jury contained a comment on the evidence. In Ragland's jury instructions, he said that although Sam Heinbach had transacted business on numerous occasions, this was irrelevant unless the jury determined that he "possessed a mind and memory sufficiently clear and unimpaired to take into consideration all his property, and the persons who had a natural and reasonable claim on his bounty, if any, and the disposition he desired to make of his property." The state supreme court ruled that this instruction was prejudicial to Mollie, and reversed and remanded the case.[24]

This ruling was important not only for Mollie and Feemy, but for the community as well. The *Ralls County Record* noted that "property rights at Ilasco have been unsettled on account of the result of the trial." There were those watching this case who now had to consider that Mollie and Feemy might, indeed, become joint owners of a major piece of Ilasco real estate next to the cement plant and thus determine future property use.[25]

The expensive, lengthy appeal process had exacerbated tensions between Mollie and Feemy, but the Atlas Portland Cement Company in the meantime had strengthened its influence in the area through even greater ties to local elites. On December 22, 1913, A. G. Croll, Atlas's assistant general manager, married New London's Ann Conn. This created tighter, interlocking family relationships and social networks that wedded Atlas more firmly to local bankers and politicians. Conn, a public school teacher, was the niece of Charles T. Hays, Hannibal's outgoing mayor and an opposing lawyer in Mollie's suit who later became an important circuit judge in the area. In addition, the marriage of Conn and Croll, who was soon promoted to general superintendent of all Atlas plants in the country, linked the company to the Megown family in New London. Benton B. Megown, a lawyer and former mayor of New London who was in the early stages of a career in Ralls County politics, was the circuit clerk and recorder of deeds at the time of the Heinbach trial in 1911. His brother, John E. Megown, was cashier at the Ralls County Bank, where Benton, too, had once been assistant cashier. When Conn married Croll, they left New London to reside in East Orange, New Jersey, but often returned to their farm west of New London where family reunions and gatherings provided important occasions for the above families and others to come together to discuss politics, business matters, and no doubt the controversial Heinbach case.[26]

This was also an important time for Atlas's booming operations in the Midwest. Missouri had become the nation's fifth-largest cement manufacturing state in 1910, and Atlas had appointed John R. Morron of Chicago to replace John Rogers Maxwell as president of the company. Thanks to the construction of a dam and power project on the Mississippi River at Keokuk, Iowa, with cement furnished by the Ilasco plant, Atlas officials had converted the plant from steam to electricity. This led to the formation of the North Missouri Light and Power Company, which by 1914, thanks to Atlas's granting of right-of-way, had extended the electrical current from Ilasco to other Ralls County towns.[27]

The activities of the North Missouri Light and Power Company encouraged real estate speculation in the Ilasco area by New London lawyers and officials who had figured prominently in efforts to prevent Mollie from inheriting the Heinbach tract. James Allison, who had provoked the dispute over Heinbach's will, and his brother, Judge Thomas E. Allison, who had rejected the will in probate court, were the largest individual stockholders in the company. James also represented the new company before the Public Utilities Board in Jefferson City to obtain a certificate granting the right to build a plant in New London.[28]

Jack Briscoe, another member of the legal team that opposed Mollie, became co-owner of 120 acres near the Heinbach tract shortly after the trial in 1911. Benjamin E. Hulse, a former prosecuting attorney in Ralls County, had bought this land from Herman Schwartz on June 3, 1911, and then three months later sold an undivided half-interest in it to Briscoe. Hulse and Briscoe then granted easements for the construction of power lines to the North Missouri Light and Power Company, in which they, too, owned stock.[29]

Through such actions, these lawyers could facilitate the county's access to electricity and make money for themselves, but there was an additional public interest that they could serve: to cooperate with Atlas's efforts to encourage the growth of Ilasco churches and schools. For at least four years before Hulse bought this tract of land from Schwartz, William True and the Ilasco Supply Company had been trying to drive Schwartz out of business in Ilasco, where Schwartz operated a tavern described by a local newspaper as a "regular hell hole." Finally, Schwartz sold his 120 acres in the Ilasco area and left for Kansas City. When Hulse purchased the tract, he first recalled the leases on lots being used for a tavern. He then donated land for the construction of a Slovak Lutheran Church, which held dedication ceremonies in Ilasco on November 5, 1911. This action by Hulse dovetailed with efforts already underway by Ilasco's Slovak Lutherans to form a congregation in the community.[30]

According to such plans, churches and schools would provide a healthy antidote to Ilasco's saloons, and to what Atlas officials regarded as low work productivity rooted in the heavy consumption of alcohol by cement plant workers. Atlas, of course, could enforce its anti-alcohol policies against workers who lived in company-owned housing, but the availability of liquor on non-company land in the community limited policing efforts. Until 1914, when a local option law closed Ilasco's saloons, this was a matter of growing concern in Ralls County, particularly among officials and native-born residents whose opposition to liquor mingled with hatred of Ilasco's Slavic immigrants. Reverend Thomas Wallace, a prohibition advocate, put his finger on the problem that confronted the public and the cement company soon after Sam Heinbach's death in 1910: half of the community was company-owned and half was not. Atlas, he observed, "keeps all clean and orderly within its limits, but beyond this lawlessness, profanity, drunkenness and fighting are common."[31]

Given the multitude of private and public interests in the Heinbach tract, it is not surprising that Mollie and Feemy barely had time to celebrate the state supreme court's decision before a new legal threat surfaced. Following a hearing presided over by Judge Ragland, Ralls County commissioners Charles T. Weaver, C. K. Gillum, and James T. Eales were appointed to survey, condemn, and set a price on part of a tract of land in Ilasco as the future site of a schoolhouse. They chose the Heinbach tract. In the circuit court on November 16, 1914, Marble Creek School District Number One initiated condemnation proceedings against several lots that formed the heart of the Heinbach tract. Board members Frank Moore, Frank Loomis, and Nelson Brown, who managed Atlas's company stables at the Ilasco plant, filed the suit.[32]

A recent Missouri law had given school boards the authority to condemn private land for such purposes provided they compensated owners of land that was confiscated. On grounds that there were too many contending parties to reach an agreement on the price to be paid for the lots, Judge Ragland set the compensation at $550. He allowed William K. Longmire and the Ilasco Supply Company to withdraw funds from that amount immediately as compensation for leases on the condemned tract, but he ordered the county treasurer to deposit the rest of the money in the circuit clerk's office until litigation of Sam Heinbach's will ended.[33]

This move revealed at least one important public motive of those who opposed Mollie's attempt to acquire most of the town site of Ilasco, but as county officials moved to shrink the Heinbach estate, she took steps to enlarge it. On January 30, 1915, she went on the offensive and retaliated by presenting a claim against the estate of Theodore Johnson, who had died a year earlier. In dispute was a strip of 2.23 acres on which Ilasco's major business section was located. This lucrative section, she claimed, in reality had belonged to Sam Heinbach but was mistakenly claimed by Theodore when he and Sam divided their tract in 1906. On this strip, the Ilasco Supply Company and several other store owners and merchants had leased several lots. Mollie claimed that she had asked Theodore and Eliza Jane to turn over rents collected from these lots, but that they refused. In her claim against Theodore's estate, she included copies of the original deeds and asked for restitution in the amount of $985.48. She calculated the amount based on monthly rental income of $14.50 from lots in this section, plus annual interest at 6 percent over the last five years.[34]

It soon became clear, however, that Mollie was no match for those poised to snatch Johnson's land, for James Allison was waiting astride Sam Heinbach's mysterious white horse to gallop across the Johnson tract, too. Allison had a long-standing, close relationship with Theodore and Eliza Jane Johnson; in fact, he had arranged for Eliza Jane to appoint him as executor of her will. Eliza Jane, who had no children, bequeathed one-half of her real estate to Theodore and the other half to Seymour Tranum, her nephew.[35]

Litigation had ensued just a few days after Eliza Jane died on September 11, 1911. A niece, Florence Thompson, sued the estate, claiming that Eliza Jane's sister and three brothers should each receive a share of one-fourteenth of the fifteen acres of land that Eliza Jane owned separately when she married Theodore. Thompson also claimed that she, Tranum, and other nieces and nephews were entitled to a one-twenty-eighth share of this land. She further charged that Theodore had used Eliza Jane's separate money in 1899 to buy what had become the most lucrative strip in Ilasco—the 2.23 acres which Mollie now sought. Theodore, she alleged, had used none of his own money for this and in fact had bought the land without Eliza Jane's written approval.[36]

Thompson urged the court to sell the fifteen acres that Eliza Jane had owned before the marriage and to divide the proceeds among all of Eliza Jane's heirs. She also urged the sale of the 2.23 acres on which many businesses were located, but requested that this strip be held by Theodore in trust for Eliza Jane's estate.[37]

What happened thereafter in the Johnson case provided a good indication of what the ultimate fate of the Heinbach tract might be. James Allison and New London officials were in a position to control the disposition of all of the Johnsons' land. When

Theodore Johnson died on January 28, 1914, he left no heirs. Neither did he leave a will. New London Mayor C. T. Lamb, who was also in the real estate business with a special expertise in bottoms land, was appointed by probate judge Thomas Allison as administrator of Theodore's estate. James Allison was one of Lamb's securities when the appointment was made.[38]

Until now, Thompson's suit against Eliza Jane's estate had gone nowhere. As executor, James Allison had kept Eliza Jane's will out of probate. In fact, it was not until February 28, 1916, more than four and a half years after her death, that Judge Benton B. Megown admitted it into probate. After Lamb's appointment, all of Eliza Jane's heirs, including Thompson, now sued Theodore's estate.[39]

Allison, Atlas, and an Atlas intermediary were about to enjoy the fruits of this manipulation. As the result of litigation involving so many contending interests, the Ralls County circuit court ruled that the Johnsons' tract could not be divided, and ordered that it be sold at a cash-only sheriff's sale at the New London courthouse on November 8, 1916. James Allison helped himself to Eliza Jane's separate estate of fifteen acres of farmland next to Ilasco for $685 and sold it four months later to Severino Fiorella for $1,000. The rest of Theodore Johnson's Ilasco tract went to Theodore Rendlen, a Hannibal lawyer and merchant who was the brother of Mollie's attorney. The business strip of 2.23 acres, which the Atlas Portland Cement Company had refused to buy from Johnson for $200 when it built its plant in 1901, now went for $2,010. The other twenty-six acres, which contained many residential lots, sold for $7,700.[40]

Theodore Rendlen was a mere intermediary in the purchase. He immediately handed over the land to Atlas. According to deed records, he sold it for exactly what he paid for it. This was undoubtedly a prearranged deal, given Rendlen's tight connections to the Hannibal National Bank, Atlas's Hannibal attorney George A. Mahan, and other members of the Chamber of Commerce. Using local intermediaries was Atlas's preferred method of acquiring land. The end result was beneficial to both parties in this case; Rendlen soon joined Mahan on the Hannibal National Bank's board of directors, and Atlas tightened the noose around the Heinbach tract, which was now surrounded by Atlas property.

The fact that Atlas paid more than $901 per acre for the business strip of 2.23 acres and more than $296 per acre for the rest of Johnson's twenty-six-acre tract was a good indication of just how badly company officials wanted to own Ilasco.[41]

Mollie's major concern in 1915–1916 was not the fate of the Johnson tract, however, but rather how to finance and present a stronger case in the next trial of Sam Heinbach's will. Toward those ends, she once again turned to Feemy for help, signing a new agreement with her on March 2, 1915. According to this agreement, Feemy agreed to pay one-third of the attorney fees in exchange for one-third of the rental income from the tract if they won the case. Mollie would retain for her own exclusive use and income the house and orchard tract on the hill, Sam's old log cabin, and the right to build new houses with the rental income she derived.[42]

With an even greater stake in the case's outcome, Feemy went to work feverishly in Ilasco, where she now lived most of the time with Mollie, to prepare for the next circuit trial. Given Mollie's near deafness, Feemy assumed major responsibility for gathering evidence in the community and shoring up her sister's case. With pencil and paper in hand, she became a familiar sight in the stores and shops, interviewing prospective witnesses, taking notes, procuring affidavits, and helping witnesses to "stand hitched." As one of her lawyers later put it, "She was on the job in the season and out of the season . . . Her zeal was unquestioned, her energy dynamic, and in her efforts to win the case she was as tireless as the law of gravitation."[43]

Feemy's own legal problems, due in part to her financial involvement in the Ilasco case, kept her tied up part of the time, however. In the summer of 1914 she had arranged for Fred Exter, a Hannibal concrete contractor, to lay a gutter, curbing, and sidewalk on her property in Hannibal pursuant to a city ordinance. According to her, a city engineer, William Smiley, had told her that she did not have to do the work until the spring of 1915, when she "hoped to have some ready cash." Smiley also allegedly told her that she could select her own contractor for the work. In late 1914, however, contractor J. H. Dunlap suddenly did the work without Feemy's permission, and on May 18, 1915, he obtained a special tax bill from the City of Hannibal in the amount of $90.27 charged against her property.[44]

Dunlap then assigned the tax bill to T. J. Cousins, a Hannibal businessman who brought a suit against Feemy for $90.27 plus 8 percent annual interest since June 18, 1915. She received a summons to appear in the Hannibal Court of Common Pleas on the second Monday in January 1916. On April 20, 1916, the court ordered her to pay Cousins a total of $141 in judgment and costs.[45]

Feemy now decided to take over this case from her Hannibal attorney, Roy Hamlin, in an attempt to appeal the judgment. She complained, in fact, that it was M. L. Farres, her first attorney in this case, who was to blame for her legal problems in the first place. According to her, he told her that he would attend to her interests to ensure that she would be held "harmless against any judgment." Furthermore, she pointed out that spring rains had already wiped out the shoddy gutter and curbing work done by Dunlap and that as a result, water had run down her lot and damaged the property. She denounced the entire case as "a cheat and a fraud."[46]

About a week after Feemy filed an "Action to Set Aside Judgement for Fraud" against Cousins in the Hannibal Court of Common Pleas, the second trial in the Heinbach will suit opened in Bowling Green. A local newspaper described it as "one of the most hotly contested suits in this section in years."[47] The trial took place in the Pike County circuit court between August 28 and September 2, 1916. Mollie once again mortgaged Wildwood Farm to borrow $125 just before going to Bowling Green for the trial. Although more than five years had lapsed since the first trial, the case still generated great interest among area residents. Most of Ilasco's native-born population and many from Hannibal came to Bowling Green for the trial. Sam Heinbach's daughters, represented now by James Allison, C. T. Hays, David A. Ball, and Jefferson D. Hostetter, had tried but failed to block Mollie's request to move the trial there. Mollie, who retained Rendlen but replaced Neeper with Eugene Pearson as a trial lawyer, had requested a change of venue to Pike County. She alleged that she could not get a fair trial in New London because of the prejudice of Judge William T. Ragland and residents of Ralls County.[48]

During the trial presided over by Judge Edgar B. Woolfolk, the extent of Feemy's hard work soon became evident. With her gathering evidence, there would be no replay of Neeper's lackluster performance at this trial. Rendlen used the witnesses whom she enlisted. Calvin Bulkley, owner of a meat business in Hannibal who had not testified at the first trial, testified that Feemy had come to his house to interview him. The testimony of new witnesses for the plaintiff revealed that Feemy had earlier interviewed Thomas Hedges, E. S. Stewart, Arthur A. Taylor, Samuel P. Young, Mitchell T. Smashey, Josephine Freeman, and several others. In the case of Freeman, who was too sick with rheumatism to travel to Bowling Green, Feemy picked her up in a taxi and took her to the second floor of the Hannibal Bank Building for the taking of a deposition on March 31, 1916.[49]

Feemy's energetic role in the case disturbed the opposing attorneys, who then tried to divert attention to her activities and her stake in the property during the trial. The jurors' eyes found her when Calvin Bulkley, at the behest of attorney J. D. Hostetter, pointed her out during cross-examination as the woman with a big hat in the courtroom. Hostetter complained before the jury that she "has been scouring the neighborhood up there [in Ilasco and Hannibal] getting people to sign papers."[50]

James Allison imputed sinister motives to Feemy's role in the case, suggesting that she possessed some type of coercive power over witnesses. Arthur Taylor, under questioning by Allison, acknowledged that in the presence of a judge he had signed an affidavit that Feemy had written, but he denied that she had threatened him if he did not show up for the trial. Mitchell Smashey, too, denied that she had forced him to sign any papers. Hostetter even insinuated that Feemy, herself, had written answers for witness Samuel Young.[51]

Unlike in the first trial, the defense attorneys introduced several women to paint a less than flattering view of Mollie and Sam Heinbach. They may have shot themselves in the foot, however, with the testimony of Mary Baker, who seemed overly eager to contradict everything said by any of Mollie's witnesses. Several witnesses had testified that Sam spruced up a bit and enjoyed a higher quality of life after he married Mollie, but Baker, who had cleaned Sam's house for him before his marriage to Mollie, disputed that. She insisted that Sam did not even like his new house or piano.[52]

Baker's credibility and stormy past were quickly called into question on cross-examination. In December 1905, she had shot and killed her husband, Joseph, in Ilasco while they both were reportedly heavily under the influence of alcohol. With James Allison as her attorney at that time, she claimed that she killed her husband in self-defense in a domestic dispute, that Joseph was charging her with a fork when she shot him. After the second-degree murder charge against her was dropped, she had then married Albert Lester, but continued to have run-ins with the law. So did Albert. In fact, both of them later fled Ilasco in order to avoid prosecution for "keeping an immoral house."[53]

In earlier testimony, Fred Jeffers had described Mary Baker as "quite a drinking woman" and recalled that she and Albert Lester were staying at Sam Heinbach's cabin at a time when he, too, was rooming there. Baker denied that Jeffers or Lester ever lived there, however, and she disputed that she was ever run out of Ilasco or Hannibal. She testified that she had seen Sam drunk and muttering to himself in his room many times. When asked on cross-examination if she in fact had ever done any drinking with Sam, she insisted, "I was always a lady."[54]

Evidence also emerged during the trial that surprised even the judge when William F. True's role as administrator of the Heinbach estate came under fire. True admitted that besides receiving his percentage of Heinbach's estate, he was getting paid an additional fifty dollars per year by Allison, Hays, and other lawyers representing Sam Heinbach's children. Judge Woolfolk, in disbelief, asked True to repeat what he had just said, but he refused to let True reveal the names of those attorneys for the court record. True, when asked on cross-examination if he had made the comment that the longer the case lasted, the better for him financially, replied, "I don't say I didn't say it; I believe I said, I didn't care of [*sic*] they didn't close it for twenty years."[55]

About forty witnesses testified that Sam Heinbach was sane at the time his will was drawn up, compared to less than half of that number who regarded him as insane. Eugene Pearson, in his closing remarks to the jury, emphasized that Sam had leased lots to "men of high degree and men of low degree to the rich and to the poor." In remarks that prompted the opposing attorneys to request that Judge Woolfolk rebuke him, Pearson called attention to the insincerity of those who had once done business with Sam but who now claimed that he was mentally unsound. "I say during all the years that this man was doing business there," he insisted, "his making leases and in his selling garden seed, and all the business that he was in with them, not one of them up until the time of his death thought that his acts were those of a man of unsound mind."[56]

Moving the case out of Ralls County paid off. The jury, after listening to fifty-two witnesses called on Mollie's behalf and to thirty-one for the defendants, quickly returned a verdict in favor of Mollie, but the battle was far from over. The financial and emotional endurance of both sisters would yet be tested further, for on November 25, 1916, Judge Woolfolk granted Edith Britton and Naomi Summers an appeal to the Missouri Supreme Court.[57]

The new verdict must have really stirred up things in Ilasco. Given Feemy's energetic role in preparing for the second trial, some who opposed her began a campaign of harassment that escalated from arguments to even sharper confrontations. Shortly after the trial, Feemy tangled with Ralls County officials who may have been part of this campaign. Thomas E. Allison, who as probate judge had rejected Sam Heinbach's will in 1910, had since left that office to become Ralls County's prosecuting attorney. At his behest, Sheriff H. A. Pritchett arrested Feemy on charges of carrying a concealed weapon—a revolving pistol. The court ordered her to appear on February 4, 1917, to answer the indictment, and appointed Frank C. Hendrix and D. M. Stout as her attorneys.[58]

It is unclear what took place between Feemy and her court-appointed lawyers, but they refused to represent her. She undoubtedly insisted on doing things her way in the case. When they showed up at the New London courthouse on February 4, they requested that the court allow them to withdraw as her lawyers. The judge chastised and fined each of them and ordered a continuation of the case, but he told Feemy in exasperation to hire her own counsel.[59]

By now, Feemy's anger and contempt for lawyers and judges were hard to contain. Insisting that her arrest was merely an attempt to harass her, she called into question the motivation and source of the concealed weapons charge. She then refused to hire a lawyer, opting to handle the case herself. On March 26, 1917, she filed her own motion to force prosecuting attorney Allison to pinpoint the place, day, and time that she allegedly had a concealed weapon in her possession. She also filed a supporting affidavit of Walter C. Fisher and other papers in the case, but Allison backed off. He did not pursue the case further, and the court dismissed charges against her.[60]

Feemy also had to refocus her attention on the lien against her Hannibal property obtained by T. J. Cousins in April 1916, in the Hannibal Court of Common Pleas. In response to Cousins's threats to force the sale of her property on Chestnut Street, she filed a suit against him, trying to make the City of Hannibal a party to the suit on January 8, 1917. The court denied her motion to set aside the judgment against her and overruled her application for a stay of execution on October 23, 1917. She then borrowed nine hundred dollars from Hannibal's George W. Pine, out of which she paid the lien against her property and court costs involved in the litigation over the gutter and curbing tax bill issued by the City of Hannibal.[61]

While Feemy attended to her own legal matters in Hannibal, the Heinbach will suit winded its way through the Missouri Supreme Court. This was the last time that Sam Heinbach's life would be put under the high court's microscope. The second trial had produced more than twelve hundred pages of transcript to review, but by April 1918 the court was ready to announce its ruling. Missouri Supreme Court Presiding Judge Robert Franklin Walker, justices Charles B. Faris and Fred L. Williams, and commissioners John Turner White and Reuben F. Roy (from New London) now knew far more about the life and habits of "the filthy old testator" than they undoubtedly cared to know. As noted in a tone of weariness by commissioner White, who wrote the court's opinion, Heinbach's

> entire life was lighted up as with Roentgen rays . . . The doctors who attended him in sickness, the lawyers who transacted business with him for other people, those who leased lots from him and paid him rent, the nurse he had, his housecleaner, washerwoman, butcher, fish peddler, those who sold him vegetables, and groceries, and tobacco; those whom he worked for, those who worked for him and with him; those who sold him drink and those who got drunk with him, were drawn upon without limit to tell what they knew about his habits and characteristics.[62]

The state court, after commissioner Roy recused himself because of his Ralls County roots and close ties to the case, upheld the Pike County circuit court's verdict in favor of Mollie. The justices rejected the appellants' complaint that Judge Woolfolk had excluded evidence that Mollie used John Hinkson, William Cutsinger, and J. T. Fisher to set her up with Sam Heinbach in order to get his property. The state court, adhering to a strict contractual assessment of Mollie's marriage to Sam, also ruled that Woolfolk had properly kept out the issue of undue influence because of a lack of evidence. "The most that can be said of the testimony excluded," wrote commissioner White, "is that Mrs. Heinbach sought the marriage with the old man because of his money. That she discharged the duties of a good wife, that his appearance and habits were much improved by the marriage, and that he entertained a true affection for his wife appears without dispute. No evidence, direct or circumstantial, was offered tending to show that she did anything or said anything which had any tendency unduly to influence Heinbach in making the disposition of his property which he made."[63]

The Supreme Court also rejected the appellants' argument that Sam Heinbach's hallucinations confirmed that he did not understand his business transactions. The court opinion noted that fifty or sixty of Sam's leases that were introduced during the trial provided good evidence that he knew exactly what he was doing. Sam may have been an alcoholic, but he knew enough not to transact business while he was drunk. In regard to Sam's infamous white horse, commissioner White observed that "the account given by the witnesses of that matter leaves one in doubt as to whether the white horse, as he spoke of it, was an apparition or a figure of speech."[64]

The appellants' attorneys had also complained that Woolfolk erred when he excluded the testimony of several witnesses for the defendants on the issue of whether Sam Heinbach was sane. The state supreme court emphasized that lawyers on both sides had been given considerable latitude in eliciting opinions about Sam's mental capacity. In some cases, even though Woolfolk had disallowed general statements by some witnesses, he then allowed those same witnesses to answer the same questions in a slightly different way. For example, when Dora Doyle testified that Sam "never had much sense to his talk," Woolfolk ordered the statement stricken out. Shortly afterward, however, he allowed this response by Doyle to the same question: "I don't recollect what he said because I don't remember, but he would say one thing that had no connection and jump off on something else." Similarly, Iva Lee's statement during the trial that Sam "would sit there and mutter, and I couldn't get any sense out of it" was disallowed by the judge, but when an attorney asked her to describe Sam's manner of talk, Woolfolk let stand her reply that "no sir, [he'd] just mutter, I couldn't understand him; that is all I know."[65]

The state court asserted that the signing and witnessing of the will conformed to statutory requirements, and rejected the argument by the appellants' attorneys that Judge Woolfolk should have rebuked the plaintiff's counsel, Eugene Pearson, for several comments to the jury during closing arguments. Woolfolk had sustained the defense counsel's objections at the time, but he did not rebuke Pearson. All in all, Supreme Court Commissioner White praised Woolfolk's role: "The case was tried with consummate ability and industry. It was fought through with pertinacious and aggressive determination on both sides, and fairly and impartially managed by the trial judge. There is no reason why the verdict of the jury should be disturbed."[66]

Finally, the state court upheld Judge Woolfolk's instructions to the jury. In their appeal of the circuit court decision, the defendants' attorneys had argued that Woolfolk misled the jury when he instructed them that Sam Heinbach had the right to disinherit his children if he so wished. Commissioner White emphasized that this instruction did not "single out facts, but is a general statement of the law as fully recognized by this court."[67]

After fighting tooth-and-nail for eight years to probate the will, Mollie and Feemy had finally gained joint ownership of land that could provide economic security in their old age. Mollie was now sixty-four years old, and Feemy was fifty-seven. All that remained was for them to pay their attorneys, collect and divide the rents now in the possession of administrator William F. True, and make plans to supervise future collections from lot rentals in Ilasco. Or, if they so chose after this exhausting battle, they could sell the entire tract to Atlas or any other potential buyer, and then split the money.

As Feemy and Mollie prepared to celebrate their hard-earned victory, they had every right to feel proud of their important role in devising a successful legal strategy to win the case. Given their contemptuous view of lawyers in general, they no doubt took most if not all of the credit for the victory. This was probably especially true of Feemy. The Heinbach tract had lost several choice lots that were sliced off by the school district, but unlike the Johnson tract, it had not ended up in the hands of Atlas. Mollie and Feemy had stood tall against the "whole crowd of the gang." For the moment, at least, they had outsmarted an alliance of area elites whose plans were to convert Ilasco into a company town.

Six

Feemy's Bloodcurdling Threats? Or Attorney Charles Rendlen's Mental Hobgoblins?

> They [Mollie and Feemy] are excusable if not justified in assuming the law is a kind of a puzzle to be worked out by craft and intrigue. From their standpoint it may absolutely seem so.
>
> —*E. L. Alford, Ralls County attorney, 1920*

By the time the Missouri Supreme Court issued its ruling in Mollie's favor, she, her attorney, and an intermediary for the cement plant were prepared to inject new drama into the Ilasco property dispute. For them, the ruling represented not the end of the case, but rather the beginning of a new round of litigation—this time against Feemy. Little did Feemy know that as she and Mollie savored their hard-fought legal victory and looked forward to the final settlement of Sam Heinbach's estate, Mollie was engaged in secret talks with Rendlen, her attorney, about the future of the Ilasco tract, now reportedly worth between twenty thousand and thirty thousand dollars.[1]

The lure of cloak-and-dagger intrigue and greed proved too seductive for Mollie. She and Feemy now owned the tract as joint tenants, but Rendlen tempted her with a deal to sell the entire tract without consulting Feemy and to keep all of the proceeds for herself. There was an important catch, however, for Mollie would receive only about half of the tract's value; Feemy's half would go to the buyer. The plan required litigation to break the joint deed, but Rendlen had lined up a buyer who allegedly offered to finance a suit against Feemy. Rendlen, of course, would steer the case through the courts, but in the meantime Mollie was to disappear and remain in hiding, allegedly out of fear that Feemy planned to kill her and assume sole ownership of the tract.

The scheme illustrated just how much the stress of the previous eight years had eaten away at the sisters' relationship. Mollie may have been exhausted from living with Feemy in Ilasco, worn down by the sheer force of her sister's personality, her confrontational politics, and her overpowering determination to fight no matter what the costs. Feemy's arrest on a concealed weapons charge in 1916 may have embarrassed Mollie in the community and contributed to her growing discomfort with how intense the conflict generated by the case was getting. Maybe she figured that it was time to get out before confrontations in the community escalated even more, or perhaps she simply seized an opportunity to profit at Feemy's expense after using her money and energies for eight years to win the will suit. She may have genuinely suspected Feemy's motives and in fact may have exaggerated her fears to Rendlen in order to play the game with him. Or, maybe selling the Ilasco tract to Atlas was what Mollie had intended all along. If this was the case, she apparently knew that she could never convince Feemy to agree to the sale. Whatever the explanation, the case took a bizarre twist when Mollie left town mysteriously after selling the entire tract for only eleven thousand dollars to Petru Sirbu, a Rumanian labor agent for Atlas who was an incorporator and former business partner of William True in Atlas's Ilasco Supply Company. Sirbu had other financial ties to Rendlen through area real estate deals.

With Rendlen as his attorney, too, Sirbu kept to the mysterious script by preparing at once for his own departure from Ilasco. For ninety-three hundred dollars, he sold to George W. Myers 188 acres of land on the outskirts of Ilasco that he had picked up for only thirty-one hundred dollars at a public auction four years earlier. He then allegedly put one thousand dollars in an escrow account in a Hannibal bank to finance a suit against Feemy to break the joint deed. Finally, as swiftly as Mollie disappeared, so did he (perhaps with her in tow)—to pursue new business opportunities in Youngstown, Ohio.[2]

For the next two and a half years, this suit kept Feemy tied up in court and ate away at what little respect she still had for the law and local officials. It jeopardized her property in Hannibal and Oklahoma, and it drove a deep wedge between her and Mollie. Feemy now recognized that the "whole crowd of the gang" that had worked to keep Mollie from inheriting the Ilasco tract would now do everything they could to cut her out of the joint deed and to back Mollie's sale of the land to Sirbu.

It is not clear exactly when Rendlen and Mollie cooked up the deal, but the evidence suggests that by late March 1918, she was preparing to double-cross her sister. When Rendlen informed Mollie of her victory in the Missouri Supreme Court, she at first concealed this from Feemy. At the time, Mollie was busy getting ready to sell Wildwood Farm, the land that once belonged to her mother. This would provide money to help sustain her during her planned disappearance, but there was a technical snag in the title to the farm that had to be cleared up before she could sell it. On May 29, 1912, Mollie had sold it for twenty-six hundred dollars to her brother, Tom, who conveyed a trust deed to J. E. Megown, cashier at the Ralls County Bank (and Mollie's future guardian), to secure a promissory note for that amount. The trust deed listed Mollie as the beneficiary, and for some reason Tom and his wife Maggie quitclaimed the land back to her on November 29, 1913. Since they never furnished evidence that the note had ever been produced or canceled, this required a signed "Affidavit of Payment, and Loss or Destruction of Note." Once this was done, the court gave Mollie clear title to the land, which she then sold for twenty-four hundred dollars on April 29, 1918.[3]

The next item of business for Mollie was to settle an old score with her former attorney, Frederick W. Neeper. This she could do with Feemy's cooperation. On May 2, 1918, the sisters appeared before Bruce Peterson, an Ilasco justice of the peace, and swore to an affidavit amending the agreement that they had signed on March 2, 1915, regarding assignment of rentals and payment of attorney fees in the Heinbach will suit. Still furious over what they regarded as Neeper's incompetent role in the first trial in 1911, they insisted in the affidavit that he "did not render the conscientious and material service therein agreed upon." They complained that he forced Mollie "to employ his assistant, and to sign a contract with said assistant to which she neither agreed, nor was [she] aware of its contents at the time of subscribing to it." They further charged that Neeper "so crippled her case with the aid of his assistant . . . that the case was lost because he refused to take a change of venue, and [refused] to use the witnesses" whom they had suggested. Since in their view this had cost Mollie the verdict in that trial in New London, they announced in their affidavit that neither Neeper nor his assistant was entitled to compensation for their services. In short, the sisters went on record indicating that they did not intend to pay Neeper's fee.[4]

After taking care of Neeper, Mollie stopped by the Hannibal Court of Common Pleas to give Feemy a little financial help with her ongoing legal problems with her property on Chestnut Street in Hannibal. Feemy, out of fear that the court would order the sale of her property because of a minor judgment and lien against it, had filed an injunction to block its sale. According to her, the clerk, Gardener S. Brockenbrough, told her that she needed to deposit $119.27 to cover possible expenses. On May 11, 1918, Mollie deposited that amount—later described by Feemy as "conscience money"—with the clerk's office for Feemy's use in the case.[5]

Mollie then made secret arrangements to slip out of Ilasco. Her victory in the state supreme court had brought William F. True's long tenure as administrator of Sam Heinbach's estate to an end on August 12, 1918. As True arranged for the final settlement of accounts to be made in the Ralls County probate court, Mollie finalized plans with Rendlen and Sirbu for her departure and the upcoming legal battle against Feemy. On August 12, Mollie met with True, apparently at a designated location in Quincy, Illinois, accepted his accounting, and left town. It is not clear whether True turned the rental income over to her at that time, or whether he gave it to Rendlen for safekeeping pending the outcome of the suit to break the joint deed. When Feemy arrived at the New London courthouse, however, probate judge Benton B. Megown, who was privy to the plan by Mollie, Rendlen, and Sirbu, refused to pay Feemy her one-third share of the rentals on grounds that "she was an interloper and had no right to said rents."[6]

Feemy returned to an empty house in Ilasco, fumed over Mollie's disappearance, and tried to figure out what had happened. Within a month, she had a clear answer. On September 11, Rendlen filed an equity suit on behalf of Mollie and Petru Sirbu in the Ralls County circuit court, charging that Feemy had forced her way into Mollie's home and coerced her into making out the joint deed in March 1911. Although there is no evidence that Rendlen over the previous seven years had expressed concern that Feemy might harm Mollie, he now claimed that Feemy had terrorized her into fleeing. He insisted that Mollie feared for her life if Feemy found out where she was hiding. He alleged that Feemy had also threatened their cousin, (Sara) Ellen Londenberg, at the time they set up the joint deed.

With a clear grasp of the full significance of her sister's abrupt disappearance, Feemy quickly went to work on the case but could not locate Sirbu or Mollie for depositions. When Rendlen notified Feemy that he intended to take a deposition from Ellen Londenberg (now Sturn), on November 1, 1918, in Bradford, Illinois, she informed him that she would be there in person for the taking of Ellen's deposition in order to cross-examine her. With less than a week's notice and short of money, she did not hire a lawyer for the trip, opting instead to conduct the cross-examination herself. According to Feemy, she told Rendlen that she would be there at five o'clock in the afternoon, but he took the deposition at four o'clock and adjourned the meeting before she got there. Thus, Feemy endured the expense and fatigue of a train ride to and from Bradford for nothing.[7]

Sensing now that she might not be able to handle this case by herself, Feemy first hired Ralls County attorney Edmund L. Alford and then Oliver C. Clay, a state representative from Lewis County, when she obtained a change of venue to nearby Canton in the Lewis circuit court. Clay's work in the Missouri legislature kept him tied up in Jefferson City until May 14, 1919, but in early June he sent a letter to Rendlen requesting him to produce both Mollie and Sirbu in either Hannibal or Canton on June 12 and 13 so he could take depositions from them. Rendlen apparently did not reply.[8]

In the meantime, a systematic campaign of harassment against Feemy intensified in Ilasco. Sirbu, after allegedly buying the land from Mollie, and before leaving Ilasco for Ohio, had leased the orchard on her property to John Lendak, a Slovak immigrant who then began pasturing livestock there. Feemy, who lived and raised chickens on this property, claimed that on April 24, 1919, Lendak threatened to sue her unless she kept her chickens out of what he now insisted was his rented pasture. She then petitioned for an injunction to keep him off the premises until the court decided who owned the land. She emphasized that since Sirbu had no legal right to the land, his lease of the orchard to Lendak was illegal. She urged the court to compel Sirbu and other parties to return the money that Lendak had paid to rent the orchard tract and to force Lendak to stay off her property. His cows had already damaged fruit-bearing trees, and he had cut down other fruit trees on the tract. Pleading that she was "under financial stress . . . and has her living to make by the sale of eggs and chickens," she drew up the petition herself and filed it in the office of the Ralls County circuit clerk and recorder.[9]

Feemy insisted that harassment of her by Lendak, who was also Rendlen's client, was only the latest indication of a broader, even physically threatening campaign against her by those who opposed her half-interest in the Ilasco tract. She now feared for her personal safety. In the petition for an injunction against Lendak, she complained that he had often "assaulted her and used profane language in addressing her." She expressed fear of him "and the class of men" who came with him onto her property, and she requested "that if it be possible, she may be protected in her home."[10]

In a reference to her arrest on charges of carrying a concealed weapon soon after she and Mollie had won the will suit in the Pike County circuit court in 1916, she argued that it was Lendak, in fact, who "designedly had her arrested under the instruction of others, for the purpose of degrading, mortifying and debasing her in the eyes of the public." Rendlen, she charged, had already introduced such evidence in the pending suit to break the joint deed in the Lewis County circuit court.[11]

Feemy and her attorney feared that it would be too risky to go to trial in Canton in mid-June of 1919 without having first cross-examined Mollie, Ellen Sturn, and Petru Sirbu. Since Clay had been working on the case for only one month, he felt especially reluctant to try the case with such inadequate preparation. On June 18, therefore, Feemy filed for a continuance in the case and formally requested that the Lewis County circuit court in the meantime appoint a receiver to take care of the Ilasco tract. She argued that the continuance would give Clay time to prepare for the case and track down Mollie for a deposition.

By now, the strain was apparently taking its toll on Feemy's health. In her request for a continuance, she presented a certificate from C. O. Shanks, a Canton physician, recommending that she not undertake a trial at that time. She emphasized to the court that "the condition of her health is such that she could not stand the strain that a trial would subject her to . . . [but that] with medical treatment she will by the next term of this court be enabled to gain strength so that she may stand the strain of a long drawn out trial such as this will be."[12]

On June 18, 1919, Judge James A. Cooley refused to appoint a receiver for the Ilasco tract and denied Feemy's request for a continuance. This convinced her that she could not get a fair trial in his court. Later that day, she obtained a change of venue to the Pike County circuit court in Bowling Green.[13]

The change of venue gave Feemy time to rest briefly before really going to work on the case, and once she did, it did not take long for her to get under Rendlen's skin. On August 13, 1919, the Lewis County circuit clerk transferred the case papers to Bowling Green, including depositions taken by Rendlen from W. F. True, Eugene Pearson, E. S. Stewart, Alice Stewart, Maybell Taylor, Harry J. Ellsworth, Melvina Ellsworth, Thomas E. Allison, Sarah Ellen Sturn, and Mark Kinder. In response, Feemy served a notice to Rendlen and Harrison White, his new law partner, on August 30 that she would be taking several depositions later that day in the office of Ilasco justice of the peace Chris E. Miller. Acting without an attorney, she conducted her own examination of six Ilasco residents. Rendlen looked on as Ida M. Shulse took the depositions in shorthand and then transcribed them. Suddenly, however, before the witnesses could sign their depositions, Feemy grabbed the depositions and left Miller's office without paying Schulse or even allowing Rendlen to have copies.[14]

Although Rendlen still refused to produce Mollie so that Feemy could take a deposition, he summoned Feemy to his office five days later to take a deposition from her. Upon being sworn, however, Feemy was defiant. "I refuse to testify," she asserted. In response, Rendlen reminded her that "when an action is pending where fraud and duress is charged to determine the validity [of] deeds, such as is the case here, that the opposing party has the right to take the deposition of such person as a witness in the case." When he warned that the court might throw out all of her pleadings if she failed to cooperate, she relented and agreed to testify. After answering all of Rendlen's questions, however, she infuriated him even more by repeatedly refusing to sign the deposition. His office mailed her the deposition, but she returned it unsigned. If she could not get a deposition from Mollie, Rendlen could not get a signed one from her![15]

Feemy struggled to raise money to protect her interests in the suit. On March 12, 1919, she mortgaged her property in Shawnee, Oklahoma, to borrow eleven hundred dollars from Mrs. E. J. Beach, a Shawnee resident, and on June 25, 1919, she borrowed eleven hundred dollars from the Shawnee Realty and Investment Company. She assigned $1,207.80—her share of the Heinbach rents—to the Shawnee Realty Company, with the rest to be used by the company to pay the 1919 taxes on her property in Shawnee. She appointed John W. Jones, of Shawnee, as trustee to handle the collection and payments.[16]

The litigation over the joint deed cost Feemy her property in Hannibal. She had earlier borrowed nine hundred dollars from Hannibal's George W. Pine to help avoid the threatened sale of her property on Chestnut Street as a result of the lien issued to T. J. Cousins, but on March 24, 1919, Pine sold the note to William S. Joseph, proprietor of the Hannibal Mercantile Company. Feemy remained in good standing with Joseph, but she refused to pay her former attorney, Oliver Clay, a fee of $234.29 plus $17.12 for costs incurred in the Lewis County circuit court. Clay, after all, had done nothing in the case as far as she was concerned, and she was not about to pay him. On January 3, 1920, the Marion County sheriff carried out a judgment on Clay's behalf against Feemy's Chestnut Street property in Hannibal.[17]

When Judge Edgar B. Woolfolk opened the equity suit in the Pike County circuit court in 1920, nearly a decade had passed since Feemy and Mollie, with the help of their cousin Ellen, had drawn up the joint deed to the Ilasco tract. Ralls County's Edmund L. Alford, a former newspaper editor of the *Perry Enterprise* and now Feemy's chief attorney, immediately called attention to the long history of the case and insisted that the equity suit was much more complex and devious than it appeared on the surface. "The suit presents some mysterious and sinister aspects," he argued. "Ostensibly it is an effort on the part of one sister to recover from another sister an undivided one half interest in the land in controversy, but in reality and in truth it is a suit prosecuted for and on behalf of Petru Sirbu, the enterprising foreigner and the hidden and concealed interest behind him, *against both sisters*" (Alford's emphasis).[18]

Alford bore in on those "mysterious and sinister aspects" of the case. First, he pointed out that although the court had upheld his motion to remove Sirbu as a proper party plaintiff in the matter, Sirbu stood to profit considerably if the court divested Feemy of her half-interest in the Ilasco tract. Her interest would then go not to Mollie but to Sirbu, even though he was no longer a party to the record and had left the state. Alford insisted that Sirbu was a mere front man for the hidden, but unnamed, interests that put up the money to prosecute the case against Feemy.[19]

Alford protested Mollie's "mysterious disappearance," which had now lasted for more than two years, and he charged that the hidden interests behind Sirbu were paying witnesses and furnishing money to keep her outside the court's jurisdiction. Alford thus had no access to her for cross-examination, since she had failed to appear in court at any time during the course of this suit. He rejected Rendlen's explanation that she was afraid to reveal her whereabouts to Feemy, and he criticized Sirbu, too, for failing to appear to testify on his own behalf. In Alford's view, this refusal on the part of both of Rendlen's clients to undergo cross-examination amounted to "a concealment of the facts."[20]

Rendlen tried the case on the ex-parte depositions of Ellen Sturn and Mollie. In Mollie's deposition, taken on February 20, 1919, in Cincinnati, Ohio, she claimed that Feemy had altered the joint deed after they notarized it. "She changed it and added words and would not show me or tell me what they were," alleged Mollie. "[She] said it was none of my God-damned business." Mollie insisted that Feemy had added the survivorship clause against her will: "I wanted to get hold of the deed and tear it up, but could not."[21]

According to Ellen's deposition, Feemy altered the deed at Mollie's home in Ilasco without permission. After they had signed and notarized the deed, Ellen claimed, the three of them returned to Ilasco on the train, and it was then that Feemy "wrote this extra on the paper." Ellen added, "I saw her write it, but I didn't know what it was . . . We didn't know what she put on [it]."[22]

Alford rejected this allegation. "This Court," he emphasized, "has been accorded an ocular inspection of the original deed at the trial of this cause and now knows to a certainty that charge . . . is absolutely groundless because the deed shows no evidence of any alteration of words or erasures whatever." He pointed out that the deeds contained the handwriting of Feemy as well as Mollie, since both sisters participated in drafting the deeds. This was consistent with Feemy's testimony. In response to Rendlen's claim that Feemy had fraudulently added the survivorship clause, Alford insisted that she had written nothing on the deeds after they were executed. Even if she had, he argued, this survivorship clause did not change the fundamental effect of the joint deed.[23]

Alford alleged that Rendlen, as part of a "carefully constructed camouflage," had shaped Ellen's deposition by coaxing and suggesting answers for her. Moreover, he suggested that Sirbu had probably paid her. Ellen testified that Feemy had made bloodcurdling threats, but Alford pointed out with sarcasm that Ellen, when asked by Rendlen to explain, replied: "Mrs. Heinbach was deaf and she scared her, she said she couldn't get through her law suit, she had to listen for her and she wouldn't help her—*that was her threats*" (Alford's emphasis). In Ellen's deposition, she criticized Feemy for opposing Mollie's suggestion to grant a one-third interest in the Ilasco tract to their brother, Tom, but Alford in response stressed that Tom was "the only one who would have a kick coming in this matter, because *he* was left out in the cold" while Feemy and Mollie each obtained a half-interest.[24]

The "smooth diction," "marvelous knowledge of the use of legal terms," and "sonorous sentences" contained in Mollie's ex-parte deposition made Alford suspicious. In fact, he argued that it was likewise Rendlen and not Ellen who was testifying in the latter's deposition. He suggested that both depositions were nothing more than Rendlen's handiwork, and he drew on biblical imagery to make that point to Judge Woolfolk: "The Court is in a position to appreciate the embarassment [*sic*] of Isaac the blind, Israelitish Patriarch, when his son Jacob approached him covered with skins to obtain the blessing which was due to his hairy brother Esau; after hearing Jacob's voice and feeling his hairy hands the blind old father pathetically exclaimed, 'The voice is Jacob's voice, but the hands are the hands of Esau.'"[25]

From Alford's perspective, another suspicious element in the case was the question of why Mollie had waited seven and one-half years to allege that Feemy had coerced her into making the joint deed. He challenged Mollie's claim that she had complained to Rendlen about what Feemy had done at that time, but that Rendlen advised her that there would be plenty of time later to bring a suit against her sister after the will suit had been won. Alford pointed out that any capable lawyer should know that the pendency of the will suit was no barrier to Mollie's prosecuting a suit against Feemy to set aside the joint deed. "But even that excuse, poor and flimsy as it is," he added, "becomes entirely invalid and insincere, when it is noted that after the will suit was actually won by Mrs. Heinbach in the Pike County Circuit Court . . . no move was made by Mrs. Heinbach or her well-versed attorney to set aside the deeds in controversy until after the case had winded its weary way thru [*sic*] the Supreme Court."[26]

What really demolished Rendlen's case, however, were the nearly one hundred letters that Mollie had written to Feemy during the period in question. Feemy, who saved the letters, introduced them as evidence. These letters contradicted allegations that she had forced her way into Mollie's home, used coercion against her and Ellen, altered the deed, and threatened to kill Mollie unless she cut her in as joint owner of the tract. In fact, the letters indicated that all three of the women maintained friendly relations after execution of the deed. Besides, as Alford noted, "It is taxing the credulity of the court to ask it to assume that Mrs. Koller could overawe and coerce two women to keep them in subjection while they were going on the train to Hannibal, and while going about the town and brow beat them into making the deeds in controversy."[27]

The letters did reveal tensions over Feemy's unilateral, headstrong decision to file the joint deed so soon after the first trial of Sam Heinbach's will, but they mainly showed deep sisterly love and affection. Since neither Mollie nor Feemy had children, they discussed in these letters how to leave property to each other when they died. Alford pointed out that the content of the letters also challenged images of Feemy as a domineering sister who completely overpowered Mollie. According to him, in fact, the letters revealed that in many respects Mollie was the "dominant character," that she was certainly not unwise to the ways of the world or "unsophisticated." After all, she boasted of her good judgment in selecting husbands and reminded Feemy that it was she who had taken the initiative to write Sam Heinbach first.[28]

Alford pointed out that Mollie was so proud of her matrimonial portfolio, in fact, that she often advised Feemy how to snag a rich husband. On one occasion, for example, Mollie had urged her to write to "a certain rich prospect called 'J.'" Apparently Mollie had already tried to act as a matchmaker with him on Feemy's behalf, for he sent Mollie a lily that she in turn passed on to Feemy. "J's" wife was terminally ill at the time, and Mollie speculated that neither "J" nor his wife might live much longer. Emphasizing the need to move fast, Mollie advised her what to say in a letter to him, and she urged Feemy to initiate the correspondence, "regardless of who might find it out."[29]

A common thread running throughout the letters was both sisters' passionate contempt for lawyers and judges. Alford pointed out that popular hatred of lawyers ran throughout the ages, and he cited New Testament scripture as well as the poetry of William Shakespeare and novels of Charles Dickens to illustrate his point. What particularly worried him, however, was that Feemy's and Mollie's low regard for the legal profession might prejudice his client's case. He admitted that Feemy fully shared the views of lawyers expressed by Mollie in her letters: "The lawyers are discussed with a freedom and an open frankness which is startling as well as amusing." He urged the judge, however, not to allow that to influence his decision. Alford argued that it should come as no surprise that Mollie and Feemy "do not entertain a high conception of the moral status of the legal fraternity. They are doubtless sincere in believing that moral delinquencies among lawyers are the rule instead of exceptions." In fact, he conceded, "They are excusable if not justified in assuming the law is a kind of puzzle to be worked out by craft and intrigue. From their standpoint it may absolutely seem so."[30]

Alford acknowledged Feemy's bitter hatred of Rendlen, but he called attention to the fact that for Rendlen, too, the case had become far too intensely personal. "Each seems to be obsessed with hatred for the other," Alford pointed out. In his view, Rendlen's antagonism toward Feemy had gotten out of hand: "Regardless of the question as to whether the attorney is justified in his intense personal antagonism towards our client we are constrained to say that we believe that his usual poise, equanimity and good judgment have been seriously affected and bent awry by his intense personal antagonism towards Mrs. Koller." Because of this, Alford concluded, Rendlen had "briefed an imaginary case . . . [that] exists only in his super-heated emotions." In the view of Alford, Rendlen was "the victim of mental hobgoblins."[31]

After a grueling suit that lasted more than two years, Feemy prevailed. On October 12, 1920, Judge Woolfolk ordered the dismissal of Mollie's equity suit, allowing Feemy to recover all costs and expenditures in the case. He denied Rendlen's motion for a new trial but granted him an appeal to the Missouri Supreme Court.[32]

As swiftly as Mollie had disappeared on August 12, 1918, she now resurfaced, allegedly surprised to discover that Feemy had won the joint deed suit. Mollie claimed that Sirbu, Rendlen's law partner Harrison White, and John Tudor, an Ilasco resident who apparently also served as an intermediary for Rendlen, told her on January 31, 1920, that she, in fact, had won the case. Through such misrepresentation, she soon alleged, her lawyers had induced her to assign all Heinbach tract rentals collected by Ilasco justice of the peace Bruce Peterson since August 12, 1918, to Rendlen for the use of Sirbu.[33]

Upon returning to Ilasco, Mollie must have faced an icy reception from Feemy, but despite the latter's combativeness and tough, penetrating critique of issues, she obviously had a blind spot when it came to her older sister. Feemy probably gave her several tongue-lashings, but they patched up their relationship and quickly made plans to supervise the collection of rentals and attend to their property. They jointly drew up two affidavits on January 26, 1921, and filed them in the office of the Ralls County circuit clerk and recorder. They insisted that William True, administrator of Sam Heinbach's estate, had never turned over to either of them rents collected between March 1, 1910, and August 12, 1918. Therefore, they demanded immediate payment of these rent monies at an annual interest rate of 8 percent, since True had allegedly used these monies for his personal use. The other affidavit likewise ordered Peterson to surrender to them all rents that he had collected since August 12, 1918, along with 8 percent interest if he, too, had used the rents for personal profit. In their new agreement, Feemy would evenly split the rent monies with Mollie instead of receiving merely a one-third share as earlier agreed upon. This compensated Feemy for some of the legal expenses she had incurred as the result of Rendlen's attempt to break the joint deed.[34]

The sisters prepared to assume joint supervision of the Ilasco tract "without any intermeddler between them." To secure the services of a trustworthy agent to collect future rents for them, they hired Ilasco constable Riley "Pappy" Hill. According to their contract with Hill, one-half of the rent income was to go to Mollie, the other half to Feemy. The contract allowed Hill to keep 5 percent of the monies for his commission. Mollie informed probate judge Benton B. Megown the next day that she and Feemy had reconciled, and she authorized him to hand over to Feemy the money that administrator True had collected for the Heinbach estate between 1910 and 1918. Finally, without Rendlen's knowledge, Mollie informed Megown that she had dismissed her pending appeal in the Missouri Supreme Court, which confirmed to the Pike County circuit court on February 7 that she in fact had withdrawn her appeal.[35]

Despite tensions created by the litigation between Mollie and Feemy, their reconciliation now offered the hope of putting aside differences and sharing their final years as co-owners of Ilasco. The eleven-year battle over the Heinbach tract had been costly, both financially and personally, but they had persevered and achieved financial security. To be sure, they still had to pay outstanding legal fees, some of which had already eaten up a significant portion of their income, but the anticipated collection of outstanding rental monies and debts owed to the estate would improve their position. At ages sixty-six and fifty-nine, respectively, Mollie and Feemy could look forward to a steady income from lot rentals and a nice house with an orchard tract where they could sell fruit and raise chickens. Each sister off and on had spent a decade of her life in Ilasco, which by now had become home, particularly for Feemy. On the other hand, if they chose, they could sell their tract to the Atlas Portland Cement Company or any other buyer, split the proceeds, and go their separate ways.

Here, too, was a chance for Rendlen to collect his fees and put the case behind him, allowing the sisters to end this costly litigation and to work on repairing their relationship. As Mollie's lead attorney, he could take great pride in having probated Sam Heinbach's will. Despite repeated irritation at what he regarded as excessive interference by both Mollie and Feemy in formulating legal strategies, he had skillfully led the case through two trials and two appeals to the state supreme court. Even though Feemy had gotten under his skin for eleven long years and so far thwarted his attempt to break the joint deed, here at last was an opportunity to close the books on a case that had occupied so much of his mental and physical energy, and a chance for an emotional respite from tangling with Feemy.

By now, however, it was clear that Rendlen had much more invested in the case than merely fees for hours logged on his client's behalf. For him, as attorney Alford had pointed out, the case had indeed become intensely personal. After all, he, too, had been thoroughly immersed in the case for eleven years. During that time he endured the death of his first wife, Lydia, as well as that of his law partner, Frederick W. Neeper, but he remarried in 1917 and soon brought Harrison White into a new law partnership. He also lost his brother Theodore, who as an intermediary had already delivered the other half of Ilasco to the Atlas Portland Cement Company after Theodore Johnson died. If Rendlen could now deliver the Heinbach estate to Atlas, this could mean untold dividends for a man with important political ambitions. Besides that, he was perhaps overinvested emotionally in the case because of his intense hatred of Feemy. After all, she had gotten the best of him to this point. The Ilasco tract still had not fallen into Atlas's hands.[36]

Seven

A Combined and Confederated Conspiracy

Mollie's Sanity Bargained Away

> She [Mollie Heinbach] is in no sense insane and outside her affirmity—deafness—she is an intelligent, normal woman having as much knowledge of business affairs and management of same as any ordinary woman of her age and experience.
>
> —*Bowling Green attorneys Jefferson Davis Hostetter and John Hardwick Haley, 1921*

The startling turn of events marked by Mollie's return to Ilasco and the withdrawal of her appeal to the Missouri Supreme Court threw the "whole crowd of the gang" into disarray. This forced a shift in tactics on the part of Rendlen, the Atlas Portland Cement Company, and county officials who regarded the sisters' reconciliation and joint ownership of valuable property next to the cement plant as unpalatable. To buy the tract outright from the sisters was not an option, for Feemy apparently was hostile toward the cement plant. Local officials, unwilling to accept that the sisters were calling the shots on Ilasco property, now had only one alternative: to strip Mollie of her legal identity and renew litigation against Feemy through a court-appointed guardian. Although cloaked in paternalism, the guardianship served as Mollie's punishment for her independent wheelings and dealings in Ilasco and for her recent reconciliation with Feemy.

This new strategy required persuading Mollie's brother that it was his patriarchal responsibility to impose a guardianship over her to protect her financial interests. It is not clear who the intermediary was, but someone "induced" Tom Sykes to step in and initiate proceedings in the probate court to declare Mollie of unsound mind. Tom petitioned the court to appoint a guardian to take charge of her money. Rendlen, of course, instead of representing Mollie as he had for the last eleven years, stepped aside temporarily according to the plan while New London attorney Joseph Barry argued the case against her in Tom's name.

Mollie, now alienated from Rendlen, hired lawyers with important political connections in Jefferson City to resist the guardianship. Her main attorneys were Jefferson Davis Hostetter and his partner and brother-in-law, John Hardwick Haley. Hostetter, who had opposed Mollie during the second trial of the Heinbach will in the Pike County circuit court, was a Bowling Green Democrat. Born near Frankford, Missouri, on November 13, 1861, he became a member of the Missouri bar in Bowling Green in 1884. He had served since 1917 in the Missouri House of Representatives, where he was floor leader and chair of the Appropriations Committee. After two terms in the house, he was elected to the state senate from the Eleventh District in 1921.[1]

Assisting Hostetter and Haley in the case were New London's Drake Watson and Mack Stout. Watson was Democratic Speaker of the Missouri House of Representatives and a bitter critic of the cement company's overreaching influence in the New London courthouse. In fact, he would soon spearhead a highly publicized campaign to call attention to Atlas's failure to pay its fair share of taxes in the county. In addition to these lawyers, of course, Mollie relied heavily on Feemy's counsel. By now the case had become a tangled web, and area residents geared up for what the *Hannibal Courier-Post* described as "another chapter in the celebrated Heinbach litigation."[2]

When Mollie's insanity hearing opened on February 21, 1921, the presiding probate judge was Benton B. Megown, another member of the tightly interlocked, influential families whose role in New London politics extended back to the Civil War era. His grandfather, Samuel Megown, was a Democrat who converted to Republicanism during the Civil War and disenfranchised those who refused to take loyalty oaths to the Union immediately after the war. This created deep bitterness in the family, for several of his sons remained Democrats. One of those sons was John, Benton's father, who once was a Democratic county assessor and probate judge. Benton's mother was a member of the Conn family, which in turn was linked through marriage to the general superintendent of the Atlas Portland Cement Company.

Benton, a former mayor of New London, had built a career on local banking and county Democratic politics. Admitted to the bar in 1905, he worked as assistant cashier at the Ralls County Bank until elected as circuit clerk in 1910. After one term in the circuit clerk's office, he was then elected as probate judge. He owned a herd of purebred Jersey cattle, and he was also a hog breeder, as well as an amateur historian, for he later wrote a brief "History of the Democratic Party in Ralls County." In addition, he was certainly well familiar with this case, for it was he who had cooperated with Rendlen to deny Feemy her share of the rental monies in August 1918 after the state supreme court recognized the validity of Sam Heinbach's will.[3]

As Mollie's hearing began, it became clear how complicated the financial implications of the case had become as the result of the litigation to date. The nearly deaf Mollie, with her ear trumpet, strained to hear what was going on in the courtroom and to make sense of the discussions that centered around whether she was competent to understand and manage her finances. As she looked to Feemy and her lawyers for help in understanding the full extent of her liability in the 1918 contract with Sirbu, she also had to confront the confusing matter of the outstanding rents from the Ilasco tract. Debtors had withheld several thousand dollars from the Heinbach estate, claiming that they did not know to whom they should pay the money.[4]

The heated confusion and strain of the hearing were too much for Mollie. After nearly two days of vigorous legal arguments and courtroom "interruptions and objections as thick as bees in a hive," she suddenly broke down. Without consulting her lawyers or Feemy, she sent a note to the judge as they neared the lunch break, indicating that she would no longer resist a guardianship. Judge Megown showed the note to Mollie's attorneys and told them to discuss it with her over lunch.[5]

When the court reconvened in the afternoon, Hostetter and

Haley informed the judge that they would not introduce any further evidence, that their client would no longer resist the appointment of a guardian to take care of her business affairs. Although the lawyers acquiesced, they complained about the "insincerity" and material motives of those who had pushed the guardianship: "She is in no sense insane and outside her affirmity—deafness—she is an intelligent, normal woman having as much knowledge of business affairs and management of same as any ordinary woman of her age and experience."[6]

For those accustomed to drama in this eleven-year-old legal saga, the sudden turn of events should have surprised no one. Judge Megown appointed his brother, John E. Megown, cashier at the Ralls County Bank in New London, as Mollie's guardian. The latter Megown, a Democrat who had been on the bank's board of directors since 1893, was a former county treasurer. The *Ralls County Record* immediately bestowed its paternalistic blessing on his appointment as Mollie's guardian, assuring the public that he would "administer the affairs of this unfortunate woman in a way that will be to his credit." The newspaper insisted "that this step should have been taken several years ago," that Mollie had "lost much of her property because of the fact that she was unable to attend to it."[7]

Now that Mollie could no longer conduct her own legal affairs, Rendlen stepped back into the picture to work in tandem with her guardian in regard to the Ilasco tract. On March 4, 1921, Rendlen, now reemployed by Mollie's guardian, appeared before the Missouri Supreme Court in an attempt to reinstate her appeal in the equity suit to break the joint deed. He filed an affidavit emphasizing that Mollie had withdrawn her appeal under pressure from her sister without consulting his firm. According to him, Mollie had told him shortly before the motion was filed that she intended to go forward with her appeal in the high court. Rendlen alleged that Feemy had intimidated her into filing the motion to dismiss the appeal. In his view, Mollie did not have the "mental capacity" to protect her interests against her sister. He submitted a sworn affidavit from Mollie drawn up at the request of her guardian, insisting that Feemy had forced her way into her home, "exercised a domination and control" over her "by threats, compulsion and fear," and continued to live there against her wishes.[8]

As Mollie's guardian, John E. Megown signed the motion to redocket the case. In that motion he stressed that she at one time fled the state out of fear that Feemy would kill her. He further asserted that when Mollie reappeared in Ilasco in December 1920 and January–February 1921, she was of unsound mind. As alleged proof of Feemy's mercenary motives, he pointed to how hard she had worked to resist the appointment of a guardian over her "feebleminded" sister.[9]

As further evidence of Mollie's alleged mental incapacity, Megown introduced affidavits by L. H. Tutt and Reuben F. Roy. Tutt was a Hannibal doctor and businessman linked to Atlas through the Ilasco Supply Company. Roy was a former New London judge married to Maggie Hays, the sister of area circuit judge Charles T. Hays, who was also related through marriage to Atlas's general superintendent. In addition, Roy was a recent appointee to the Missouri Supreme Court as a commissioner, and he had once represented Atlas's interests in the county court in New London. At one time he had also acted as Mollie's attorney. Tutt claimed that Mollie's "mind and mental condition" was "now so unsettled . . . and has been in the same condition for the last several months as it is at this time," that she was "incapable of managing her affairs." Roy went even further, alleging that Mollie had been mentally unsound for years.[10]

By now, it had become quite tricky trying to sort out who was feebleminded in this case, and who was not! Was this "feebleminded" Mollie the same Mollie portrayed earlier in the courts as a master manipulator who cleverly preyed on Sam Heinbach's feeblemindedness to get his money and land? Was this the same woman who daringly sold the tract to Sirbu and helped Rendlen to cook up the case against Feemy? The same woman who fled the state surreptitiously in August 1918, hid out for two and one-half years, and betrayed her sister for financial gain? Had she now been stripped of all human agency, reduced to a mere "feebleminded" victim of Feemy's machinations?

The motion to redocket the case in Jefferson City raises other important questions. If, in fact, Mollie really was mentally unsound, how long had she been in that condition? The same tough question that Rendlen had put to opposing attorney Jack Briscoe in regard to Sam Heinbach's alleged incompetence ten years earlier might well be put now to Rendlen. In the first trial of the Heinbach will, Rendlen pressed Briscoe that if he honestly believed Sam was incompetent, why had Briscoe continued as a county official to accept legal transactions to which Sam affixed his name? After the case's many twists and turns, however, this had now become an appropriate question for Rendlen. If he did believe that Mollie was incompetent, why did he facilitate her sale of the Ilasco tract to Sirbu and lay out a suit against Feemy? Was Mollie a client who did not understand what she was doing? If so, did this mean that he was taking advantage of her? Why did he, Sirbu, and others who knew where Mollie was hiding during her absence from the state not express concern that they were doing business with an incompetent?

If Rendlen and others now believed that Mollie was feebleminded, why would they necessarily believe her allegations that Feemy was trying to kill her? Had Mollie been feebleminded even longer, perhaps as long as Rendlen had been on the case? Had he represented a mentally incompetent client for eleven years? If so, why had there been no effort to establish a guardianship over her earlier? Finally, why did Mollie not become feebleminded until after she came out of hiding when Feemy won the joint deed suit in the Pike circuit court?

For Feemy, the answers to these questions were all too clear. She smelled a rat. Only ten years earlier, she had heard rumors and allegations that it was she who was plotting to set up a guardianship over Mollie. Now, however, she was under attack by Rendlen and Megown, not for supporting but rather for opposing Mollie's guardianship. By their terms of the game, sinister motives underlay everything that she did.

Feemy hired Hostetter and Haley, Mollie's former lawyers in the insanity hearing, to oppose the redocketing of the appeal by her sister's guardian. Whereas Megown and Rendlen impugned Feemy's motives, Hostetter emphasized the suspicious nature of their carefully coordinated effort to continue the litigation. To a state supreme court that must have been exasperated by a case which seemed doomed never to go away, Hostetter insisted that Mollie's guardianship and appeal were being manipulated for the benefit of others. "I wish to invite the fullest investigation of this matter," he urged in a letter to state justice Robert F. Walker, "and if there be an African in the wood pile you will find it in the other fellow's fuel."[11]

In Hostetter's "Suggestions in Opposition to Motion to Reinstate Appeal," dated March 10, 1921, he reviewed the long history of the case and for the first time specifically implicated cement plant officials in the litigation. Pointing out the suspicious circumstances surrounding the attempted sale of the Ilasco tract to Petru Sirbu, he emphasized that in August 1918, Mollie had been "mysteriously and surreptitiously spirited away" from her Ilasco home and "sent to some unknown place in Ohio." Hostetter linked the entire matter to Sirbu's connections with the Atlas Portland Cement Company, "which traditionally desired to acquire ownership of the 26 acres on account of its convenience and its contiguity to its immense plant."[12]

In Hostetter's view, Rendlen's renewed effort to reinstate the appeal did not grow out of a genuine concern for Mollie's best interests. Rather, he pointed out, those who stood to benefit from Sirbu's contract with her were the same ones who had pushed to establish a guardianship over her. He reminded the court that Rendlen was also Sirbu's attorney, and suggested that it was not on Mollie's behalf but on Sirbu's "and the hidden and sinister forces behind him" that Rendlen had filed the motion to reinstate the appeal.[13]

Hostetter again disputed that Mollie was mentally incompetent. He emphasized that she was perfectly capable of taking care of her own affairs. He praised Judge Woolfolk's ruling in the equity suit, and urged the state court to refuse to redocket the appeal. Hostetter insisted that it was time at last to stop the litigation. "It would certainly be a useless expense," he argued, "to permit Mrs. Heinbach's money to be spent in prosecuting a fruitless case against her sister."[14]

In April 1921, the Missouri Supreme Court agreed. It overruled the motion by Rendlen and Megown to reinstate the case. This handed Feemy a clear-cut legal victory. At long last the courts had vindicated her. She was now a rightful co-owner of the Ilasco tract.[15]

Feemy faced limited options, however, as she considered how to carry on a joint business relationship with Mollie through the latter's guardian. On the one hand, she could try to share supervision of the tract with her sister, but this would require a business relationship with Megown and Rendlen. She hated both of them, of course, and they in turn hated her. Harassment of her would probably continue under such arrangements, and it would undoubtedly be difficult to collect her share of the rentals that had accrued over the last three years.

Now the joint tenancy that Mollie and Feemy had created in 1911 to preserve the entire tract became a problem for Feemy. Had they created a tenancy in common, it would have been easier to manage or sell her half of the estate. Instead, her attorneys advised her that a partition suit against Mollie was now the best course to pursue. Perhaps they sensed the hopelessness of trying to continue supervision of the property under the joint tenancy, considering the latest developments and animosities created by the litigation. Perhaps, too, they shared the underlying assumption that the tract would be better off under the supervision of Atlas, that it would inevitably wind up under the company's control anyway. After all, wouldn't it be far better for both sisters to sell the property, split the proceeds, and get on with their lives, free at last of this conflict?

On April 4, 1921, Hostetter and Haley filed a suit in the circuit court to partition the tract on Feemy's behalf. She needed money desperately, and she apparently rejected any thought of cooperating with Megown and Rendlen in the future management of her Ilasco interests. By now she had heavily mortgaged her property in Oklahoma, and she had lost her Hannibal property.[16]

After Megown filed a similar partition suit on behalf of Mollie, Judge Charles T. Hays ruled on May 24, 1921, that the land was not susceptible of partition in kind. Hays, a former mayor of Hannibal and relative of Atlas general superintendent Croll, was one of the lawyers who had represented Sam Heinbach's adult children in the original litigation over the tract. For several years he had been the senior partner in a Hannibal law firm with H. Clay

Heather and Berryman Henwood. He then was appointed to replace William T. Ragland as judge of the Tenth Judicial Circuit in 1919, when Ragland joined the Missouri Supreme Court as a commissioner. Hays ordered Ralls County Sheriff E. S. Holt to conduct a cash-only sale of the former Heinbach tract on the steps of the courthouse. The proceeds of this sale were to be divided between Feemy and Mollie as joint tenants.[17]

In the meantime, Feemy's anger at the way Mollie had been used in the long history of the case did not subside, and she set out to protect her sister's interests as well as her own. For example, she sniffed out what she believed was a trail of corruption that led across the river to Quincy, Illinois, where Mollie had apparently stopped en route to Ohio in 1918. On May 14, 1921, Feemy notified Mollie's guardian that William F. True, administrator of Sam Heinbach's estate until August 12, 1918, had extorted two hundred dollars from Mollie at some point while she was in Quincy. She called attention to the fact that this two hundred dollars was an overpayment to the law firm of Pearson and Pearson for services during the second will trial in Bowling Green. As Feemy later complained, however, Megown showed a lack of concern over her revelations, even though this overpayment had hurt Mollie's estate: "His only office, as guardian, it seems, was to sell the Heinbach land—which he at once proceeded to do."[18]

The sheriff's sale of the Ilasco tract was set for November 7, 1921, but Feemy in the meantime became suspicious that lawyers had manipulated the partition suit. On October 26, she inexplicably filed a motion to dismiss the suit. She did this without the advice of her attorneys, who were so disturbed by her erratic behavior that on the day of the sale, they asked the court for permission to withdraw as her counsel. The court consented, but Hostetter and Haley agreed to stay on the case after they prevailed upon Feemy to withdraw her motion to dismiss the suit.[19]

During the sale, however, the face of the Atlas Portland Cement Company revealed itself clearly to an enraged Feemy for the first time. Ray E. Hoffman, superintendent of the Atlas plant in Ilasco, stepped from the shadows and bought the tract for ten thousand dollars. It's not clear if Feemy had a verbal confrontation with Hoffman at the courthouse, but something happened there to set her off. By now, she would do anything rather than concede the loss of the Ilasco tract to the company. When the sheriff's report of the sale came before the circuit court for approval later that day, she urged Judge Hays to reject it, insisting now that she was once again dropping her partition suit. An exasperated Hays warned Feemy of the costs involved but had no choice but to dismiss her suit. He then nullified the sale, assessing the costs against her.[20]

What this meant, of course, was that a new sale would be necessary based on a partition suit now to be initiated by Mollie's guardian. Although this bought Feemy time to try to raise money to compete with Atlas's bid, she still failed to prevent Atlas's acquisition of the tract. On December 16, 1921, Sheriff Holt again conducted a sale at which Feemy tried to bid against Atlas. She bid ninety-five hundred dollars in an attempt to hang on to the tract, but did not have enough cash. After Holt reminded her that it was a sale for cash only, Atlas plant superintendent Hoffman again took the land for only ten thousand dollars. Even the supportive *Ralls County Record* expressed a bit of sarcasm at how little money the land brought at the sale: "The price paid was cheap enough and the Atlas company has a bargain."[21]

Atlas's purchase of this tract at a bargain-basement price came at a time when the company's public image was in trouble. First, Mill Number 5 at the Ilasco plant had been shut down for an entire year as the result of the depression of 1921. This had left one thousand people out of work in the area and led to wage cuts of 25 percent for those who still held onto their jobs in Mill Number 6. To make matters worse, Atlas and other cement manufacturers were under attack for high prices and monopolistic practices. In fact, Missouri lawmakers had appointed a committee in 1921 to explore the feasibility of creating state-owned cement manufacturing plants to give taxpayers a break as the state launched a new highway construction program. In addition, Atlas was among several cement firms targeted in criminal and civil suits brought by the U.S. Department of Justice for allegedly conspiring to restrain trade.[22]

Perhaps to repair its public image and soften possible criticisms of its role in the Heinbach case, Atlas demonstrated that it intended to use the tract in part to benefit the education of Ilasco's children. The company, which during World War I had used Ilasco schools to promote patriotism and Americanization of its largely immigrant labor force, now aimed to continue such efforts through the schools. On land that was condemned and appropriated from the Heinbach tract by the county school district in 1914 for a new school but that somehow was now given by county officials to Atlas, the cement plant provided land and equipment for a new playground next to the grade school. In April 1921, just as the Missouri Supreme Court was preparing to deny the motion by Mollie's attorney and guardian to reinstate the appeal against Feemy, school officials and Atlas representatives staged a big celebration to publicize Atlas's generosity. The company worked even more closely with the local school board in the early 1920s to devise plans for the further expansion of Ilasco's school facilities.[23]

Atlas's paternalism also revealed itself in other ways. Only a month before Atlas bagged the Heinbach tract, the *Ralls County Record* had praised A. G. Croll, the company's general superintendent, and Ray E. Hoffman, Ilasco plant manager, for their contributions to a Ralls County float to celebrate Homecoming Day at the University of Missouri. In cooperation with students at the university, each county was to sponsor a parade float that represented the most important industry in the county. Onie Newlon, a law student from Ralls County who was a friend of Croll's and a soon-to-be prosecuting attorney, reported in appreciation that Atlas officials responded "very generously and went the limit in time, expense and trouble in assembling and sending a great deal of material for the occasion."[24]

Such paternalism did not impress Feemy. Furious, she went outside the county to hire new attorneys J. W. Matson and C. E. Cowherd, of Louisiana, Missouri, in an attempt to set aside the sale. She complained that Atlas had bought the tract for less than one-third of its intrinsic value, despite the fact that as "a responsible bidder," she had worked out an agreement with Mollie beforehand to buy the land for fifteen thousand dollars. Mollie, because of her recent guardianship, of course, no longer had control over her own financial affairs, but Feemy alleged that the sale was conducted "over the protest" of both sisters. She further insisted that the court had erred in rejecting her bid. In her view, the entire conflict that led to the sale in the first place was "the result of a combined and confederated conspiracy" by Atlas officials, their "secret agent"—Petru Sirbu—and a supporting cast of lawyers and county officials.[25]

Feemy also contended that the lawyers failed to comply with regulations regarding the sale of land in a partition suit. She claimed that they did not ask the court to appoint three commissioners to determine whether the Ilasco tract, in fact, was not susceptible of partition. These lawyers instead simply agreed among themselves that Feemy and Mollie's guardian could not reach a partition agreement, she charged. According to her, the lawyers then misled the court into ordering that the land be sold. She complained that they secured an execution against the entire tract to prevent either Mollie or her from using the land as collateral for a loan so that they could raise twenty thousand dollars in cash. This would have let Feemy use her half of the loan to support a fifteen-thousand-dollar cash bid at the sale, but the sheriff rejected her bid on grounds that she could not cover it in cash.[26]

The court overruled Feemy's motion to set aside the judgment and order of sale. On March 7, 1922, the court also denied her request for a new hearing, but granted an appeal to the Missouri Supreme Court, fixing her appeal bond at five thousand dollars.[27]

For both Mollie and Feemy, the litigation up to this point had been very costly. The probate records of Mollie's estate do not indicate how much money she had at the time John E. Megown became her guardian in February 1921, but they do contain numerous canceled checks indicating payments between then and the date of the court-ordered sale. The court allowed Rendlen to collect a large fee of $1,501.20 from Megown on July 23, 1921, for legal services rendered during the suit to break the joint deed. This, despite the fact that Sirbu and Rendlen had worked out an agreement to finance and prosecute that suit. In transactions that were legal according to guardianship laws, Megown quickly loaned $700 of Mollie's money and later an additional $500 to his son Edward. Probate Judge Benton B. Megown collected $190.25

in costs for the insanity hearing, and Joseph Barry collected $100 as Tom Sykes's lawyer. Finally, Mollie had granted Hostetter and Haley a lien on her tract to ensure payment of $500 at 6 percent interest for their services as her lawyers during the insanity hearing. As the *Ralls County Record* observed, "There have been so many claimants against the Heinbach estate that the widow . . . has been almost bankrupted. From a disinterested standpoint it looks like many lawyers and some who are not lawyers regard the Heinbach estate as legitimate pickings."[28]

This also had been an expensive litigation for Feemy. To pay attorneys Hostetter and Haley, she, too, had drawn up two separate trust deeds of $500 and $250 at 6 percent interest. In addition, she owed them $125 for services in a suit brought against her and Mollie by Leigh Neeper to recover a fee which Feemy and Mollie had refused to pay her husband, Frederick W. Neeper, now deceased, during the Heinbach will suit. A jury in the Ralls County Circuit Court had awarded $1,000 plus costs to Neeper's widow on November 10, 1920, but Feemy rejected the judgment as "a cruel fraud" and dismissed it as "a debt never earned, or due, nor never attempted to recover during the lifetime of the husband of Leigh A. Neeper."[29]

Fees and court costs also devoured a significant portion of the proceeds from the court-ordered sale of the tract. On the date of the sale, the Ralls County circuit court ordered the sheriff to set aside $1,500 for Neeper, whose victory in that court was now being appealed by Feemy as well as by Mollie's guardian to the St. Louis Court of Appeals. From the $10,000 in proceeds from the sale, the court authorized a payment of $500 to Rendlen and White for representing Mollie during the partition suit. Other costs totaled an additional $229.10, leaving a sum of $7,770.90 to be divided evenly between Feemy and Mollie, subject to several liens. The court deducted $725.80 from Mollie's share to satisfy liens by Hostetter and Haley against her. This left her with $3,159.65, while Feemy's share came to only $2,520.16 after the court had deducted money to cover the costs of the second sheriff's sale and additional fees charged by Hostetter and Haley.[30]

All in all, it is clear that as Sam Heinbach had once anticipated with his white horse imagery, lawyers had a field day with the property case. Mollie and Feemy received only about 56 percent of the proceeds of the sale at the time, but that percentage later shrank even further as others got in line to file claims. For example, Sirbu came back to town to sue Mollie through her guardian for money that he had put into an escrow account on her behalf when he tried to buy the entire tract from her in 1918. On November 14, 1924, the Ralls County circuit court, in a case tried without a jury, awarded Sirbu $825.[31]

The circuit court at once distributed Mollie's share of the proceeds from the sheriff's sale to her guardian, but withheld Feemy's. This made it hard for Feemy to continue contesting the sale in court. Nevertheless, while she was waiting for the Missouri Supreme Court to rule on her appeal of the sheriff's sale, she drew up a suit to recover money from her sister's guardian—John E. Megown—as well as from his brother, Benton, William F. True, Charles E. Rendlen, George Elam, and Ray E. Hoffman. Acting as her own attorney, she filed the suit in the Ralls County circuit court on January 24, 1923.[32]

Because of the complex financial entanglements and the absence of other financial record-keeping, it is hard to measure the accuracy of Feemy's allegations and calculations laid out in this suit. First, she named county treasurer George Elam in the suit because when the school district condemned a strip of the Heinbach tract for the new school site in November 1914, the county had retained the five hundred dollars in compensation for the condemned land until the courts determined rightful ownership of the Heinbach tract. Feemy now demanded that the county pay her one-half of the five hundred dollars plus interest that had accrued over the last eight years.[33]

She accused True, administrator of Sam Heinbach's estate, of corruption and mismanagement. She charged that he had used rents from the estate for his personal use—to buy and sell real estate in the Hannibal area in his wife's name. In fact, Feemy emphasized that he had admitted this while testifying during Mollie's insanity hearing in 1921. This was legal, of course, but the law required administrators to pay interest if they used money from estates for personal financial transactions. Based on True's annual report of settlements, she also accused him of preferential treatment of Atlas's Ilasco Supply Company. True, a former incorporator of the company who in the meantime acquired extensive real estate investments in Hannibal, had allowed representatives of the company to collect and keep a record of their own rent due on thirty-five special leases on the Heinbach tract. They did so without paying interest on those rents for the entire eight-year period of True's tenure as administrator of the estate. Furthermore, True even paid a commission of 10 percent to the company's bookkeeper, Frank Cable, for separately collecting these rents. Feemy also charged that True had failed to keep a record or collect rents from many of Heinbach's lots that had been leased for summer gardens.[34]

According to Feemy, Charles E. Rendlen had testified at Mollie's insanity hearing that after he began to collect rents on behalf of Petru Sirbu on August 13, 1918, he deposited the rent monies into an interest-bearing bank account. She now requested that the court force Rendlen to produce a certified bank statement of such sums. According to her, Rendlen had never made an effort to turn over the rents that he collected for Sirbu. She also complained that Judge Megown had allowed Rendlen to collect an exorbitant legal fee of fifteen hundred dollars from Mollie. This fee amounted to between one and two years of annual income from rentals on the Heinbach tract. Feemy requested that the court adjust Rendlen's fee to a more reasonable figure to benefit her sister.[35]

Feemy protested that Mollie had been "lured by the interferance [*sic*] and criminal designs of others to throw the Heinbach estate into litigation, and so cover it with judgements, liens, and deeds of trust, thereby to enforce its sale." She complained, in fact, that Mollie's mind had been "'Bargained away' for the sole purpose of money graft," and charged that Megown had "appropriated to his own use and profit" unspecified but significant sums of money. According to her, when she requested her share of rents from the tract, he replied disingenuously that "'the lawyers won't let me.'"[36]

As Feemy understood the case, certain lawyers and county officials may have played a sleazy role in what she regarded as "an open case of Grand Larceny & Embezzlement," but they were merely pawns on the chessboard of corporate politics. In her view, they were nothing more than instruments of the Atlas Portland Cement Company, which she charged had "incited the havoc." She claimed that the financial burden of the lengthy case had resulted in the loss of her property in Hannibal and Shawnee, Oklahoma. Blaming Atlas "for all this loss of real estate, vitality, time, talent, and despair," she sued the company for twenty-five thousand dollars as the "instigator," including a claim for punitive damages. Feemy complained that as a result of this case, she had dissipated all of her energy "in hard mental and physical labor." In perhaps tragic recognition of the devastating toll that the case had taken on her, she described herself as a "talented and gifted writer" whose "mental vitality has been for 14 years, consumed in the struggle to live, and to keep her realty intact—But now, she is homeless—because all she owned is gone."[37]

From Feemy's vantage point, it was absolutely crucial to remove the case from Ralls County. Atlas superintendent Croll, linked closely by his wife's family ties to county officials, often hosted family reunions and other social events that brought together several of the key men who were directly involved in the case. Although the Crolls lived in East Orange, New Jersey, they owned the "Running Brook Farm" west of New London, where they at times held such gatherings. For example, the Conn family reunion became an annual event on their farm attended by Benton and John E. Megown, as well as by Judge Charles T. Hays. In fact, in December 1923, while Feemy was wrapped up in her appeal of Atlas's purchase of the Ilasco tract, Croll treated Hays to a turkey dinner at his New London home.[38]

It was also important for Feemy to attain free legal help as she prepared to prosecute her own suit, for she continued to wage war and defend herself on several legal fronts. Gardener S. Brockenbrough, former clerk of the Hannibal Court of Common Pleas, still held the sum of $119.27 that Mollie had deposited on Feemy's behalf on May 11, 1918. That sum was to cover expenses in case the lien against Feemy's Hannibal property led to a court-ordered sale. The anticipated expenses did not materialize, however, and upon Mollie's return to the Ilasco area, she gave written authorization for the court to release the money to Feemy on December 20, 1920. When Feemy then asked Brockenbrough for the funds, however, he refused, insisting that court expenses in the case had eaten up the total amount.[39]

With Rendlen as his attorney, too, Brockenbrough initiated litigation in early 1923 to challenge Feemy's claim to the money in question. Perhaps this was to clear the matter up once and for all or perhaps it was simply to keep her tied up and distracted, both financially and emotionally, on different fronts. Benton B. Megown, now the Ralls County prosecuting attorney and one of the defendants charged with corruption in Feemy's damages suit in New London, also appeared in the Hannibal court to represent Mollie's interests through her guardian, John E. Megown. Hannibal attorney Roy Hamlin represented Feemy, who yet again faced one of Rendlen's clients in a court presided over by Judge Hays.[40]

When Brockenbrough filed the suit on March 16, 1923, he deposited $106.37 with the court clerk. This amounted to the sum deposited by Mollie in 1918 minus his costs in the case involving the lien against Feemy's property in Hannibal. Judge Hays, after allowing Brockenbrough to take twenty-five dollars for his attorney fees in the matter, released him from all further liability and then disqualified himself as judge in order to let someone else decide whether Feemy or Mollie would get what was left. Byron Bigger, acting as a special judge in the case, issued his decision on May 16, 1923. He determined that after court costs were deducted, Feemy would get what little was left—a moral victory for her but one that did little to compensate for the harassment and distraction provided by Brockenbrough's suit.[41]

On the heels of this Hannibal distraction, a strapped-for-cash Feemy again turned her attention to the suit against Atlas and other county officials in New London. On June 7, 1923, she unsuccessfully requested a change of venue on grounds that Judge Hays was prejudiced against her and under the undue influence of the former probate judge, Megown. To defray costs, she also asked the court to allow her to prosecute the case as a poor person. In response, the court merely appointed New London attorney Drake Watson to examine her petition to see if it was in the proper form. Watson observed that the only problem was that there was no return of the sheriff's summons in her papers to indicate that the defendants had been duly notified as required by the law. The court then ordered the sheriff to deliver a notice of summons to the defendants, and extended Feemy's time for filing an amended petition to January 1924.[42]

On February 25, 1924, the court ruled that Judge Hays was disqualified from presiding over the case, and called for a special judge. One of Feemy's former attorneys, Edmund L. Alford, replaced Hays on the case, and granted Feemy another leave to file an amended petition. He apparently refused, however, when she again requested a change of venue on June 6, 1924.[43]

For Feemy, the outcome of this case was crucial to the prosecution of her appeal that was pending in the Missouri Supreme Court. Trying to handle both of these cases by herself with limited resources, however, put her at a clear disadvantage. As a result, she requested and received from the state court a continuance on December 29, 1923, and another on April 7, 1924. She emphasized in her requests that she did not have the money to pay for the transcribing of evidence, the printing of the Bill of Exceptions, and her abstract and legal brief. Megown, she explained, refused to release her share of the Heinbach rental monies until ordered to do so by the Ralls County circuit court. Therefore, she needed a continuance first to prosecute the other suit against Atlas, Megown, True, and Rendlen; then, she argued, she would devote her full attention to the appeal before the state court.[44]

By June 1924, this case had therefore reached a critical stage for Feemy, as well as for county and cement company officials infuriated by her dogged refusal to accept Atlas's purchase of the Ilasco tract. After all, those who had pulled strings to orchestrate and guide this case over the last fourteen years now found themselves on the defensive as the result of her damages suit. To date, the circuit court had denied Feemy a change of venue, but what if her case went to a jury? Would she tap into swelling anti-Atlas resentments among the county's farmers (and potential jurors)? To be sure, farmers' anger at that time was reaching a boiling point over the company's favored tax treatment and cozy relationship with the county's Board of Equalization. Several hundred farmers, in fact, led by the Ralls County Farm Bureau and attorney Drake Watson in a highly publicized campaign, had recently signed a petition protesting tax assessments that protected Atlas and consequently put a bigger bite on farmers. Would this make potential jurors more likely to believe Feemy's allegations about the company? Would her charges of corruption and collusion between Atlas and county officials seem so outrageous and far-fetched, or would they resonate with potential jurors up in arms over closed-door meetings between Atlas attorneys and the Board of Equalization?

For those with financial and political interests at stake in this case, these were clearly unsettling questions to ponder. If jurors believed Feemy's charges, what would happen to the Ilasco tract if she won damages against Atlas and then used that money to pursue her appeal of the sheriff's sale to the state supreme court? Lastly, what would be the fate of county officials and others charged with corruption if she pressed forward with her suit?[45]

Eight

Probate Judges and "Old Nuts"

The Politics of Euphemia B. Koller's Insanity

> The insane were disturbing, peculiar, or incomprehensible. They were in many cases out of touch with reality and in a small number of cases violent or destructive. But they became insane not when they crossed some well-defined boundary between health and sickness, between normality and abnormality. They became insane when other individuals decided they could no longer be tolerated.
>
> —Richard W. Fox, *So Far Disordered in Mind: Insanity in California, 1870–1930*

The case entered a new, more dangerous phase in the summer of 1924. Feemy was convinced that from the time Mollie had tried to probate Sam Heinbach's will in 1910, powerful forces opposing her, as well as Mollie's own attorneys, had manipulated the law to continue the litigation and further their own interests. In effect, the county probate court had become a rat's nest for both sisters, particularly Mollie, whose guardianship was manipulated to force a sheriff's sale of their Ilasco tract. For Feemy, who now stood alone in a desperate battle to deny her enemies the spoils of victory, this was a bitter reminder that the law was a dirty business designed for those with enough money and influence to manipulate it. By suing Atlas and other officials, she had dramatically raised the stakes in the game; she had, however, underestimated just how high those stakes had become. Indeed, she was about to learn a costly lesson in the law of politics and the politics of insanity—Ralls County style.

The Missouri Supreme Court sustained Feemy's motion for a continuation of her appeal of the court-ordered sale of the tract until the October term of 1924, but a new, more ominous threat quickly faced her. Benton B. Megown, a target of her damages suit who had followed a familiar trail in Ralls County politics by leaving the probate court to become prosecuting attorney, went after her in his new position of authority. On May 14, 1924, he and Sheriff E. S. Holt secured Probate Judge Harry G. Weaver's authorization for a petition of inquiry into her mental condition. They did not file it with the court until June 14, the week after Feemy filed a new motion in the circuit court for a change of venue in her damages suit. The petition, which emphasized that she owned a "considerable amount of property," urged the appointment of a guardian "for the proper conservation of her said property, and for the proper care" of her.[1]

By now it was clear that Ralls County officials had run out of patience with Feemy's continued interference with efforts to finalize the extension of Atlas's full legal control over Ilasco. Unlike in Mollie's case, however, they bypassed her brother Tom Sykes, who may have refused to have anything to do with efforts to place a guardianship over Feemy. After his role in Mollie's insanity hearing, perhaps he had lost the stomach for it. Whatever the case, it was a county official, not a member of Feemy's family, who initiated her insanity hearing proceedings.

On June 25, 1924, Holt and Megown appeared in probate court, along with Feemy, who claimed to have no money for a lawyer. Judge Weaver scheduled an insanity hearing to be held on December 29, 1924, and appointed attorney Joseph F. Barry, a New London former state representative, to represent her. Barry tried but failed to get the case dismissed on grounds that the court had failed to give Feemy proper notification of the preliminary hearing and complaint against her.[2]

It was clear from the probate court's procedure for selecting jurors that the hearing would be an uphill battle for Feemy. Many of Missouri's county courts at that time used methods of obtaining jurors that gave added leverage to the officials who had filed the petition for an insanity hearing. In some cases, courts left the selection of jurors up to the sheriff, while in others the court "selected" jurors rather than draw names from a box. Although the Missouri Supreme Court had invalidated a method in which prosecuting attorneys picked jurors, an appellate court had subsequently upheld a jury selected as the result of discussions between a county court and prosecuting attorney. In Feemy's case, Judge Weaver empowered the constable of New London's Spencer township to summon twelve prospective jurors for the occasion. As a result, Feemy's jurors would come from the New London area, not from Ilasco.[3]

Feemy was already wrapped up in litigation, but this latest action posed an even graver threat. The petition for an inquiry into her mental condition came at a critical time. The impending insanity hearing absorbed her energy and resources at a time when she needed to devote full attention to the pending appeal in the state supreme court and her suit in the Ralls County circuit court. At stake now was the loss of her very legal identity and financial independence. If Megown succeeded in having her declared mentally incompetent, she could no longer sue him or anyone else under the law without the consent of a court-appointed guardian.[4]

In the suit to recover money from Megown, Atlas, and others, she managed to file an amended petition on August 2, 1924, but time was running out on her appeal before the Missouri Supreme Court. On October 18, attorney Charles E. Rendlen on behalf of Mollie, or rather on behalf of her guardian, filed a motion to dismiss Feemy's appeal on grounds that she had needlessly failed to make progress toward prosecuting the appeal. He emphasized that Mollie was "being continually deprived of the enjoyment of her share of the proceeds of the [sheriff's] sale," and that the Atlas Portland Cement Company, which had already deposited ten thousand dollars in cash with the Ralls County sheriff, was "awaiting disposition of the appeal before making contemplated permanent improvements on the property."[5]

Although Rendlen complained that Mollie had not yet received her share of the proceeds from the sale of the Ilasco tract, circuit court records indicate otherwise. The sheriff's office had released Mollie's share to John E. Megown, her guardian, on December 16, 1921, the same date of the sale. It was Feemy's share, not Mollie's, that was still being withheld by the sheriff. This deprived Feemy of badly needed money to challenge the sale in the courts.[6]

As the date for Feemy's scheduled insanity hearing approached, her options were quickly narrowing. On November 6, 1924, the state court sustained Rendlen's motion and threw out Feemy's appeal because of failure to comply with the rules of the court. This upheld Atlas's clear title to the Heinbach section of Ilasco, including the tract on which Feemy and Mollie were still living.[7]

At the insanity hearing on December 29, 1924, Feemy faced an assembled jury of six distinguished men of Spencer township—Raymond E. Weaver, John W. Keach, Henry H. Glascock, Edward B. Beshears, Arthur W. Guttery, and John Lefever. This jury was tightly connected to the judge and other area officials and bankers through kinship, marriage, and social and economic ties. For example, Raymond E. Weaver (the presiding judge's cousin) was married to Mary Carstarphen, the niece of Ezra T. Carstarphen, who had long been on the board of directors of the Bank of New London. Raymond, recently an insurance agent in Hannibal, was the brother of Walter L. Weaver, cashier at the Hannibal National Bank, where the Atlas Portland Cement Company did its banking. Juror Henry H. Glascock was the son of Stephen and Henrietta Glascock and grandson of Virginia-born James and Davilla Woodson Glascock. His grandfather had been one of the wealthiest slaveholding planters in the county. The Glascock family, too, had long-standing connections to the Bank of New London, where W. H. Glascock sat on the board of directors. Henry was married to Ruth Wood, a member of another prominent New London family with important political and economic connections. For example, John S. Wood, formerly assistant cashier at the Bank of New London, was the chief national bank examiner for the Eighth Federal Reserve District in St. Louis. Moreover, Judge Weaver himself was linked to the Wood family through his wife, Winifred.[8]

The prosecution produced several witnesses, some of whom were businessmen with close ties to Atlas who testified that they regarded Feemy as mentally incompetent. William True, one of those named in Feemy's suit because of his alleged financial improprieties as the administrator of Sam Heinbach's estate, also testified for the prosecution, as did Curd Fisher of Atlas's Ilasco Supply Company. Chris E. Miller and Bruce Peterson, Ilasco justices of the peace, also testified in favor of a guardianship. Two Hannibal doctors—L. E. Fisher and J. J. Bourne—bolstered the case against Feemy by offering that she was mentally incompetent.[9]

Joe Barry, Feemy's New London attorney, had six months to prepare for the hearing, but for some reason he called only five witnesses on her behalf, compared to ten who testified against her. This may have been at least partly attributable to the fact that he received only fifty dollars from the county for attorney fees, thus limiting how much time he put into the case. The defense witnesses generally were neighbors such as Loren Kennedy and Neal Smashey and other men with whom Feemy had conducted business transactions in Ilasco and Hannibal. They objected to the campaign against her.[10]

The jury determined that Feemy was of unsound mind and incapable of managing her own affairs. Instead of following the law's general tendency to consider close relatives as natural guardians over those found to be mentally incompetent, Judge Weaver used the court's discretion to appoint Sam Elzea rather than Feemy's brother, Tom Sykes, as her guardian. Whereas the Ralls County Bank held Mollie's money through the guardianship of its cashier, John E. Megown, the rival Bank of New London now became the repository of Feemy's funds through Elzea, its assistant cashier. The well-connected Elzea had held previous positions with the Hannibal Trust Company and the Federal Reserve Bank in St. Louis. The *Ralls County Record*, in a clear misrepresentation of the forces driving the long history of litigation over the Ilasco tract, praised the court's actions, blaming Feemy alone for all of the money wasted in the suit: "She has squandered thousands of dollars that belonged to her and her sister . . . and the verdict of the jury was a just one, both to Mrs. Koller and those with whom she has been associated."[11]

Now that Elzea controlled Feemy's financial affairs, the court finally released $2,490.04—her share of the proceeds from the sale of the Ilasco tract—more than three years after the sale. In the meantime, the interest from her share had apparently gone into someone else's pocket or into the county treasury. The records indicate that she received no interest on her money over the entire three-year period, since the amount transferred to Elzea on January 8, 1925, was the same as that determined by the court to be hers shortly after the sale in December 1921.[12]

Until now, Feemy and Mollie had lived together in Ilasco. Despite Rendlen's earlier contention that Mollie feared that Feemy would kill her, concerns for Mollie's safety apparently vanished as soon as the court established a financial guardianship over her and ordered the sale of the Ilasco tract in 1921. There was no further mention of this alleged threat in any of the court records after the sale, apparently not even in Feemy's insanity hearing. The sisters had lived together since 1921 without the intervention of authorities to protect Mollie. To be sure, their relationship was strained. In fact, they rarely even spoke to each other, but Feemy's insanity hearing must have driven the final wedge between them. Mollie, also influenced by the recent legal confirmation of Atlas's title to the land, soon moved out. Two weeks after Feemy's hearing, Mollie moved with many of her household goods into the Mankopf Hotel in New London until a house that she had bought there was ready. This left Feemy alone on Atlas property in Ilasco with little but her dogs, a few chickens, a lot of bitterness and rage, and the loss of her financial independence.[13]

Because of the guardianship, Feemy could no longer sue, but the fight had still not gone out of her. Although the circuit court struck her damages suit from the docket on March 2, 1925, for failure to prosecute, she geared up for an appeal of the verdict at her insanity trial. Thanks to a 1921 statute in Missouri's probate law that clarified the right of an alleged incompetent to appeal a probate court decision to the circuit court, Feemy's lawyer obtained an appeal to the circuit court, and then a change of venue to the Hannibal Court of Common Pleas. He emphasized that she could not get a fair trial in Ralls County.[14]

Feemy's guardianship did little to improve the low standing of lawyers in Ilasco or in the eyes of the general public. In fact, at the time of her insanity hearing, public cynicism toward attorneys had become a matter of increasing concern to the Missouri Bar

Association. Edmund L. Alford, Feemy's former attorney who had recently served as a special judge in her case, called the bar association's attention to the problem just a couple of months before her hearing. In a welcoming address to the state bar association's 1924 convention in Joplin, he noted, "In all my experiences as a lawyer I have never noticed as much criticism leveled at the administration of justice as during the past year." He pointed out that many newspaper editorials, although often biased, reflected the public's cynicism in regard to lawyers. Urging his associates to "remedy those things and remove from public view and public concern those things that are giving rise to this talk," he expressed a sense of urgency in his plea that lawyers reform their behavior: "We are confronted with the proposition with the fact we must either do something along that line or rapidly lose the respect of the people of the State; and we ought to lose it. These are not theories, but they are conditions that confront us."[15]

Many of Feemy's Ilasco neighbors, when given an opportunity, rushed to her defense when her long-standing nemesis, Judge Charles T. Hays, presided over the opening of her second insanity hearing in the Hannibal Court of Common Pleas on April 27, 1925. Since the case was so well known in the area, several jurors were dismissed because they already held opinions. Ralls County Prosecuting Attorney Benton B. Megown claimed in his opening statement that Feemy was afflicted with "monomania," a label long used to describe reformers and critical thinkers, particularly if they were women. Feemy, he argued, was gripped by a single-minded obsession with money and filing lawsuits.[16]

According to the law at that time, there were two general classes of mania: intellectual and moral. Monomania was a form of intellectual mania that often "grows out of a perversion of the intelligence, or reasoning powers." In effect, monomania amounted to partial insanity, either permanent or temporary. The prevailing legal view was that monomania usually led to delusions and paranoia. As one legal expert explained it, monomania "affects the mind of the subject as to one subject, or a limited number of subjects . . . The person so affected may be perfectly rational, and even unusually bright, as to all other subjects; and be insane as to the particular subject which incites the mania."[17]

According to the legal definition of monomania-related delusions at the time, such alleged delusions could not be related to more abstract questions such as legal and political theories. Neither could these alleged delusions be related to a person's unorthodox religious beliefs such as spiritualism, but Feemy's prosecutor apparently disregarded this and made some of her unorthodox views an issue at the insanity hearing. Unfortunately, a transcript of the hearing does not appear in the records, but a newspaper reported that a witness asserted during testimony that Feemy had "peculiar ways." It is not clear whether the witness was referring perhaps to Feemy's interest in spiritualism, hypnotism, astrological forecasting, water-cure treatments, or to some other alternative view of hers. Whatever the case, Feemy felt compelled to interrupt the proceedings at this point. According to the reporter covering the hearing, she "demanded to be heard, and made a short talk on the subject upon which the witness was giving testimony."[18]

The prosecution called twelve witnesses, none of whom was a doctor. Although one of Feemy's neighbors, Dan Mack, testified against her, most prosecution witnesses were either Ralls County officials such as E. S. Holt, W. E. Conn, Chris E. Miller, and J. A. Palmer, or lawyers such as Charles Rendlen and his partner, Harrison White, who had tangled with Feemy for years. Of these, only Miller lived in Ilasco. Others were businessmen such as Frank Cable and William F. True, both of whom were connected to the Ilasco Supply Company, Atlas's subsidiary. Of course, True, now a Hannibal businessman with real estate interests, had been one of those sued by Feemy for alleged mismanagement and embezzlement of funds as the administrator of Sam Heinbach's estate.[19]

The defense, which called eighteen witnesses, presented a much stronger case, due in part to the testimony of Dr. Robert Heavenridge, of Hannibal, and Hannibal businessmen William H. Fisher, Richard M. Stillwell, and Charles O. Mayes. Feemy had conducted financial transactions with these businessmen and apparently enjoyed less antagonistic relationships with them. Perhaps even more importantly, many of her witnesses were Ilasco neighbors and supporters—farmers and/or cement plant workers, including Loren Kennedy, Phillip Stewart, Ernest M. Sanders, Vasilie Gherman, George Myers, and William Smashey.[20]

Once again, getting the case out of Ralls County paid off. It took the Hannibal jury less than twenty-five minutes to conclude on April 28, 1925, that Feemy was of sound mind, thus reversing the earlier verdict in the Ralls probate court.[21] Ralls officials refused to acknowledge defeat, however, and filed a motion for a new trial on grounds that a doctor who was out of state during this hearing would have testified that Feemy was "really an old nut" obsessed with filing lawsuits. The Hannibal court denied the motion, but granted an appeal.[22]

With the appeal apparently pending for the next year and a half, Feemy continued to live in Ilasco, but without direct access to her own money. Although the Hannibal jury had ruled that she was mentally competent, her guardian Elzea and the Bank of New London continued to control her money pending the outcome of the appeal. In September 1925, Elzea left the bank for a new position with a real estate company in Florida, but by April 1926 he had returned to his old position as assistant cashier of the Bank of New London. At times, Feemy was reduced to begging him, Probate Judge Harry Weaver, and others at the bank to release payments or to honor checks that she had written to creditors so she could continue to buy food and other necessities on credit in Ilasco. On November 5, 1926, for example, she desperately requested that Elzea pay a bill in the amount of $14.39 that she owed to C. E. Miller, an Ilasco merchant and justice of the peace. "Mr. Elzea," she pleaded, "please honor this request. It means my bread and butter. I want credit of Mr. Miller."[23]

Elzea's record of transactions and final settlement indicates that Feemy had anything but a luxurious existence during this period in Ilasco. In fact, the evidence suggests that the guardianship further marginalized her. During the first year of the guardianship, the balance of her estate only dropped from $2,490.04 to $2,219.67. According to these figures, she spent only $270.37 for the entire year, including a guardian's commission of $30 to Elzea and probate fees of $8.15. On average, she spent only about $20 per month on living expenses—mainly food and supplies from the Ilasco Supply Company, clothing from John Fleurdelys, and wood and coal from Phillip Stewart and the Hehmeyer Transfer and Coal Company. There is no indication in her probate file that Elzea or cashiers at the Bank of New London credited any payments of interest to her estate.[24]

Feemy's living expenditures did not change much in 1926 under the continued guardianship. The biggest bite out of her estate came when a Ralls County justice of the peace ordered Elzea to pay $394.65 to Edmund L. Alford, one of Feemy's former attorneys. This payment was for a long overdue fee, that she had contracted in the form of a promissory note.[25]

Squeezed by the guardianship, Feemy's mode of dress and spartan living conditions reflected her descent into broken health and spirits. If her guardian and Ralls County officials were concerned about her physical and mental health, they apparently did nothing to ensure that she had access to medical care. Her guardian's record does not show a single payment to a doctor for the entire period of her guardianship. The collective memory of Ilasco residents and relatives reveals vivid images of the desperate, impoverished living conditions that she endured during the final phase of her life in the community. Melvin Sanders and Angelo Venditti recalled that she wore ankle-length dresses made of gunnysacks as she gave legal advice to neighbors who sought her out in Ilasco's stores, lecturing them about how powerful interests manipulated the law. Anna Venditti remembered that she often went about the town dirty with several dogs that lived with her, and Fay Scheiner, one of Feemy's great-nieces, recalled that her aunt, in fact, often traveled between Ilasco and Hannibal looking like a "rag picker."[26]

This provided authorities with images that they could later manipulate in a campaign to hospitalize her. It is not clear when some of the county officials and area elites first considered involuntary commitment as an option for her. As a result of state politics and important changes in the governance of Missouri's mental institutions, Hannibal and New London interests had gained considerable influence in the management of the state's hospitals for the insane in the early 1920s. In 1921, the legislature had created a governor-appointed State Eleemosynary Board with authority to appoint superintendents and stewards. Arthur M.

Hyde, the newly elected Republican governor, named Hannibal Republican attorney Charles E. Rendlen, Feemy's bitter enemy, to the bipartisan board. Perhaps at Rendlen's request, he also appointed Joseph W. Elliott, a former postmaster and one of New London's leading, if rare, Republicans as the steward of State Hospital No. 1 for the Insane in Fulton. Elliott, a farmer from whom Atlas officials bought hay for their horses and mules at the Ilasco plant's company barn, had once been in the mercantile business. He, too, had close ties to the Bank of New London.[27]

Elliott may have served as an important conduit of information between Ralls County officials and Fulton hospital administrators and supervisors. On one occasion shortly after Feemy sued Atlas, Rendlen, and others in 1923, Elliott drove over to the New London courthouse accompanied by Rendlen, Atlas attorney George A. Mahan, and George V. Brown, the manager of the Fulton state hospital's farm. The newspaper reporting this did not indicate the purpose of the trip, but it may have been related to Feemy. Elliott was also in New London when the petition for her first insanity hearing was filed in June 1924, and again during the hearing at the end of December. The timing of these developments may have been a mere coincidence, but at the very least, Elliott was in a position to familiarize himself with Feemy's case and to strengthen the line of communications between county and hospital officials. After all, discussions of a person's alleged insanity in this era often took place between judges and hospital authorities long before an insanity hearing was held. In other words, state hospital officials usually agreed beforehand to accept a specific patient.[28]

Discussions about Feemy's mental health may have taken place between local authorities, lawyers, and Fulton hospital officials on these occasions, but Republican intraparty squabbles in Missouri later led to the removal of Elliott as steward of State Hospital No. 1 for the Insane, and to the subsequent resignation of Rendlen from the State Eleemosynary Board. Shortly after the Hannibal jury found Feemy to be of sound mind, the new Republican governor, Sam A. Baker, found a replacement for Elliott as steward. Rendlen, whose term on the board did not expire until June 19, 1926, then resigned in protest, complaining that Governor Baker, a fellow Republican, was simply playing patronage politics with the board. When Elliott returned to New London, he accepted a position on the board of directors of the Bank of New London—the repository of Feemy's money.[29]

What, if anything, precipitated the county's final action against Feemy in 1927 is not clear. On February 13, 1926, the sheriff had filed the final settlement of the partition suit that led to Atlas's purchase of the Ilasco tract.[30] This meant that Feemy continued to live on land to which Atlas now had clear title. Perhaps for public relations purposes, Atlas tolerated this arrangement for awhile, since the house in which she lived did not stand directly in the way of company quarrying or manufacturing operations. In fact, officials might well have continued to tolerate this arrangement as an option, simply ignoring her and allowing her to live out her remaining years on Atlas property in Ilasco. This certainly would not have hurt Atlas financially, since the company charged other residents only a nominal fee of one dollar per month in ground rent.

At stake in this case, however, was much more than mere ground rent. Feemy had become consumed with passionate, perhaps obsessive hatred for the alliance of male elites whom Mollie had years earlier referred to as "the whole crowd of the gang." For many years, Feemy had helped to thwart their designs to prevent the Heinbach estate from falling into the hands of her and her sister. Ilasco had been her home for nearly two decades, after all, and she was now sixty-six years old. It is possible that plant officials tried to run her off the property but found her defiant and perhaps even armed in the doorway of her house. As a critical-minded spiritualist and angry woman with "peculiar ways" and a continued resistance to local authorities, she stuck out like a sore thumb in what was clearly now Atlas's town.

To local officials, Feemy had become more than a mere nuisance; she stood in the way of Atlas's plans to promote community institutions on land that once belonged to the Heinbach estate. On July 26, 1926, for example, Atlas established a gift deed to Ralls County's Marble Creek School District No. 1 in order to build a new high school in Ilasco. The land would revert to Atlas if the county ever stopped using the land for school purposes. In addition, Atlas sponsored a Church of the Nazarene on company land in 1926, and it deeded land for the new Ilasco Methodist Church in 1928. The private interests of the cement company in Ilasco had thus become synonymous with the community's interests, but Feemy was a reminder that land once belonging to her and Mollie made Atlas's largesse possible. In a community now dominated by company paternalism, she was a symbol of defiance against the methods by which the nation's top cement corporation wielded power.[31]

From the perspective of county officials, they had run out of options in regard to removing Feemy from Ilasco. In most cases, it was at the request of a relative or guardian that private patients were involuntarily committed to state mental institutions, but if Feemy's brother, Tom Sykes, would not call for confinement proceedings, county officials would have to take the initiative to remove her from the community. If no male would step forward to assert patriarchal authority over her, the state then would have to assume that function.[32]

In many cases of alleged insanity around the country, state hospitals screened potential patients in advance. Statutes required judges, physicians, or families to respond first to a list of interrogatories about the individual in question before any hearing could be scheduled. State hospitals put forth the interrogatories to learn as much as possible about the behavior of the individual in advance. This meant that insanity hearings usually took place only after hospital superintendents had already agreed to admit the patient. In this context, the very fact that a hearing took place at all predisposed the judge and others involved in the case to conclude even before the hearing that the person at the center of the inquiry was insane. Doctors were more likely than not to endorse commitment if the individual in question exhibited any behavior that might be construed as strange, particularly if that person seemed disrespectful or antagonistic. Given this presumption of insanity, such hearings were often nothing more than mere formalities.[33]

Of course, such procedures were costly, and this is perhaps what deterred Ralls County officials from pushing forward their appeal of the verdict in which a Hannibal jury had vindicated

Feemy in 1925. On April 5, 1927, however, the Missouri General Assembly amended a statute to allow county officials to recover money from the estate of insane persons to compensate for their maintenance, support, or confinement. This opened the door to new proceedings against Feemy without the county's having to bear any of the expenses.[34]

Ralls County officials acted quickly, first by closing the books on the appeal of the Hannibal jury verdict. Elzea, now her former guardian, then handed over to her the balance of her estate—$1,280.94—on August 6, 1927, but four days later, the authorities went after her again. Sheriff J. A. Palmer and new Prosecuting Attorney Oney D. Newlon, also a friend of Atlas officials, petitioned for a new inquiry into her alleged insanity. Sheriff Palmer served a writ on her the following day, and Probate Judge Weaver hurriedly scheduled a hearing for August 18, giving Feemy only one week to prepare her defense. Six male jurors—W. R. Carstarphen, Earl E. Naylor, Asa Glascock, Dick Hamilton, John A. Gaumer, and C. H. Tompkins—were summoned to determine the county prosecutor's case. Once again, not a single juror was from Ilasco.[35]

Feemy apparently had neither the time nor inclination to get an attorney for the hearing. As a result, jurors heard only the testimony of prosecution witnesses W. H. Hays, who was a Hannibal doctor, and a supporting cast of Judge E. T. Cameron, Chris E. Miller, Curd Fisher, Dan Mack (who had testified against Feemy in an earlier insanity hearing), and Mrs. Russell Mack. In the case of the Mack family—residents of Ilasco—there may have been long-standing tensions with Feemy, or commonly shared perceptions and family discussions of her as someone who was crazy. Whatever the case, jurors concluded that Feemy, age sixty-six, was not only mentally incompetent but also "so disordered in her mind as to endanger her own person and the lives and property of others." Judge Weaver ordered Sheriff Palmer to haul her to the State Hospital for the Insane at Fulton as a private patient as soon as possible. This meant that the county would bear none of the financial responsibility in the case; to add insult to injury, the court required Feemy to pay the expenses of her own confinement.[36]

The probate court's action did not necessarily mean, however, that she could not continue to have control over her money. According to the law, unless the court ruled further that she was mentally incompetent and appointed a guardian, she still had the right as a patient to dispose of her property and enter contractual relationships. In other words, she might have continued to file lawsuits even as a patient in Fulton. Therefore, the Ralls County probate court further determined that she was mentally incompetent, and Judge Weaver reappointed Elzea, not her brother Tom, as guardian. Elzea's fellow directors at the Bank of New London—James Allison and cashier Harry C. Wood, who was also chairman of the Ralls County Democratic Party—were put up as sureties for his bond.[37]

Feemy's confinement raises several troubling questions. Was she, in fact, clinically insane? Six New London male jurors who were lay persons decided her fate, influenced by the opinions of a handful of other hostile lay witnesses and a single doctor. Most doctors, in fact, could hardly qualify as "expert" witnesses in such matters at that time, for even they often had only a limited, superficial understanding of insanity.[38] Most Ralls County officials, lawyers, and Atlas officials probably had no trouble believing that Feemy was crazy, indeed, for continuing to protest the sale of the Heinbach tract and her sister's guardianship. From this perspective, what else could explain her rebellious, eccentric, and defiant behavior?

Of course, there were plenty of "old nuts" in Ilasco and every other community, but most did not end up in institutions for the insane. Why Feemy? To what extent was her alleged insanity based on the interactions of class and gender in the history of this dispute? In many cases of women's insanity around the turn of the century, doctors attributed it to their forceful personalities and to their willful, open resistance to male authority and socially proscribed roles. For years, in fact, many American doctors, politicians, and other male professionals had insisted that women such as Feemy who pursued education, autonomy, and independence did so at the risk of their own emotional and physical well-being.[39]

If Feemy was a "monomaniac" obsessed with money and filing lawsuits, couldn't the same be said about some of the male lawyers who seemed equally obsessed with initiating and continuing the litigation against both Mollie and Feemy? Lawyers such as James Allison and Charles E. Rendlen, Sr., of course earned a good living through manipulation of litigation, acquired status, and built political careers in the courts. Not so with Feemy! The law was a man's game, and for defending herself and counterattacking in response to litigation against her and Mollie, she in contrast became an old nut obsessed with filing lawsuits.

Was this a clear-cut case of wrongful confinement? Would Feemy have been confined to the state hospital if she had not defied the Atlas Portland Cement Company? Was she really a threat to anyone's life or property, or was this an ambiguous case based on concepts of insanity that prevailed at the time but that would fall short of meeting our standards today? Would Feemy have experienced a different fate if she had simply taken her share of the proceeds from the sale of the Ilasco tract in 1921 and left town? Or, what if she had then melted quietly into the community, asking with appropriate deference and gratitude to remain in her former house and pay rent to Atlas, like so many others in Ilasco? Would her peculiar ways have disturbed county officials enough to take her off to Fulton?

In 1946, sociologist Edwin M. Lemert pointed out that rural communities at that time generally found more flexible ways to absorb and take care of eccentric residents, even if they were clinically insane. Why, then, could a community such as Ilasco, a popular place for folk superstitions, ghost stories, hypnotists, traveling medicine shows, and other peddlers of unorthodox remedies, no longer make room for Feemy? What was the source of opposition to her continued presence in the community? Certainly not Loren Kennedy, Phillip Stewart, Ernest Sanders, or others who testified successfully on her behalf at the Hannibal insanity hearing in 1925! Certainly not Melvin Sanders and other children who in the wintertime with Feemy's permission went sleigh-riding and toasted marshmallows on her property, and accepted invitations to come into her house to get warm.[40]

Ilasco was far from representative of rural communities, however, and Feemy's broad-based defiance of male authority and corporate class prerogatives tested the paternalism of county officials and "Old Man" Atlas beyond endurance. In the view of many doctors at that time, female insanity typically resulted when forceful, defiant women such as she rejected male authority or deviated from conventional roles. As sociologist Lemert explained in 1946, "It is the deviations of the psychotic person from customary role expectancies which increase his [her] social visibility and put strains upon others that provide the impetus to insanity proceedings."[41]

Feemy's scrappiness and harangues against area elites and Atlas officials had indeed increased her social visibility in Ilasco. Her perpetual attacks on the New London courthouse as a den of thieves in the service of Atlas were constant, vivid reminders of the "iron fist" inside the "velvet glove" that dispensed company paternalism in Ilasco and other tightly controlled company towns around the nation. The cement and steel industries, in particular, were bastions of the Open Shop at that time, and executives did not tolerate interference in class relations in the autocratic towns that they dominated. Just seven years later in the steel company town of Aliquippa, Pennsylvania, for example, authorities arrested a labor organizer and threw him into a state insane asylum before a state investigation later led to his release. Although Feemy was not a labor organizer, she nevertheless stood in the way of Atlas's plans to consolidate its paternalistic approach to labor relations. From the standpoint of county authorities, only a show of state-delivered force in the form of hospital confinement could silence her and put an end to the turmoil that had lasted for seventeen years.[42]

Although this study does not examine the daily internal workings of the State Hospital for the Insane in Fulton, Feemy's case reinforces the argument of certain sociologists and historians that mental institutions have functioned more as instruments of social control rather than as humanitarian centers where enlightened professionals dispense badly needed care to the mentally ill. In her case, confinement served the controlling interests of a well-integrated network of New South elites anxious to put Ilasco under the firm control of the Atlas Portland Cement Company. This in turn consolidated Atlas's power in the Midwest and facilitated the wider expansion of big business in the 1920s.[43]

In certain respects, Feemy's case reinforces the findings of historian John S. Hughes in his study of Alabama's state hospital for the insane in the late nineteenth and early twentieth centuries. Hughes emphasizes that many patients in Tuscaloosa's Bryce Hospital were "peculiar and eccentric" women who had "simply embarrassed other family members." One such patient, for example, was Andrew Sheffield, a woman whose drug addiction, deviancy, and criminal behavior prompted relatives to have her committed to the asylum rather than endure an even greater embarrassment by watching her serve an almost certain stretch in prison for arson. For Hughes, Sheffield's case in some ways strengthens the "social-control" interpretation of asylums, but in other ways undermines the notion that her confinement served the interests of a controlling elite in society. Hughes stresses that Sheffield's confinement mainly benefited her family.[44]

Feemy, too, embarrassed family members in northeast Missouri because of her persistent, defiant challenge to well-entrenched authorities, but there is a very important distinction in her case. County officials, not family members, were the ones who put her away, and it was some of these very officials, along with the Atlas Portland Cement Company, who benefited the most from her guardianship and confinement. The state, not a brother, husband, or father, became her patriarch, all in the service of private interests now cleverly transformed into the public's interests. Feemy's intellect, antiauthoritarian outlook, and combative personality—packaged in spiritualist beliefs—spelled trouble as she confronted powerful forces eager to tame the town that had turned the world of Tom Sawyer and Huckleberry Finn upside down.

Epilogue

An Unmarked Grave and a Buried Community

Insanity's Outcomes and Legacies

> My prayer is, that for the bitter drops moneyed-might, sex-might, and law-might press into my cup, I may have strength to drink them to the dregs,—without flinching,—and then have strength enough remaining to hurl the empty cup, with my fiercest denunciation and deathless defiance, into the face of such shameless injustice.
>
> —*Mrs. J. W. [Marietta] Stow, Probate Confiscation: Unjust Laws Which Govern Woman, 1876*

> The central question raised by women's history is: what would history be like if it were seen through the eyes of women and ordered by values they define.
>
> —*Gerda Lerner, The Majority Finds Its Past: Placing Women in History, 1979*

When the doors to Missouri's State Hospital No. 1 for the Insane closed behind Feemy in August of 1927, she became one of thirty-eight women, along with thirty-four men, admitted that year as private patients. Like other private patients, she was a paying customer. She had to pay the rate of forty dollars per month in advance, as well as the costs of clothing and transportation to and from the hospital. This compared to a monthly rate of eighteen dollars for the 142 individuals admitted as county patients in 1927.[1]

After what must have been a long, traumatic ride with the sheriff to Fulton, Feemy entered an institution that like many others at the time had been plagued for years by overcrowding, understaffing, and abuse of patients, even after the creation of a bipartisan board of control and the hiring of Dr. George Ard as medical director of Missouri's hospitals for the insane in 1921. The board, in its first biennial report, called attention to some of the problems that plagued Missouri's mental hospitals. Of special concern was the fourteen-hour workday put in by employees who also slept where they worked. As the board warned, this jeopardized the well-being of patients: "It is wrong to expect men and women to remain on duty on a ward for the insane twelve and fourteen hours a day and then be obliged to sleep on the same ward in which they are employed . . . Employees who spend fourteen hours amidst insane patients are worn out physically and nervously, long before the expiration of their term of duty, they lose their patience and release their self control and do things which they would not do under other conditions."[2]

As the result of better medical care, the reclassification of patients, and the removal of bars from windows of patients' rooms on the lower floors, the prisonlike atmosphere of these hospitals (formerly asylums) had somewhat improved by the time of Feemy's admission, but serious problems still existed. The Fulton hospital had an average daily resident population of 1,495 in 1927, and understaffing still plagued daily operations. There was a ratio of 7.3 patients to each employee and officer. As the state board acknowledged with a sense of urgency at the end of 1930, "The present overcrowded condition is alarming."[3]

The abuse of patients by Fulton hospital staff remained a shocking problem during Feemy's confinement. In fact, abuse and neglect of patients in the hospital aroused public attention around the time of her death in early 1930. In March, a patient died, reportedly after slashing his wrists with a knife. Public concern quickly mounted, capped off perhaps by newspaper reports in May that Charles Tolka, a diabetic patient for twenty-one years, had allegedly committed suicide by drowning himself in a pond at the hospital's water tower. Two months later, forty-nine-year-old George Stone's body was found in the tall grass near the hospital's barn. According to newspaper reports, Stone apparently had suffered injuries in an escape attempt after he broke a lock, pried open bars on the windows, and fell while lowering himself from an upper-floor window with the aid of sheets tied together. A "model" patient who had been missing for six days, Stone reportedly wandered into the barn lot, dazed by his fall, and then died.[4]

Reports of patient abuse disturbed public officials in the Hannibal area, particularly Marion County judges Henry G. Riedel, E. H. Disselhorst, and Calvin F. Bulkley. The judges, accompanied by clerks and county health doctor E. M. Lucke, visited Fulton on May 29 to investigate the conditions of patients from the Hannibal area. They told a local newspaper that they intended to bring some of the patients back to the county infirmary or to release them to their homes if possible. In response, the state eleemosynary board tried to calm fears, reassuring the legislature that "brutality in the handling of patients has been investigated, and those responsible have been summarily discharged from duty."[5]

Whether Ralls County officials expressed similar concern over their patients in Fulton is unclear, but if they did, it was too late for Feemy. Without access to her patient records at the state hospital, it is hard to ascertain the circumstances that led to her death. What is clear, however, is that a few days after a "fall" in which Feemy fractured her left hip, she contracted lobar pneumonia and died at the age of sixty-eight on February 24, 1930.[6]

Shortly after Feemy's fall, hospital superintendent D. H. Young quickly notified Samuel Elzea, her guardian, that she was in bad shape. Young emphasized that she was suffering from hardening of the arteries as well as pneumonia. On February 28, 1930, the weekly *Ralls County Record* featured two stories on her in the same edition, one of which mentioned the fall, and the other contained her obituary. The same newspaper that had blasted her just a few years earlier now assumed a much more benevolent tone of paternalism. After pointing out that "many years ago she was a brilliant woman, being well-educated, refined, and a fluent talker," editor Guilford Harris bestowed a final blessing upon his sister's sister-in-law: "Peace to her troubled soul."[7]

By comparing the estates of Feemy and Mollie, who had died two years earlier from burn injuries sustained when she caught on fire from a house stove, we see the material results of the divergent strategies that they pursued in the lengthy dispute over the Heinbach tract. Mollie's entrepreneurial, manipulative strategy clearly paid more dividends. Based on an appraiser's report, Mollie had $2,645.99 in cash and other personal property valued at $493.07 when she died on January 23, 1928. This included many middle-class accoutrements, such as a piano, china closet, carpet sweeper, silverware, brass bed, gold watch and chain, and many jewelry items. In addition, she owned a lot in New London appraised at $700. The total value of her estate before funeral expenses was $3,839.06.[8]

Even after funeral and administration expenses, Mollie's estate still contained a significant amount of money. H. M. Piper, a New London undertaker who was the administrator of her estate, took $251.95 to cover his costs of administration. Mollie's funeral expenses amounted to $447.35, and Piper deducted an additional $75 for a marker to decorate her grave in the Harris family plot in New London's Barkley Cemetery. After paying taxes on the estate, Piper subtracted in total $778.73. This left $3,060.33 to be distributed among Feemy's guardian and her brothers, Tom Sykes and Harry Eby in Oklahoma.[9]

In contrast, the inventory and appraisal of Feemy's estate revealed a portrait of a broken woman with few worldly possessions. In an American decade that worshiped business heroes and big stock market deals, her determination to challenge the mighty and powerful on matters of principle and ethics produced financial as well as emotional ruin. Shortly after she was committed to the state hospital, she still had $1,159 in the Bank of New London but did not possess any jewelry or other items of substantial value. This may have reflected Feemy's nonacquisitive values and itinerant lifestyle as well as the economic toll that litigation had taken on her. The most expensive item in her house was a coal stove appraised at eight dollars. Chickens that were worth ten dollars and an old hoe appraised at twenty-five cents further symbolized the kind of subsistence that she was trying to scratch out when the authorities grabbed her for the trip to Fulton. Perhaps the most vivid, painful reminder of Feemy's earlier life of travel, education, and independence was an old suitcase appraised at twenty-five cents.[10]

By the time of Feemy's death, there was little left in her estate, even after the distribution of $1,224.12 from Mollie's estate to Samuel Elzea, her guardian. Upon Feemy's death, Elzea turned over the estate to Tom Sykes, who received $405.18—barely enough to bury his sister. H. M. Piper collected $216.20 for a casket and undertaker services. Unlike Mollie, however, Feemy did not get a steel vault or even a grave marker when they lowered her, too, into the Harris family plot alongside "the whole crowd of the gang" in Barkley Cemetery. After the deduction of all expenses, Feemy's estate left only $69.30.[11]

At the time of her death, Feemy still owned property in Shawnee, Oklahoma, and may still have been receiving rents from that property, even after she was committed to the state hospital. Missing from her probate file is a guardian's record of disbursements and assets for the period of her confinement, but someone, presumably Elzea, since he was her guardian, had continued to pay the interest on a loan in which she had mortgaged this property in March 1919, during the thick of the Ilasco litigation. Court records in Shawnee show that interest payments were made on this loan in March 1925 and again in October 1927—during Elzea's tenure as guardian. This kept the interest paid up until October 1, 1929, and avoided foreclosure, but no payment was made after that. Had Elzea used the resources of Feemy's estate to pay off the mortgage, it would have benefited Tom Sykes and Harry Eby, of course, but it might have forced Ralls County then to bear the financial burden of her confinement because of insufficient funds in her estate. What was in the best interests of county officials and the Bank of New London was not in the best interests of Feemy's heirs.[12]

As a result, Tom Sykes and Harry Eby lost the property in Shawnee. On February 25, 1930, the day after Feemy's death, a judgment and foreclosure suit was filed against her property in the district court of Pottawatomie County, Oklahoma. Tom, who became the administrator of her estate, hired New London attorney Joe Barry to try to stop the foreclosure. On August 5, 1930, however, an Oklahoma judge ordered Tom to pay $1,136.66 from Feemy's estate to Wilma Wallace, who now held the lien against the property in Shawnee. When Tom failed to do so, the court ordered a sheriff's sale of the property. At this sale on October 13,

1931, Wallace paid only $100 for the land that Feemy had bought for $2,100 in 1902.[13]

Having watched Feemy and Mollie come to tragic ends, Tom Sykes must have felt great anguish, conflicted emotions, and perhaps even guilt as he looked back on the previous twenty years. At someone else's behest, he had helped to establish a guardianship over Mollie, although he was not driven by the same motives as others who urged him to do so. He no doubt believed that he was acting in her best interest, given her complicated financial circumstances and strained relationship with Feemy at the time. Whether anyone ever approached him about initiating similar proceedings against Feemy is uncertain, but if they did, he apparently refused to have anything to do with it. Through his wife, Maggie, he had close family, political, and social ties to politicians and business leaders in New London. He no doubt felt pressured by those connections at times to participate in and to keep quiet about machinations behind the scenes to control the disposition of the highly coveted Ilasco tract. In the end, however, he did not participate in county efforts to seek Feemy's involuntary commitment as the final option for removing her from Atlas's town.

Tom's health deteriorated sharply after R. Alex Jones, a New London Baptist preacher, conducted services for Feemy as she was lowered into her grave on February 26. On October 20, 1930, while in the middle of legal efforts to prevent a judgment and foreclosure on her property in Shawnee, a sick, worn-out Tom Sykes died after being in poor health for some time.[14]

Tom apparently went to his grave a bitter man. According to Maxine Harris, who married Clifford ("Tip") Harris, Jr., the son of Zella Pearl Sykes and Clifford Harris, Maggie was the source of much of that bitterness. Tom, on his deathbed, hinted that he had important secrets to reveal, but Maggie refused even to allow any of his children to be alone with him in the hospital room. According to Maxine, as soon as Maggie entered the room, Tom would then "screw up his face in disdain and turn to look at the wall."[15]

Whether it was Tom or his wife, Maggie, who refused to buy a tombstone for Feemy is not clear, but Tom was his sister's only surviving sibling in the area, as well as the administrator of her estate. If he and Maggie argued over a grave marker, he clearly lost, for after his death, she had the final word. Tom joined Feemy and Mollie in the Harris family plot in Barkley Cemetery, but Feemy's spot remained anonymous to grave site visitors. The family drama that so profoundly shaped Ilasco's history and the consolidation of the Atlas Portland Cement Company's power in the Midwest had finally come to an end.

The fate of some of the main lawyers, politicians, and intermediaries in the case suggests that their contributions to Atlas's acquisition of the Heinbach tract certainly did not hurt their future careers. Charles E. Rendlen's stature and influence grew steadily in Hannibal, as did his reputation as a skilled Republican lawyer. He made an unsuccessful bid for the U.S. Senate in 1944. When he died on April 7, 1957, he left behind three sons who had joined the family law firm. Branham, Charles E., Jr., and Albert L. Rendlen also developed distinguished practices with extensive business, civic, and Republican political interests. Albert, in fact, served on the Missouri Supreme Court from 1977 to 1992.[16]

James Allison, the chief instigator of the litigation that set this case in motion in 1910, continued to play an important role in Ralls County Democratic politics. In 1920, he was honored by his selection as the permanent Democratic chair of the county organization. He became a member of the Missouri constitutional convention of 1922–1923 and a member of the Board of Regents of the Northeast Missouri State Teachers College. He died on January 24, 1930.[17]

Benton B. Megown—the presiding probate judge at Mollie's insanity hearing and later prosecuting attorney who initiated Feemy's first insanity hearing—made a long career out of officeholding in the New London courthouse. As Oney Newlon, his opponent in the 1924 election, sarcastically pointed out, Megown believed in the principle of "rotation in office." Newlon noted that Megown first spent four years in the circuit clerk's office, then "rotated" to the office of judge of the probate court, where he spent eight years before "rotating" to the office of prosecuting attorney, where he was still "rotating" at that time. After Megown stopped rotating in office, he wrote a history of the county Democratic Party and received an appointment as

U.S. Conciliation Commissioner in 1935. He died on July 23, 1941.[18]

Perhaps more gratifying to Feemy was the ultimate fate of Atlas's "secret agent," Petru Sirbu. After Sirbu's departure from Ilasco in 1918, he moved to Youngstown, Ohio, where he again opened a butcher business. It is not clear how much he profited from his role in Mollie's attempted sale of the entire Ilasco tract and her subsequent disappearance and lawsuit against Feemy. It is clear, however, that his years in the butcher business and his ties to Atlas were lucrative. By the time he retired and returned to the Ralls County circuit court in early 1925 for an awarded judgment of $825 to be paid him by Mollie's guardian, he had accumulated savings of at least $100,000.

For a man on the make such as Sirbu, however, the same financial temptations that drew him into the Heinbach tract case soon lured him yet again. This time, however, he would lose more than half of his savings. After picking up the money from Mollie's guardian, he and his wife went to the spas in Hot Springs, Arkansas, for health purposes in March 1925. There Sirbu was befriended by a man who claimed to be a confidential agent for the "International Exchange," which was allegedly trying to drive smaller stock exchanges out of business around the country. The man offered to let Sirbu in on an inside deal to make millions, and Sirbu went for it. Sirbu's wife hurriedly took a train to Hannibal to withdraw sixty thousand dollars in cash from a local bank for the transaction, and when she returned, her husband turned the "investment" over to the confidence man. At a prearranged time after the stock market closed the next day, Sirbu was to meet with his newfound friend and pick up his anticipated bonanza profits from the quick deal.

It would have come as no surprise to Feemy that Sirbu fell for a scheme to clean up on a big stock market deal. She probably received more than a bit of pleasure to learn of his victimization, for on March 19, 1925, the front page of the *Hot Springs Sentinel-Record* featured a headline reporting that Sirbu had been taken by a gang of swindlers for sixty thousand dollars. Several newspapers, including the *Hannibal Courier-Post* and the *Ralls County Record* picked up the story and brought the news to area residents.[19]

No doubt less gratifying to Feemy was the fate of Charles T. Hays, the circuit judge who ordered the sheriff's sale of the Ilasco tract in 1921. As one of the attorneys who along with James Allison had tried to block Mollie's inheritance of the tract in 1910, his career and political connections had steadily grown throughout the period. From mayor of New London to mayor of Hannibal to circuit judge in the area, he had strengthened his political and family ties to the Atlas Portland Cement Company. His conservative judicial philosophy benefited the company in important ways in district courts. This was especially true in damages lawsuits by injured Atlas workers in which he kept the case from jurors because he regarded the suit as a threat to property rights.

Hays, reelected as judge of the Tenth Judicial Circuit in 1922 and 1928, went on to enjoy a distinguished career of public service on the bench of the Missouri Supreme Court. His career as a state justice, which peaked in 1937 when he became chief justice of the state's high court, stretched from 1932 until his retirement in 1942. He followed in the footsteps of his predecessor, William T. Ragland, who retired from the state court in 1932. Ragland, too, before joining the state bench had represented the Tenth Judicial Circuit, where he had presided over the first trial of Sam Heinbach's will.[20]

In the last analysis, however, it must be remembered that jurors, not judges such as Hays and Ragland, delivered the courtroom verdicts. In 1925, in fact, a Hannibal jury sitting in a courtroom presided over by the same Judge Hays determined that Feemy was *not* mentally incompetent, thus reversing on appeal the findings of a Ralls County jury a few months earlier. Moreover, Hays rightfully recused himself on a couple of occasions when Feemy came before him in the courtroom.

The patterns of the case suggest that it was the Ralls County courthouse that was the real snake pit for Mollie, and later for Feemy. When Mollie secured a change of venue to Bowling Green for the second trial of the will, she won, and the Missouri Supreme Court upheld that victory. Likewise, when Feemy moved Rendlen's equity suit against her to Bowling Green, she prevailed, and the state court refused to redocket Rendlen's appeal of Judge Woolfolk's decision. Finally, by taking an appeal of her New London insanity hearing to Hannibal, Feemy was vindicated by jurors in 1925.

What this suggests, in part, is the overwhelming influence of the Atlas Portland Cement Company upon a small but highly influential group of interlocked county officials and elites whose influence over New London jurors was remarkable, if not at times downright frightening. This was especially true if a case involved Ilasco, for many New Londonites were frightened by the cultural and class composition of the community's predominantly Slavic working-class residents. Through the Democratic Party, a handful of prominent political families (or as some might prefer, a "ring") had held a lock on the New London courthouse since before the Civil War. This power grew primarily out of agrarian (formerly slaveholding) landed wealth, but these elites in the early 1900s quickly put themselves at the service of Atlas. Since Atlas was the county's major provider of industrial jobs and a rich source of related revenues, company officials cultivated clientelist relationships with county politicians to ensure that nothing interfered with cement operations in the area. They may have wielded power in a more sophisticated and less conspiratorial way than Mollie and Feemy presumed, but at bottom the sisters certainly understood what they were up against with "the whole crowd of the gang."

Little did Feemy know at the time she was embroiled in the controversy that she was fighting for the very future of the community itself. Had she reappeared in Ilasco only thirty-five years later, she might have caught a fleeting glimpse of Sam Heinbach's legendary white horse in full gallop. This time, however, Sam's unsaddled, unbridled horse had a new corporate rider—the community's new landlord, the Universal Atlas Cement Company. A couple of months before Feemy's death, the United States Steel Corporation had put together a merger of the Atlas and Universal Portland Cement companies—industry leaders at that time. By the early 1960s, Universal Atlas and the State of Missouri had already begun to dissolve Ilasco to make room for a new plant and a highway that would serve the interests of Hannibal's Mark Twain tourist industry. On the tract that Feemy battled so long to preserve, she now would have found highway construction engineers, demolished buildings, bulldozers, hollowed-out earth, and cement company vehicles speeding over dirt roads to and from new quarries. Under construction nearby was a huge smoke-stack—a towering symbol not only of the cement plant's new single-kiln manufacturing process but also of Atlas's unmistakable power in the area. In the shadow of this smokestack, Feemy would have found a ghost town—a buried community whose history until very recently remained condemned to the same obscurity as the unmarked grave in which her body rests.[21]

Notes

Introduction. Pennsylvania Yankees in "Old Man Atlas's" Courts

1. Molly Heinbach, Certificate of Death, January 23, 1928, Missouri State Board of Health, Bureau of Vital Statistics, Jefferson City; *Ralls County Record,* December 3, 1927, and January 27, 1928.
2. *Hannibal Courier-Post,* February 26, 1930; Euphemia B. Koller, Certificate of Death, February 24, 1930, Missouri State Board of Health, Bureau of Vital Statistics, Jefferson City; *Ralls County Record,* February 28, 1930.
3. On the history of Ilasco, see Gregg Andrews, *City of Dust: A Cement Company Town in the Land of Tom Sawyer.*
4. *Hannibal Courier-Post,* February 26, 1930; *Ralls County Record,* February 28, 1930.
5. *Hannibal Morning Journal,* August 1, 1901.
6. U.S. Federal Manuscript Census, 1910, Saverton township, Ralls County.
7. Andrews, *City of Dust,* 8–9, 63. On the history of Ralls County, see Goldena Howard, *Ralls County Missouri.* Some authors have included Ralls County in "Little Dixie." See, for example, Robert M. Crisler, "Missouri's 'Little Dixie.'" More recently, however, R. Douglas Hurt, *Agriculture and Slavery in Missouri's Little Dixie,* has excluded Ralls from this classification.
8. Gregg Andrews, "Ilasco Cement Workers and the War on Booze in Ralls County, Missouri, 1903–1914"; Andrews, "Immigrant Cement Workers: The Strike of 1910 in Ilasco, Missouri."
9. Andrews, *City of Dust,* 112–14.
10. On Mark Twain's reaction to Atlas's transformation of the area next to the cave hollow, see Charles Neider, ed., *The Autobiography of Mark Twain,* 82. On the appropriation of Mark Twain by Atlas, see Gregg Andrews, "From Robber Caves to Robber Barons: New South Missouri and the Social Construction of Mark Twain, 1910–1935."
11. Marriage of Samuel Heinbach and Mollie Scott, December 18, 1908, Marriage License Record, book H, 77, Ralls County, Office of the Circuit Clerk and Recorder, New London. On the Cult of True Womanhood in the nineteenth century, see especially Barbara Welter, "The Cult of True Womanhood: 1820–1860," and Nancy F. Cott, *The Bonds of Womanhood: "Woman's Sphere" in New England, 1780–1835.*
12. *Mary Alice Heinbach, Appellant, vs. Jesse Heinbach et al.,* November 24, 1914, *Missouri Reports: Reports of Cases Determined by the Supreme Court of the State of Missouri,* vol. 262; Andrews, *City of Dust,* 21–22, 26–27.

13. For penetrating contemporary critiques of marriage and women's economic dependence on men around the turn of the twentieth century, see Charlotte Perkins Gilman's classic works, *Women and Economics* and *The Yellow Wallpaper.* On women's use of marriage as a survival strategy, see especially Carroll Smith-Rosenberg, *Disorderly Conduct: Visions of Gender in Victorian America*, 13.
14. Gerald W. Gawalt, ed., *The New High Priests: Lawyers in Post–Civil War America*, provides a broader discussion of the role of lawyers in the post–Civil War era.

One. Coming to Mark Twain's Salt River Country

1. U.S. Federal Manuscript Census, 1870, Saverton township, Ralls County; U.S. Federal Manuscript Census, 1850, 1860, Shrewsbury township, York County, Pa. I wish to thank Don Sykes and Jane Hemeyer for providing me with copies of inscriptions in Sarah J. Sykes's Family Bible.
2. U.S. Federal Manuscript Census, 1860, Carlisle East Ward, Cumberland County, Pa.; U.S. Federal Manuscript Census, 1850, 1860, Shrewsbury and Fawn townships, York County, Pa.; Joseph Sykes and Co., Rockford Factory, "We Have Leased for Five Years a Mill," Wilmington, Del., 1818, Early American Imprints, 2d series, Shaw-Shoemaker Bibliography, 1801–1819; Kathryn Jordan and Mary Hellen Emery, "Records of Fawn Grove Quakers (York County, PA)," 250, 254–55.
3. U.S. Federal Manuscript Census, 1850, 1860, Hopewell township, York County, Pa.; U.S. Federal Manuscript Census, 1860, Towsontown, Baltimore County, Md.; George R. Prowell, *History of York County Pennsylvania: Biographical, Vol. II*, 127–29.
4. Prowell, *History of York County Pennsylvania: Biographical, Vol. II*, 129; *Ralls County Record*, May 10, 1866. For the earliest date of the Sykes family's arrival in Ralls County, I have used Samuel Megown, "A List of Qualified Voters for Jasper Election District," 41, Ralls County Supervisor of Registration Ledger, Western Historical Manuscripts Collection–Columbia (hereafter cited as WHMC–Columbia).
5. U.S. Federal Manuscript Census, 1850, Shrewsbury township, York County, Pa.; U.S. Federal Manuscript Census, 1870, Jasper township, Ralls County; Joseph B. Sykes to Andrew Wasson, January 24, 1870, trust deed, book V, 131, Ralls County, Index to Deeds, and Marriage of William Johnson and Ellen J. Sykes, January 14, 1870, book B, 1943, Ralls County, Index to Marriages, 1821–1897; both in Missouri State Archives, Jefferson City (hereafter cited as MSA).
6. David D. March, *The History of Missouri*, vol. 1, 810; Howard, *Ralls County Missouri*, 57–58; Crisler, "Missouri's 'Little Dixie'"; *Ninth Census—Volume I: The Statistics of the Population of the United States, 1870*, 43–45, 356; 1860 Census Population Schedules, Missouri: Slave Schedules, Ralls County, microfilm roll 146.
7. 1860 Census Population Schedules, Missouri: Slave Schedules, Ralls County, microfilm roll 146; Mary Harris Davis, comp., "From the *Ralls County Record*, 1865–1912," prepared by Kay Detweiler, 1995, 49, 65; Mary Harris Davis, comp., "Cemetery Inscriptions from Ralls County, Missouri," pre-

pared by Kay Detweiler, 1995, 11; U.S. Federal Manuscript Census, 1870, Saverton township, Ralls County. Stephen, Charles, and Harrison Glascock were the earliest clerks and ex officio recorders and deputies of the Ralls County circuit court. They also served as probate and county court judges. Stephen and French, Jr., served in the state legislature. See Howard, *Ralls County Missouri*, 316, and Roy D. Blunt, Missouri Secretary of State, *Historical Listing of the Missouri Legislature*, 46. I wish to thank John Graves, of St. Louis, for providing me with the following materials on the Glascock family, of which he is a descendant: Mrs. Oliver Howard, "Old House in Ralls Sheltered Famous Romance," *Hannibal Courier-Post*, December 14, 1953; Mable Daniels, "Fire Blackens Glascock Home's Historic Past," *Hannibal Courier-Post*, March 16, 1971, and an undated family genealogy entitled "Thomas Woodson and Annie Gentry Glascock," written by Thomas E. Fenner.

8. Michael Fellman, *Inside War: The Guerrilla Conflict in Missouri during the American Civil War*, 70; Howard, *Ralls County Missouri*, 104; *Ninth Census—Volume I: The Statistics of the Population of the United States, 1870*, 193. For Twain's view of his role as a Confederate volunteer, see "The Private History of a Campaign That Failed," published twenty years after the war. See also Neider, ed., *The Autobiography of Mark Twain*, 111.
9. "Ralls County Historical Sketch," March 23, 1938, collection no. 3551, microfilm roll 574, folder 17494, U.S. Work Projects Administration—Historical Records Service, Missouri, 1935–1942, WHMC–Columbia (hereafter cited as U.S. WPA-HRS, followed by microfilm roll and folder numbers). On the state convention of 1865, see William E. Parrish, *Missouri under Radical Rule, 1865–1870*, 14–35. See Martha Kohl, "Enforcing a Vision of Community: The 'Test Oath' and Missouri's Reconstruction," for a discussion of loyalty oaths in Missouri.
10. Eric Foner, *Reconstruction: America's Unfinished Revolution, 1863–1877*, 42.
11. *Ralls County Record*, December 14, 1865, and January 25, 1866; *Portrait and Biographical Record of Marion, Ralls, Pike Counties Missouri, 1895*, 272–73. On the differences between Radical Unionists and Conservative Unionists, see Parrish, *Missouri under Radical Rule*, 1–13.
12. *Portrait and Biographical Record of Marion, Ralls, Pike Counties Missouri*, 453–54, 549–50. On Missouri's new registration law, see William E. Parrish, *A History of Missouri: Volume III, 1860 to 1875*, 136–38. For attacks on Samuel Megown, see, for example, *Ralls County Record*, November 22, 1866, and Howard, *Ralls County Missouri*, 106, 111. According to county historian Goldena Howard, because of the bitterness over Samuel Megown's Republican Reconstruction activities, there was not much communication between the different branches of the family for more than two generations. See Goldena Howard to State Historical Society of Missouri, Manuscripts Collection, undated letter, in Supervisor of Registration Ledger, 1866, WHMC–Columbia.
13. *Ralls County Record*, August 2, 9, 1866; Ralls County, Circuit Court Record, vol. F, 290–95, 329–31, MSA; Parrish, *A History of Missouri, Volume III*, 136–39.
14. U.S. Federal Manuscript Censuses, 1870, 1880, Spencer township, Ralls County; 1860 Census Population Schedules, Missouri: Slave Schedules,

Spencer township, Ralls County; Mary Harris Davis, comp., *From the Ralls County Record,* 32, 46, 84. William E. Harris's obituary is in the *Ralls County Times,* February 2, 1906.

15. 1860 Census Population Schedules, Missouri: Slave Schedules, Ralls County; U.S. Federal Manuscript Census, 1870, Jasper township, Ralls County; *Portrait and Biographical Record of Marion, Ralls, Pike Counties Missouri 1895,* 649–50, 700–701; Howard, *Ralls County Missouri,* 64, 69, 120. William T. Briscoe is quoted in Joanne Chiles Eakin and Donald R. Hale, comps., *Branded as Rebels: A List of Bushwhackers, Guerrillas, Partisan Rangers, Confederates and Southern Sympathizers from Missouri during the War Years,* 43. On James W. Allison's disfranchisement, see Eakin and Hale, comps., *Branded as Rebels,* 5.
16. Parrish, *A History of Missouri: Volume III,* 140; *Ralls County Record,* November 15, 22, 1866, and January 3, February 21, 1867.
17. "A List of Qualified Voters in Jasper Election District," 41, in Megown, Ralls County Supervisor of Registration, WHMC–Columbia. One of those banned from voting was Thomas R. Dodge, coeditor of the *Ralls County Record.* Dodge had served in the Union army but became a leading critic of Radicalism and was disqualified as a voter. See Parrish, *Missouri under Radical Rule,* 282.
18. *Ralls County Record,* February 4, May 13, 1869. See Laura F. Edwards, *Gendered Strife and Confusion: The Political Culture of Reconstruction,* 220–22, 230–44, for a discussion of similar tactics employed by the Democratic Party to regain power during Reconstruction in Granville County, North Carolina. Edwards shows that the local Democratic Party likewise tried unsuccessfully to throw out all of the ballots from a township that had voted Republican.
19. On the opening of the new steam mill in New London, see *Ralls County Record,* July 15, 1869.
20. James T. Matson and Neil Cameron to Sarah Jane Sykes, September 24, 1870, quitclaim deed, book T, 734, Ralls County, Index to Deeds, MSA. I would like to give a special thanks to Dorothy F. Eichenberger for providing me with notes that she and her deceased husband, J. Allen Eichenberger, an amateur archaeologist, took on the history of this Saverton property after they bought it in 1946.
21. U.S. Federal Manuscript Census, 1870, Shrewsbury Borough, York County, Pa. On Sarah Sykes's property transactions in Ralls County, see Noah Sykes to Sarah J. Sykes, April 29, 1873, general warranty deed, and James T. and Eliza V. Matson and Neil and Berthenia Cameron to Sarah Jane Sykes, September 24, 1870, quitclaim deed; both in vol. C, Ralls County, Index to Deeds, MSA. A table showing the evolution of Missouri's Married Women's Property Acts is in Joan Hoff, *Law, Gender, and Injustice: A Legal History of U.S. Women,* 381.
22. *E. H. Sykes vs. John D. James,* August 28, 1869, legal action on account, and *E. H. Sykes vs. Hannibal and St. Joseph Railroad Company,* March 29, 1870, garnishment, Ralls County, Index to Circuit Court Records, vol. G, MSA. See also Ralls County, Circuit Court Record, vol. G, 222, 237, 297, 341, 406, 409–10, 413, 463, 474, and vol. H, 53, 134; both in MSA. Bailey was among those denied the right to vote in the 1866 elections because of his Confederate sympathies. See Eakin and Hale, comps., *Branded as Rebels,* 13.

23. Davis, comp., "Cemetery Inscriptions from Ralls County, Missouri," 129; Ralls County, Circuit Court Record, vol. F, 194, vol. G, 222, 233, 237, 297, and vol. H, 444, MSA; *Ralls County Record*, March 5, May 21, 1874.
24. U.S. Federal Manuscript Census, 1870, 1880, Saverton township, Ralls County; U.S. Federal Manuscript Census, 1900, Mason township, Hannibal, Marion County; Marriage of Benjamin F. Eby and Sarah J. Sykes, September 1, 1874, book B, 409, Ralls County, Index to Marriages, MSA.
25. Marriage of Seth Gilman Eby and Emma Sykes, April 2, 1889, Ralls County, Marriage Record E, 16, and Marriage of Charles D. Eby and Laura J. (Sarah) Sykes, October 10, 1877, Ralls County, Marriage Record D, 2489; both in MSA; U.S. Federal Manuscript Census, 1870, Jasper township, Ralls County.
26. *Missouri: The Center State, 1821–1915*, 26–28; U.S. Federal Manuscript Census, 1850, District 37, Rock Island, Ill.; U.S. Federal Manuscript Census, 1860, Andalusia, Rock Island County, Ill.; Walter Williams, ed., *A History of Northeast Missouri*, vol. 3, 2032–33; *Portrait and Biographical Record of Marion, Ralls, Pike Counties Missouri 1895*, 327–28. On the Eby family, I have relied on Ezra E. Eby, *A Biographical History of the Eby Family, Being a History of Their Movements in Europe during the Reformation and of Their Early Settlement in America*. See also Alex H. Harris, *A Biographical History of Lancaster County: Being a History of Early Settlers and Eminent Men of the County*, 176–86.
27. Thomas H. Bacon, *A Mirror of Hannibal*, 371; *Missouri: The Center State*, 26–28; *Portrait and Biographical Record*, 327–28; Hannibal City Directory, 1871–1872, 66; Williams, ed., *A History of Northeast Missouri*, vol. 3, 2032–33; "Historical Notes and Comments," *Missouri Historical Review* 34 (April 1940): 424; *History of Marion County, Missouri*, 923.
28. Saverton Methodist Church, Church Records Form, July 21, 1941, U.S. WPA-HRS, reel 573, folder 17457, WHMC-Columbia; U.S. Federal Manuscript Census, 1900, 1910, Saverton township, Ralls County; "Persons Who Served in the Army, Navy and Marine Corp. of the U.S. During the War of the Rebellion Who Are Survivors, and Widows of Such Persons," Saverton township, Ralls County, Special U.S. Census Schedule, June 1890.
29. Saverton Methodist Church, Church Records Form, July 21, 1941, reel 573, folder 17457, U.S. WPA-HRS, WHMC-Columbia; "Persons Who Served in the Army, Navy, and Marine Corp. of the United States During the War of the Rebellion," Saverton township, Ralls County, Special U.S. Census Schedule, June 1890; Howard, *Ralls County Missouri*, 330. Dalton, attracted by the Progressive reforms of Theodore Roosevelt's wing of the Republican Party, switched parties in the early 1900s, but by 1912 Woodrow Wilson had won him back to the Democratic Party. Dalton's obituary is in the *Ralls County Record*, September 4, 1925.

Two. Designing Women: The Lady and the Hypnotist

1. Marriage of John Kellogg and Mary A. Sykes, March 29, 1870, book B, 1963, Ralls County, Index to Marriages, and Missouri State Penitentiary, Register of Inmates, vol. D, 27; both in MSA. On the tradition of brawling on the southern frontier, see Elliott J. Gorn, "'Gouge and Bite, Pull Hair and Scratch': The Social Significance of Fighting in the Southern Backcountry";

and Charles C. Bolton and Scott P. Culclasure, eds., *The Confessions of Edward Isham: A Poor White Life of the Old South.* On the itinerant lifestyle of Mollie and John Kellogg, I have relied on the 1870 U.S. Federal Manuscript Census, Ralls County. They were enumerated twice in that census, first in the Spencer township household of William Caldwell on July 26, and then on August 22 in the Center township household of William Shannon near Cincinnati, Mo. The *Ralls County Record,* August 25, 1870, also described him as an itinerant painter.

2. *Ralls County Record,* July 7, 21, 1870.
3. *Ralls County Record,* August 25, 1870.
4. *Ralls County Record,* March 23, April 20, 27, August 24, 1871; Ralls County, Circuit Court Record, vol. G, 466, and vol. H, 23, 43–44, 79; Missouri State Penitentiary, Register of Inmates, vol. D, 27; all in MSA.
5. *Ralls County Record,* September 21, 1871, and June 11, 1874; Missouri State Penitentiary, Register of Inmates, vol. D, 27, MSA. On his second stretch in the penitentiary, see Ralls County, Circuit Court Record, vol. K, 77, 78, 81, 86–87, MSA.
6. E. H. Sykes and wife to Noah Sykes, February 4, 1871, general warranty deed; Noah Sykes to John R. Self, October 12, 1871, trust deed; Noah Sykes to James A. Gilliland, January 18, 1873, trust deed; Noah Sykes to Sarah J. Sykes, April 29, 1873, general warranty deed; all in vol. C, Ralls County, Index to Deeds, MSA. I have been unable to find a record of Mollie's divorce from John Kellogg, or of her marriage to Noah Sykes. They perhaps never formalized these arrangements.
7. U.S. Federal Manuscript Census, 1880, city of Louisiana, Pike County; Bank of Pike County to Noah Sykes, February 25, 1885, General Warranty Deed, book 73, 46–47, Pike County, Index to Deeds, vol. 5, MSA. The census taker who enumerated district 132 that included Mollie, Noah, and Bertha Sykes on June 10, 1880, spelled their last name as "Sycks." The hotel was kept by Allison Beth Hall. Only a week earlier, a census enumerator in district 131 recorded Noah Sykes as a boarder in a different Louisiana household. The census profile fits him, however, and I have concluded that they are the same person. During that week, Noah apparently found living accommodations that would make it possible for Mollie and Bertha to join him.
8. U.S. Federal Manuscript Census, 1900, Mason township, city of Hannibal, Marion County; Noah Sykes and Mrs. Mary A. Sykes, deed of adoption, April 18, 1887, Deed Record, book 79, 14–14, Pike County, Recorder's Office, Bowling Green. The last reference to Bertha Kellogg that I have found is in the section entitled "Saverton Items" in the *Ralls County Record,* May 23, 1888.
9. *Louisiana Journal,* August 11, 1887.
10. Ibid.
11. Cynthia A. Brandimarte, "Somebody's Aunt and Nobody's Mother: The American China Painter and Her Work, 1870–1920," 203–6.
12. Ibid., 207–11.
13. Ibid., 216–20.
14. Peter W. Bardaglio, *Reconstructing the Household: Families, Sex, and the Law in the Nineteenth-Century South,* 202–3; *Louisiana Journal,* September 6, 1889.

15. Noah Sykes to Wm. C. Freeman, April 7, 1890, Deed Record, book 83, 565, Pike County, Recorder's Office, Bowling Green.
16. Ibid. If Mollie and Noah never formalized their marriage, this also might explain why her name was not on the deed.
17. Hannibal City Directory, 1894–1895, 1897–1898. I have been unable to find a record of her marriage to Broome.
18. Marriage of John M. Scott and Mollie A. Broome, August 12, 1903, Pike County Marriages, vol. 12, 285, MSA. See also John M. Scott's obituary in the *Bowling Green Times*, January 24, 1907. On the death of Nannie Tinsley, see *J. E. Scott et al. vs. Perry Tinsley et al.*, February term, 1909, box 168, reel 67, no. 20, Pike County, Office of the Circuit Clerk, Bowling Green.
19. U.S. Federal Manuscript Census, 1870, Bowling Green and Louisiana, Pike County; U.S. Federal Manuscript Census, 1880, Louisiana, and Hartford township, Pike County; *Portrait and Biographical Record*, 465–66; Karen Schwadron, comp. and ed., *Pike County, Missouri: People, Places and Pikers*, 646–47. In 1860, Lafayette Tinsley had owned thirty-four slaves and $20,500 in personal property. See Population Schedules of the Eighth Census of the United States, 1860: Missouri [Slave Schedules], Cuivre township, Pike County; and U.S. Federal Manuscript Census, 1860, Cuivre township, Pike County.
20. Sarah J. Eby to John M. and Mary Alice Scott, February 9, 1905, Deed Record, book 73, 576, Ralls County, Office of the Circuit Clerk and Recorder, New London; *Ralls County Times*, March 17, 1905. I would like to thank Ruth Pickett, the current owner of Wildwood Farm, for providing a copy of the "Abstract of Title" to this property—the south half of the southwest quarter of section twenty-five, township 56, range four, in Ralls County. On land values in Ralls County, see Bureau of the Census, *Thirteenth Census of the United States Taken in the Year 1910, Volume VI: Agriculture, 1909 and 1910*, 914.
21. Estate of John M. Scott, January 25, 1907, case no. 2244, Ralls County, Office of the Probate Clerk, New London; *Ralls County Times*, October 19, 1906, January 18, 1907.
22. *Bowling Green Times*, January 17, 24, 1907; *Hannibal Courier-Post*, January 18, 1907; *Ralls County Times*, January 18, 1907.
23. *Bowling Green Times*, May 30, 1907; *Perry Tinsley, executor, vs. Illinois Life Association*, June term, 1907, box 165, reel 67 (numbers 15, 16), Pike County, Office of the Circuit Clerk, Bowling Green.
24. *Tinsley vs. Illinois Life Association*, June term, 1907, box 165, reel 67 (numbers 15, 16); Circuit Court Record, book 37, 191, 198, 204, 302–3, 349, 432, 471, 634, and Circuit Court Record, book 38, 4; all in Pike County, Office of the Circuit Clerk, Bowling Green.
25. Saverton Methodist Church, Church Records Form, July 21, 1941, reel 573, folder 17457, U.S. WPA-HRS, WHMC-Columbia; *Louisiana Journal*, May 8, 1889. On Laura's death, see Roberta and J. Hurley Hagood, comps., "A List of Deaths in Hannibal, Missouri, 1880–1910," rev. ed., 23.
26. Mt. Olivet Cemetery Records, Hannibal, Missouri; Sykes Family Bible; *Ralls County Record*, January 10, 1890. On the Saverton Literary Society, see, for example, *Ralls County Record*, April 20, May 4, 1887.
27. Smith-Rosenberg, *Disorderly Conduct*, 258. For recent works on women in

the New South, in particular, see Marjorie Spruill Wheeler, *New Women of the New South: The Leaders of the Woman Suffrage Movement in the Southern States;* LeeAnn Whites, *The Civil War as a Crisis in Gender: Augusta, Georgia, 1860–1890,* 199–224; Elizabeth Hayes Turner, *Women, Culture, and Community: Religion and Reform in Galveston, 1880–1920;* and Judith N. McArthur, *Creating the New Woman: The Rise of Southern Women's Progressive Culture in Texas, 1893–1918.*

28. U.S. Federal Manuscript Census, 1880, city of Baltimore, eighth precinct, seventh ward, Baltimore County, Md.; Baltimore City Directory, 1877, 388; *Baltimore Sun,* June 7, 1871; Marriage of John A. Koller and Georgianna Medinger, May 15, 1871, book 1865–1873, Folio 349, Baltimore City Court, 1851–1885, Marriage Index, Male, Maryland State Archives, Annapolis. Georgianna's obituary is in the *Baltimore Sun,* December 22, 1874.
29. U.S. Federal Manuscript Census, 1900, Mason township, city of Hannibal, Marion County.
30. *Euphemia B. Koller v. John A. J. Koller,* August 5, 1993, book 33-B, 116, Baltimore City Circuit Court, Equity Papers A, Miscellaneous, Maryland State Archives, Annapolis; *Euphemia B. Koller, Plaintiff, v. John H. Woodbury Dermatological Institute and Frederick S. Kolle, Defendants,* April term, 1907, Cases and Exceptions, 1896–1911, book 2316, 34, Supreme Court of the State of New York, Appellate Division—First Department, New York State Library, Albany.
31. Charles D. Eby to Euphemia B. Koller, November 19, 1900, and "Sheriff's Deed under Trust Deed Sale," Miscellaneous Deed Record, book 162, 78–81, Marion County, Office of the Circuit Clerk and Recorder, Palmyra; Hagood and Hagood, comps., "A List of Deaths in Hannibal, Missouri, 1880–1910," 23.; U.S. Federal Manuscript Census, 1900, Mason township, Hannibal, Marion County. J. Allen Eichenberger, "Eichenberger Place," March 1946, Eichenberger Papers. On Benjamin F. Eby's death, see Mt. Olivet Cemetery Records, Mt. Olivet Cemetery, Hannibal.
32. Marriage of Henry T. Sykes and Sarah F. Murphy, January 24, 1881, book D, 2741, Ralls County, Index to Marriages, MSA; Jane Hemeyer, telephone conversation with author, October 30, 1994. On the death of Sarah Murphy Sykes, see Tom Sykes's obituary in the *Hannibal Courier-Post,* October 20, 1930.
33. Jane Hemeyer, telephone conversation with author, October 30, 1994; Jane Hemeyer to Gregg Andrews, October 29, 1994, and February 10, 1995; Marriage of Cora E. Sykes and Andrew J. Lusk, August 10, 1900, book F, 61, and Marriage of H. T. Sykes and Maggie Harris, June 9, 1904, book F, 216; both in Ralls County, Office of the Circuit Clerk and Recorder, New London. On Mabel's death and burial in Ralls County's Salem Baptist Church Cemetery, see Davis, comp., "Cemetery Inscriptions from Ralls County, Missouri," 117.
34. Kent Ruth et al., comps., *Oklahoma: A Guide to the Sooner State,* 205; Marion M. Kerfoot and Ida M. Kerfoot to Mrs. E. B. Koller, April 30, 1902, Warranty Deed Record, book 22, 210; Miscellaneous Record, book 11, 605; Euphemia B. Koller to John W. Jones, May 27, 1907, Warranty Deed Record, book 37, 497; Jno. W. Jones to Mrs. Euphemia B. Koller, June 21, 1907, Warranty Deed Record, book 50, 450; all in Pottawatomie County, Office of the Court Clerk, Shawnee, Okla. On Harry Eby's move to Tecumseh, Okla., see

Hannibal Morning Journal, December 17, 1901. For the occupations and moves of Feemy's brothers, see U.S. Federal Manuscript Census, 1900, Mason township, city of Hannibal, Marion County, and U.S. Federal Manuscript Census, 1920, Wilson City, Carter County, Okla.; Tulsa, Tulsa County, Okla.; and Reno township, Grant County, Okla. The Historical Society of Pottawatomie County in Shawnee, Okla., provided the information on Feemy's boardinghouse at 232 Union Avenue to me over the telephone.

35. For a fuller discussion, see John S. Haller, Jr., and Robin M. Haller, *The Physician and Sexuality in Victorian America*, 141–87, and Kathy Lee Peiss, *Hope in a Jar: The Making of America's Beauty Culture*.
36. *Koller v. Woodbury Dermatological Institute and Kolle*, April term, 1907, Cases and Briefs, 1896–1911, book 2316, 24–25, New York Supreme Court, Appellate Division—First Department, New York State Library, Albany.
37. Ibid., 30–31.
38. Ibid., 1–2; *Euphemia B. Koller, Respondent, v. John H. Woodbury Dermatological Institute and Fred S. Kolle, Appellants*, First Department, April, 1907, *Reports of Cases Heard and Determined in the Appellate Division of the Supreme Court of the State of New York*, vol. 119, 865.
39. *Koller v. Woodbury Dermatological Institute and Kolle*, April term, 1907, Cases and Briefs, 1896–1911, book 2316, 36, New York Supreme Court, Appellate Division—First Department, New York State Library, Albany.
40. Ibid., 45–49.
41. Ibid., 33–34.
42. See, for example, Erika L. Murr, "Exploring the Myths of the Southern Lady through the Writings of Elizabeth Scott Neblett," 79–81. On the spiritualist movement, see especially R. Laurence Moore, *In Search of White Crows: Spiritualism, Parapsychology, and American Culture*; Ann Braude, *Radical Spirits: Spiritualism and Women's Rights in Nineteenth-Century America*; and Peter McCandless, "Mesmerism and Phrenology in Antebellum Charleston: 'Enough of the Marvelous.'"
43. In the suit against the Woodbury Dermatological Institute, Feemy testified that she enrolled in this course, although the trial transcript refers to the Nevada center as the "Welcome Institute." This is a typographical error in the court record. Feemy clearly was referring to the Weltmer Institute. See ibid., 35. On the Weltmer Institute in Nevada, see Patrick Brophy, "The Weltmer Institute and Magnetic Healing in Nevada, Missouri," in Gene Fowler, ed., *Mystic Healers and Medicine Shows: Blazing Trails to Wellness in the Old West and Beyond*, 111–26; and J. O. Crone, *The Magnetic Healer's Guide or Personal Experiences in Magnetic and Suggestive Healing*.
44. Brophy, "The Weltmer Institute," 111–26. For a discussion of unorthodox medical theories and practices at the time, see John S. Haller, Jr., *American Medicine in Transition, 1840–1910*, 100–149.
45. Brophy, "The Weltmer Institute," 116; *American School of Magnetic Healing and J. H. Kelly, Appts., v. J. M. McAnnulty*, November 17, 1902, *United States Supreme Court Reports*, book 47, 90–97.
46. Crone, *The Magnetic Healer's Guide*, 78–84.
47. Maxine Harris to Gregg Andrews, January 11, 1998.
48. On the Milling brothers and operators of other water-related health establishments in Texas, see Gene Fowler, *Crazy Water: The Story of Mineral Wells*

and Other Texas Health Resorts, and Fowler, "The Milling Brothers: Texas 'Outlaw' Medicine Men," in Fowler, ed., *Mystical Healers and Medicine Shows,* 127–40.

49. Jane Hemeyer, telephone conversation with author, October 30, 1994; Erna Fergusson, *Our Southwest,* 227–44; Billy M. Jones, *Health-Seekers in the Southwest, 1817–1900,* 174–98.
50. Jane B. Donegan, *Hydropathic Highway to Health: Women and Water-Cure in Antebellum America,* 185–201; Susan E. Cayleff, *Wash and Be Healed: The Water-Cure Movement and Women's Health,* 29–31; Kathryn Kish Sklar, *Catharine Beecher: A Study in American Domesticity,* 205–9.
51. For a discussion of nineteenth-century women's "fashionable diseases," see Ann Douglas Wood, "'The Fashionable Diseases': Women's Complaints and Their Treatment in Nineteenth-Century America." On the use of hydrotherapy in hospitals for the insane, see "Water to Quench the Fires of Mania," 1109–10.
52. For a discussion, see Braude, *Radical Spirits,* 157–61; Wood, "'The Fashionable Diseases'"; Carroll Smith-Rosenberg and Charles Rosenberg, "The Female Animal: Medical and Biological Views of Woman and Her Role in Nineteenth-Century America"; and Haller and Haller, *The Physician and Sexuality in Victorian America,* 24–43.
53. Quoted in Braude, *Radical Spirits,* 160.
54. George M. Beard, *Sexual Neurasthenia: Its Hygiene, Causes, Symptoms and Treatment, with a Chapter on Diet for the Nervous,* 58–59. For a fuller discussion of neurasthenia, see Haller and Haller, *The Physician and Sexuality in Victorian America,* 5–13.
55. In *The Yellow Wallpaper,* which came out in 1890, Charlotte Perkins Gilman, one of Weir's best-known patients and a leading critic of women's economic dependency at that time, wrote a damning indictment of what he put her through when she underwent the rest cure after bouts of depression and nervous exhaustion. For further discussion, see Wood, "'The Fashionable Diseases,'" 31–32, 42–43; and Carol Ruth Berkin, "Private Woman, Public Woman: The Contradictions of Charlotte Perkins Gilman."
56. Angelo Venditti, interview by author, July 9, 1993.
57. Janette Barnes, "Women and Entrance to the Legal Profession"; D. Kelly Weisberg, "Barred from the Bar: Women and Legal Education in the United States, 1870–1890"; Karen Berger Morello, *The Invisible Bar: The Woman Lawyer in America, 1638 to the Present,* 11–21, 44–49; Hoff, *Law, Gender, and Injustice,* 161–70; Nancy T. Gilliam, "A Professional Pioneer: Myra Bradwell's Fight to Practice Law"; Glenda Riley, *Inventing the American Woman: A Perspective on Women's History,* 169. On the history of women lawyers in St. Louis, see Lucile Wiley Ring, *Breaking the Barriers: The St. Louis Legacy of Women in Law, 1869–1969.*
58. For a blistering attack on such masculine assumptions and the special disadvantages of married women in California's probate courts after the Civil War, see Mrs. J. W. [Marietta] Stow, *Probate Confiscation: Unjust Laws Which Govern Woman.*
59. For a discussion, see Michael Grossberg, "Institutionalizing Masculinity: The Law as a Masculine Profession." On Conkling-Whitney, see Ring, *Breaking the Barriers,* 39–47.

60. *Koller, Respondent, v. Woodbury Dermatological Institute and Kolle, Appellants*, April term, 1907, Cases and Exceptions, 1896–1911, book 2316, 47, Supreme Court of the State of New York, New York State Library, Albany.
61. *Hannibal Courier-Post*, May 6, 1909.
62. *J. E. Scott et al. vs. Perry Tinsley et al.*, February term, 1909, box 168, reel 67 (no. 20); Circuit Court Record, book 38, 552; both in Pike County, Office of the Circuit Clerk, Bowling Green.
63. *Scott et al. vs. Tinsley et al.*, February term, 1909, box 168, reel 67 (no. 20); Circuit Court Record, book 38, 562; both in Pike County, Office of the Circuit Clerk, Bowling Green.
64. Quitclaim Deed Record, book 137, 47; Miscellaneous Deed Record, book 145, 168; both in Pike County, Recorder's Office, Bowling Green. See also Estate of John M. Scott, case no. 2244, January 25, 1907, Ralls County, Office of the Probate Clerk, New London; and Circuit Court Record, book 38, 564–65, Pike County, Office of the Circuit Clerk, Bowling Green.
65. For a discussion, see David Thelen, *Paths of Resistance: Tradition and Democracy in Industrializing Missouri*, 182–89.
66. Andrews, *City of Dust*, 292–93.

Three. Marrying "Down" for Money: Mollie and Samuel Heinbach

1. Stow, *Probate Confiscation*, 6, 66.
2. Braude, *Radical Spirits*, 120–21.
3. For a fuller discussion, see Welter, "The Cult of True Womanhood."
4. Mary A. Scott to Wm. H. Dodd, lease, January 25, 1908, Miscellaneous Record, book 78, 589, Ralls County, Office of the Circuit Clerk and Recorder, New London.
5. To sample some of these eugenic studies, see, for example, Nicole Hahn Rafter, ed., *White Trash: The Eugenic Family Studies, 1877–1919*. For a recent study of the eugenics movement in the Deep South, see Edward J. Larson, *Sex, Race, and Science: Eugenics in the Deep South*.
6. Andrews, *City of Dust*, 23–24; "Persons Who Served in the Army, Navy and Marine Corp. of the U.S. during the War of the Rebellion Who Are Survivors, and Widows of Such Persons," Special U.S. Census Schedule, June, 1890, Saverton township, Ralls County; *Molly Heinbach vs. Jesse Heinbach, Edith Britton and Naomi Summers, and William F. True, Administrator of the Estate of Samuel Heinbach, deceased*, April term, 1914, case no. 14178, trial transcript, 181–82, 388–91, Missouri Supreme Court Files, MSA (hereafter cited as MSCF–MSA).
7. Andrews, *City of Dust*, 24; *Heinbach vs. Heinbach et al.*, April term, 1914, case no. 14178, trial transcript, 391–98, 406, MSCF–MSA.
8. Andrews, *City of Dust*, 25; *Heinbach vs. Heinbach et al.*, April term, 1914, case no. 14178, trial transcript, 166, 245–46, 276–77, 286–87, 397–407, MSCF–MSA; *Ralls County Record*, May 23, 1888.
9. *Heinbach, Appellant, v. Heinbach et al.*, November 24, 1914, *Missouri Reports*, vol. 262, 77–78; *Samuel Heinbach vs. Sarah Heinbach*, case no. 8816, filed January 14, 1906, Ralls County, Office of the Circuit Clerk and Recorder, New London; *Heinbach vs. Heinbach et al.*, April term, 1914, case

no. 14178, trial transcript, 181–82, MSCF–MSA; *Mary Alice Heinbach v. Jesse Heinbach et al.*, April 26, 1918, *Missouri Reports*, vol. 274, 308. See also Andrews, *City of Dust*, 20–21, 25–26.

10. *Heinbach vs. Heinbach et al.*, April term, 1914, case no. 14178, trial transcript, 185–88, MSCF–MSA; "Statement and Brief on behalf of Defendant Euphemia B. Koller," 6, *Molly Heinbach vs. Euphemia B. Koller et al.*, October 15, 1919, case no. 1219, Pike County, Office of the Circuit Clerk, Bowling Green.
11. *Heinbach vs. Heinbach et al.*, April term, 1918, case no. 20303, trial transcript, 1156–57, MSCF–MSA.
12. Ibid., 75–76, 91, 1158–59.
13. Ibid., 1161.
14. Marriage of Samuel Heinbach and Molly Scott, December 18, 1908, Marriage License Record, book H, 7, Ralls County, Office of the Circuit Clerk and Recorder, New London; *Ralls County Times*, January 1, 1909.
15. *Heinbach vs. Heinbach et al.*, April term, 1918, case no. 20303, trial transcript, 15–16, 1161; *Heinbach vs. Heinbach et al.*, April term, 1914, case no. 14178, trial transcript, 157–58, 164, 166, 181–82, 292, 300–304; both in MSCF–MSA. See also Andrews, *City of Dust*, 27.
16. *Heinbach vs. Heinbach et al.*, April term, 1918, case no. 20303, trial transcript, 1095–96, MSCF–MSA.
17. Ibid., 742–43.
18. *Mary Alice Heinbach, Appellant vs. Jesse Heinbach et al.*, November 24, 1914, *Missouri Reports*, vol. 262, 80.
19. *Heinbach vs. Heinbach et al.*, April term, 1914, case no. 14178, trial transcript, 65, 148–49, 169, 567; *Heinbach vs. Heinbach et al.*, April term, 1918, case no. 20303, trial transcript, 684–85; both in MSCF–MSA.
20. Ibid., 43–44, 130, 295, 305–8, 314, 474–78, 518.
21. Ibid., 508–14.
22. Ibid., 146; *Heinbach vs. Heinbach et al.*, April term, 1918, case no. 20303, trial transcript, 537–51, MSCF–MSA.
23. Jane Hemeyer, interview by author, July 11, 1996; *Heinbach vs. Heinbach et al.*, April term, 1918, case no. 20303, trial transcript, 442, MSCF–MSA.
24. Angelo Venditti, interview by author, July 9, 1993.
25. *Heinbach vs. Heinbach et al.*, April term, 1914, case no. 14178, trial transcript, 130, MSCF–MSA.
26. *Heinbach vs. Heinbach et al.*, April term, 1914, case no. 14178, trial transcript, 287, and *Heinbach vs. Heinbach et al.*, April term, 1918, case no. 20303, trial transcript, 57–58, 64, 273–77, 440; both in MSCF–MSA.
27. *Heinbach vs. Heinbach et al.*, April term, 1918, case no. 20303, trial transcript, 148, MSCF–MSA.
28. Ibid., 289, 614–19; *Heinbach vs. Heinbach et al.*, April term, 1914, case no. 14178, trial transcript, 553–54, 557–58, MSCF–MSA.
29. *Heinbach vs. Heinbach et al.*, April term, 1918, case no. 20303, trial transcript, 182–83, 575–78, 590–91, MSCF–MSA.
30. Ibid., 458–71.
31. *Heinbach vs. Heinbach et al.*, April term, 1914, case no. 14178, trial transcript, 191–92, MSCF–MSA.
32. Ibid., 167–68, 173.

33. Ibid., 16–17, 40–41, 76–77.
34. Ibid., 16–17, 26–32.
35. Estate of Theodore Johnson, Charles T. Lamb, administrator, case no. 4183, January 31, 1914, Ralls County, Office of the Probate Clerk, New London.
36. *Heinbach vs. Heinbach et al.*, April term, 1914, case no. 14178, trial transcript, 146, MSCF–MSA.
37. Ibid., 517–18.
38. Ibid., 305–7.
39. Ibid., 307–8, 313; *Heinbach vs. Heinbach et al.*, April term, 1918, case no. 20303, trial transcript, 464–65, 852, 856, MSCF–MSA.
40. *Heinbach vs. Heinbach et al.*, April term, 1914, case no. 14178, trial transcript, 313–14; *Heinbach vs. Heinbach et al.*, April term, 1918, case no. 20303, trial transcript, 852–53; both in MSCF–MSA.
41. *Heinbach vs. Heinbach et al.*, April term, 1914, case no. 14178, trial transcript, 306–9, MSCF–MSA.

Four. Samuel Heinbach's White Horse

1. *Ralls County Record*, January 7, 1910; *Heinbach vs. Heinbach et al.*, April term, 1918, case no. 20303, trial transcript, 70–71, MSCF–MSA.
2. *Heinbach vs. Heinbach et al.*, April term, 1914, case no. 14178, trial transcript, 458, MSCF–MSA.
3. Andrews, *City of Dust*, 15–16; *Hannibal Courier-Post*, March 15, 18, 21, 26, 1907; Guy D. Helmick, "The Hannibal Cement Plant Story," Guy D. Helmick Manuscript (January 1952), WHMC–Columbia.
4. On Atlas's wider campaign to control Ilasco at this time, see Andrews, *City of Dust*, chap. 3. See also Andrews, "Ilasco Cement Workers and the War on Booze."
5. Andrews, *City of Dust*, 90–91. For the flavor of area newspaper coverage of the strike and editorial attacks on Ilasco's immigrants, see the *Hannibal Courier-Post*, August 3, 1909.
6. Andrews, *City of Dust*, 92–106, 113–15; Andrews, "Immigrant Cement Workers."
7. *Hannibal Courier-Post*, December 5, 1908.
8. On the context in which Atlas sought to take a more active role in shaping Ilasco's cultural institutions, see Andrews, *City of Dust*, chaps. 1–6. On lawyers as a "strategic elite" in the New South, see Gail Williams O'Brien, *The Legal Fraternity and the Making of a New South Community, 1848–1882*.
9. *Heinbach vs. Heinbach et al.*, November 24, 1914, *Missouri Reports*, vol. 262, 79.
10. *Portrait and Biographical Record of Marion, Ralls and Pike Counties Missouri*, 700–701; Blunt, *Historical Listing of the Missouri Legislature*, 3; Howard, *Ralls County Missouri*, 316; "Historical Notes and Comments," *Missouri Historical Review* (October 1929–July 1930): 463.
11. *Portrait and Biographical Record of Marion, Ralls and Pike Counties Missouri*, 700–701; Howard, *Ralls County Missouri*, 316; Williams, ed., *The State of Missouri*, 583; "Historical Notes and Comments," *Missouri Historical Review* 24 (October 1929–July 1930): 463; *Perry Enterprise*, January 6,

1910. On Allison's ties to David R. Francis, see *Ralls County Record*, August 12, 1910. See also the obituary of Thomas E. Allison in the *Ralls County Record*, November 3, 1922.

12. *Heinbach vs. Heinbach et al.*, April term, 1918, case no. 20303, trial transcript, 386, MSCF–MSA; *Hannibal Courier-Post*, August 24, 1906. On the campaign against alcohol in Ilasco, see Andrews, "Ilasco Cement Workers and the War on Booze," 2–13.
13. *Heinbach vs. Heinbach et al.*, April term, 1914, case no. 14178, trial transcript, 106–7, MSCF–MSA; *Ralls County Record*, March 5, 1909, and November 3, 1922.
14. *Heinbach vs. Heinbach et al.*, April term, 1914, case no. 14178, trial transcript, 3, 34, 52–53, 182–83, MSCF–MSA.
15. Ibid., 57–58, 240–41.
16. Ibid., 4–6, 85–86; *Heinbach vs. Heinbach et al.*, April term, 1918, case no. 20303, trial transcript, 188–89, MSCF–MSA. On the Ilasco Supply Company, see Andrews, *City of Dust*, 51–53.
17. *Heinbach vs. Heinbach et al.*, April term 1914, case no. 14178, trial transcript, 4–6, MSCF–MSA.
18. U.S. Federal Manuscript Census, 1880, New London, Ralls County; 1860 Census Population Schedules, Missouri: Slave Schedules, Spencer township, Ralls County, microfilm roll 146. George Hays, Jr., was the Ralls County treasurer during Reconstruction. See *Ralls County Record*, January 6, 1870. On Hays's kinship to Mark Twain, see Davis, comp., "From the *Ralls County Record*, 1865–1912," 1995, 46. George Hays, Jr., however, was on a list of approved voters in New London's Spencer township in 1866. When he became Ralls County treasurer in the election of 1868, however, the Missouri Supreme Court threw out three Democratic election victories, including his, because the county clerk, claiming minor voting irregularities, had refused to count the ballots of heavily Republican Jasper township. See Ralls County Supervisor of Registration, 1866, WHMC–Columbia; and the *Ralls County Record*, May 13, 1869.
19. *Ralls County Record*, April 18, 1919; *Ralls County Times*, December 8, 1905; "Historical Notes and Comments," *Missouri Historical Review* 43 (April 1949): 308; J. Hurley Hagood and Roberta (Roland) Hagood, *The Story of Hannibal*, 300; Blunt, *Historical Listing of the Missouri Legislature*, 54; Davis, comp., "From the *Ralls County Record*," 62; U.S. Federal Manuscript Census, 1880, New London/Spencer township, Ralls County. On Hays's residence next to Baker, see *W. O. Gardner vs. Atlas Portland Cement Company*, December 19, 1913, case no. 9743, trial transcript, 24, Ralls County, Office of the Circuit Clerk and Recorder, New London.
20. *Heinbach vs. Heinbach et al.*, April term, 1914, case no. 14178, trial transcript, 348–56, 364, MSCF–MSA; J. Allen Eichenberger, "Eichenberger Place," March 1946, Eichenberger Papers; Marriage of Jack Briscoe and Sarah E. Stout, May 9, 1901, book F, 120, Index to Ralls County Marriages, MSA.
21. March, *The History of Missouri*, vol. 4, 1104–5; Hagood and Hagood, *The Story of Hannibal*, 102; *Hannibal Labor Press*, April 12, 1957.
22. Bacon, *Mirror of Hannibal*, 461.
23. *Heinbach vs. Heinbach et al.*, April term, 1914, case no. 14178, trial transcript, 200–201, MSCF–MSA.

24. Defendant's exhibit no. 4, dated January 20, 1911, "Statement and Brief on behalf of Defendant Euphemia B. Koller," 3–4, *Molly Heinbach et al. vs. Euphemia B. Koller et al.*, October term, 1919, film no. 72, box 222, no. 21, Pike County, Office of the Circuit Clerk, Bowling Green. On the renting of Feemy's house at 338 Chestnut Street in Hannibal, see U.S. Federal Manuscript Census, 1910, Mason township, Hannibal, Marion County.
25. U.S. Federal Manuscript Census, 1910, Mason township, Hannibal, Marion County; Defendant's exhibit no. 24, dated March 16, 1911, "Statement and Brief on behalf of Defendant Euphemia B. Koller," 4, *Heinbach et al. vs. Koller et al.*, October term, 1919, film no. 72, box 222, no. 21, Pike County, Office of the Circuit Clerk, Bowling Green.
26. *Heinbach vs. Heinbach et al.*, April term, 1914, case no. 14178, trial transcript, 8, MSCF–MSA; *Ralls County Record*, April 7, 14, 1911.
27. *Heinbach vs. Heinbach et al.*, April term, 1914, case no. 14178, trial transcript, 16–58, MSCF–MSA.
28. Ibid., 58–70.
29. Ibid., 76–85.
30. Ibid., 85–108, 164–65, 508–14.
31. The jurors were C. S. Bowles, J. S. Small, W. P. Hays, T. R. Powell, J. W. Gentry, Ed G. Brown, J. A. B. McElroy, F. E. Fanning, J. Guy Biggs, Robert Trigg, and foreman F. E. Florey. See *Heinbach vs. Heinbach et al.*, April term, 1914, case no. 14178, trial transcript, 7, MSCF–MSA.
32. Ibid., 185–88.
33. Ibid., 188–92.
34. Ibid., 192–95, 468, 501–2.
35. Ibid., 54, 60, 179–80, 208, 294, 462.
36. Ibid., 45–46.
37. Ibid., 209, 294.
38. Ibid., 44–45, 250.
39. Ibid., 44, 130, 294, 327, 445.
40. Ibid., 232.
41. *Heinbach vs. Heinbach et al.*, April term, 1914, case no. 14178, trial transcript, 169, MSCF–MSA.
42. On Atlas's use of intermediaries to acquire property in the area, see Andrews, *City of Dust*, 15–16, and the *Hannibal Courier-Post*, March 15, 18, 21, 26, 1907.
43. *Heinbach vs. Heinbach et al.*, April term, 1914, case no. 14178, trial transcript, 93–103, MSCF–MSA.
44. Ibid., 110–11.
45. Ibid., 150–54.
46. Ibid., 165–80.
47. For a discussion of such attitudes among authors of eugenic family studies around the turn of the century, see Rafter, ed., *White Trash*, 13–17.
48. *Heinbach vs. Heinbach et al.*, April term, 1914, case no. 14178, trial transcript, 117–31, MSCF–MSA.
49. Ibid., 131–32.
50. Ibid., 348–58.
51. Ibid., 362–64, 367–71.
52. Ibid., 372–75.

53. Ibid., 358–61.
54. Ibid., 210, 252–53, 277–78, 330.
55. Ibid., 388–413.
56. Ibid., 314.
57. Ibid.
58. Ibid., 433, 443.
59. Ibid., 433–34.
60. Ibid., 468–69, 481, 499.
61. Ibid., 490–91, 537–39.
62. Ibid., 167, 502–7, 529–34.
63. Ibid., 558–65.
64. Ibid., 502–4.
65. Ibid., 528–29.
66. Ibid., 566–70.
67. Ibid., 254–55.
68. Ibid., 75–76, 558, 570–71.
69. Grossberg, "Institutionalizing Masculinity," 133–51.
70. *Heinbach vs. Heinbach et al.*, April term, 1914, case no. 14178, trial transcript, 594–95, MSCF–MSA.
71. Ibid., 8–11; *Ralls County Record*, April 14, 1911.
72. Defendant's exhibit no. 35, dated August 12, 1911, "Statement and Brief on behalf of Defendant Euphemia B. Koller," 5, *Heinbach et al. vs. Koller et al.*, October term, 1919, film no. 72, box 222, no. 21, Pike County, Office of the Circuit Clerk, Bowling Green.

Five. The Whole Crowd of the Gang

1. On the deeds, dated March 25, 1911, see Deed Record, book 92, 107–8, and on the rental income agreement, see Mary Alice Heinbach and Euphemia B. Koller, "Assignment of Rents," March 27, 1911, Miscellaneous Record, book 93, 214; both in Ralls County, Office of the Circuit Clerk and Recorder, New London.
2. Lawrence M. Friedman, *A History of American Law*, 206–7.
3. Heinbach and Koller, "Assignment of Rents," March 27, 1911, Miscellaneous Record, book 93, 214, Ralls County, Office of the Circuit Clerk and Recorder, New London.
4. "Statement and Brief on behalf of Defendant Euphemia B. Koller," 6, *Heinbach et al. vs. Koller et al.*, October term, 1919, film no. 72, box 222, no. 21, Pike County, Office of the Circuit Clerk and Recorder, Bowling Green; U.S. Federal Manuscript Census, 1910, Spencer township, Ralls County. On Atlas's promotion of Roy Sykes, see *Ralls County Times*, April 14, 1911. For a brief sketch of Tom Sykes, see his obituary in the *Hannibal Courier-Post*, October 20, 1930, and the *Ralls County Record*, October 24, 1930.
5. Jane Hemeyer, telephone conversation with author, October 30, 1994.
6. U.S. Federal Manuscript Census, 1870, Spencer township, Ralls County. On the marriage of Pearl Sykes and Clifford C. Harris on January 7, 1911, see Index, Ralls County Marriages, MSA. William E. Harris's obituary is in the *Ralls County Times*, February 2, 1906. Blunt, *Historical Listing of the Missouri Legislature*, 52; Davis, comp., "From the *Ralls County Record*," 32, 84.

Tom Sykes and Guilford Harris were officers in the Knights of Pythias. See *Ralls County Times*, December 10, 1915.

7. Defendant's exhibit no. 9, dated April 21, 1911, in "Statement and Brief on behalf of Defendant Euphemia B. Koller," 4, *Heinbach et al. vs. Koller et al.*, October term, 1919, film no. 72, box 222, no. 21, Pike County, Office of the Circuit Clerk, Bowling Green.
8. "Statement and Brief on behalf of Defendant Euphemia B. Koller," 9, *Heinbach et al. vs. Koller et al.*, October term, 1919, film no. 72, box 222, no. 21, Pike County, Office of the Circuit Clerk, Bowling Green. On Koller's trip to New Mexico, see her affidavit notarized in St. Vrain, New Mexico, on April 14, 1911, in Miscellaneous Record, book 93, 214, Ralls County, Office of the Circuit Clerk and Recorder, New London.
9. Ibid., 5; *Ralls County Times*, May 26, 1911.
10. "Statement and Brief on behalf of Defendant Euphemia B. Koller," 5, *Heinbach et al. vs. Koller et al.*, October term, 1919, film no. 72, box 222, no. 21, Pike County, Office of the Circuit Clerk, Bowling Green.
11. Defendant's exhibits no. 29, dated October 29, 1911, no. 35, dated August 12, 1911, and no. 38, dated August 6, 1911; all in ibid., 5.
12. Defendant's exhibits nos. 6, 29, 34, dated May 28, September 27, October 29, 1911, 5, 10, in ibid.
13. "Statement and Brief on behalf of Defendant Euphemia B. Koller," 6–7, *Heinbach et al. vs. Koller et al.*, October term, 1919, film no. 72, box 222, case no. 21, Pike County, Office of the Circuit Clerk, Bowling Green.
14. Euphemia B. Koller, "Affidavit," April 14, 1911, Miscellaneous Record, book 93, 214, Ralls County, Office of the Circuit Clerk and Recorder, New London.
15. Ibid.
16. Ibid.
17. Ibid.; "Statement and Brief on behalf of Defendant Euphemia B. Koller," 10, *Heinbach et al. vs. Koller et al.*, October term, 1919, film no. 72, box 222, case no. 21, Pike County, Office of the Circuit Clerk, Bowling Green.
18. "Statement and Brief on behalf of Defendant Euphemia B. Koller," 5, *Heinbach et al. vs. Koller et al.*, October term, 1919, film no. 72, box 222, case no. 21, Pike County, Office of the Circuit Clerk, Bowling Green; "Abstract of Title to the following described real estate situated in the county of Ralls and the State of Missouri towit: The South half of the South West quarter section twenty five (25) Township fifty six (56) Range four (4)."
19. Defendant's Exhibit no. 36, dated March 12, 1912, in "Statement and Brief on behalf of Defendant Euphemia B. Koller," 5, *Heinbach et al. vs. Koller et al.*, October term, 1919, film no. 72, box 222, case no. 21, Pike County, Office of the Circuit Clerk, Bowling Green.
20. Charles M. Roberts to Euphemia B. Koller, Deed of Release, September 28, 1915, Deed Release Record, book 231, 144, Marion County, Office of the Circuit Clerk and Recorder, Palmyra; Molly Heinbach to Henry T. Sykes, General Warranty Deed, May 29, 1912, Warranty Deed Record, book 92, 532; Henry T. Sykes and Maggie Sykes to Molly Heinbach, November 29, 1913, Deed Record, book 80, 543; both in Ralls County, Office of the Circuit Clerk and Recorder, New London. "Abstract of Title to the following described real estate situated in the county of Ralls and the State of Missouri towit: The

South half of the South West Quarter of Section Twenty Five (25) Township Fifty Six (56) Range Four (4)."

21. *Ralls County Record*, October 16, 1914; *Molly Heinbach, Appellant, v. Jesse Heinbach et al.*, November 24, 1914, *Missouri Reports*, vol. 262, 69–91.
22. Ibid., 83–86.
23. Ibid., 86–88.
24. Ibid., 88–91.
25. *Ralls County Record*, October 16, 1914.
26. Andrews, *City of Dust*, 118–19; *Ralls County Record*, December 26, 1913. On the marriage of Croll and Conn, see Index, Ralls County Marriages, 1827–1919, MSA. In 1910, Ann Conn was living in the Hays household at 321 Hill Street in Hannibal. See U.S. Federal Manuscript Census, 1910, Mason township, Marion County, Missouri. On Benton Megown's career, see Floyd Calvin Shoemaker, *Missouri and Missourians: Land of Contrasts and People of Achievements*, vol. 5, 266–68.
27. Andrews, *City of Dust*, 113–14, 118–20.
28. Ibid., 120; *Ralls County Times*, June 19, July 3, 1914. The *Ralls County Record*, September 26, 1913, provides a list of shareholders in the North Missouri Light and Power Company.
29. Andrews, *City of Dust*, 120.
30. Ibid., 44, 51–53, 146–47; *Ralls County Times*, April 6, 1906.
31. Quoted in *Ralls County Record*, August 26, 1910. On the campaign against Ilasco saloons, see Andrews, "Ilasco Cement Workers and the War on Booze."
32. *Ralls County Times*, October 2, 1914; Miscellaneous Record, book 97, 207–9, Ralls County, Office of the Circuit Clerk and Recorder, New London.
33. *Ralls County Times*, April 11, 1913; *Ralls County Record*, September 25, 1914; Miscellaneous Record, book 97, 207–9, Ralls County, Office of the Circuit Clerk and Recorder, New London.
34. A copy of her claim is in Estate of Theodore Johnson, case no. 4183, Charles T. Lamb, Administrator, Appointment made January 31, 1914, Ralls County, Office of the Probate Clerk, New London.
35. Estate of Eliza Jane Johnson, February 28, 1916, case no. 4273, Ralls County, Office of the Probate Clerk, New London.
36. *Ralls County Times*, September 15, 1911; *Florence Thompson et al. vs. Theodore Johnson et al.*, September 15, 1911, case no. 9484, Ralls County, Office of the Circuit Clerk and Recorder, New London.
37. Ibid.
38. Estate of Theodore Johnson, January 31, 1914, case no. 4183, Ralls County, Office of the Probate Clerk, New London. On Lamb's real estate background, see *Hannibal Courier-Post*, August 3, 1917.
39. Estate of Eliza Jane Johnson, February 28, 1916, case no. 4273; estate of Theodore Johnson, January 31, 1914, case no. 4183; both in Ralls County, Office of the Probate Clerk, New London.
40. *Ralls County Record*, November 3, 10, 1916; *Hannibal Courier-Post*, August 3, 1917; J. O. Allison to Severino Fiorella, March 12, 1917, Deed Record, book 99, 432; Quitclaim Deed Record, book 100, 135–36; Sheriff's Deed in Partition, Miscellaneous Record, book 101, 7–8; all in Ralls County, Office of the Circuit Clerk and Recorder, New London. On Atlas's earlier re-

fusal to buy the strip of 2.23 acres, see Helmick, "The Hannibal Cement Plant Story," 5.

41. Quitclaim Deed Record, book 100, 135–36, Ralls County, Office of the Circuit Clerk and Recorder, New London; J. Hurley Hagood and Roberta Roland Hagood, "History of the Hannibal National Bank, 1888–1988," 49–50.
42. *Euphemia B. Koller vs. Molly Heinbach and Her Guardian John E. Megown et al.*, January 24, 1923, case no. 11,606, Ralls County, Office of the Circuit Clerk and Recorder, New London.
43. Alford, "Statement and Brief on behalf of Defendant Euphemia B. Koller," 10, *Heinbach et al. vs. Koller et al.*, October term, 1919, film no. 72, box 222, case no. 21, Pike County, Office of the Circuit Clerk, Bowling Green.
44. *T. J. Cousins vs. Euphemia Koller*, case no. 10,902, Office of the Clerk, Hannibal Court of Common Pleas, Hannibal.
45. Ibid.
46. Ibid.; Record 38, 92, 174, 230–31, 248, Office of the Clerk, Hannibal Court of Common Pleas, Hannibal.
47. *Bowling Green Times*, September 7, 1916.
48. *Heinbach vs. Heinbach et al.*, April term, 1918, case no. 20303, trial transcript, 1–11, MSCF–MSA; *Ralls County Times*, April 2, 1915; *Bowling Green Times*, September 7, 1916; "Abstract of Title." Attorney Jack Briscoe, who had worked with Allison during the first trial, moved to Lewiston, Montana, shortly after Mollie's victory in the Missouri Supreme Court in November 1914. See *Ralls County Record*, November 13, 1914.
49. *Heinbach vs. Heinbach et al.*, April term, 1918, case no. 20303, trial transcript, 137–40, 292–96, 334, 348, 513–21, 610, 629, MSCF–MSA.
50. Ibid., 140, 336.
51. Ibid., 334–36, 518–19, 610.
52. Ibid., 1105, 1118–20.
53. *Ralls County Times*, December 22, 1905, March 23, 1906, and May 28, 1909; Circuit Court Record, book P, 279–80, Ralls County, Office of the Circuit Clerk and Recorder, New London; *Ralls County Record*, September 3, 1909.
54. *Heinbach vs. Heinbach et al.*, April term, 1918, case no. 20303, trial transcript, 1112–14, MSCF–MSA.
55. Ibid., 213, 228.
56. Pearson's remarks are in defendants' "Motion for a New Trial," 3, *Molly Heinbach vs. Jesse Heinbach et al.*, April term, 1916, microfilm no. 70, box 200, case no. 8, Pike County, Office of the Circuit Clerk, Bowling Green.
57. *Ralls County Record*, December 15, 1916; *Bowling Green Times*, September 7, 1916; *Molly Heinbach v. Jesse Heinbach et al.*, April 26, 1918, *Missouri Reports*, vol. 274, 301–26.
58. Circuit Court Record, book R, 520, 547, Ralls County, Office of the Circuit Clerk and Recorder, New London.
59. Ibid., 547.
60. Ibid., 554, 565; *Ralls County Record*, November 16, 1917.
61. Record 38, 293, 411; Record 39, 115, 206, 221, 235; *Gardener S. Brockenbrough vs. Euphemia B. Koller et al.*, case no. 12,594; all in Office of the Clerk, Hannibal Court of Common Pleas, Hannibal.
62. *Heinbach vs. Heinbach et al.*, April 26, 1918, *Missouri Reports*, vol. 274, 301, 308–9.

63. Ibid., 311.
64. Ibid., 309–10.
65. Ibid., 313–14.
66. Ibid., 321–24. On the remarks in question, see, for example, "Motion for a New Trial," 3, *Heinbach vs. Heinbach et al.*, April term, 1916, microfilm no. 70, box 200, case no. 8, Pike Co., Office of the Circuit Clerk, Bowling Green.
67. *Heinbach vs. Heinbach et al.*, April 26, 1918, *Missouri Reports*, vol. 274, 324.

Six. Feemy's Bloodcurdling Threats? Or Attorney Charles Rendlen's Mental Hobgoblins?

1. *Ralls County Record*, April 12, 1918.
2. "Suggestions in Opposition to Motion to Reinstate Appeal," March 10, 1921, 3, *Molly Heinbach vs. Euphemia B. Koller*, case no. 21498, and *Heinbach vs. Heinbach et al.*, April term, 1918, case no. 20303, trial transcript, 682–97; both in MSCF–MSA. On the financial relationship between Rendlen and Sirbu in the financing of area real estate deals, see Miscellaneous Record, book 93, 639–40; Trust Record, book 102, 171–72; and Deed Record, book 99, 574; all in Ralls County, Office of the Circuit Clerk and Recorder, New London.
3. *Mary Alice Heinbach vs. Henry Parker et al.*, March 27, 1918, case no. 11,135; Mary Alice Heinbach to Henry T. Sykes, May 29, 1912, book 92, 532; Henry T. Sykes and wife Maggie to J. E. Megown, use of Mary Alice Heinbach, May 29, 1912, book 87, 249; Henry T. Sykes and wife Maggie to Mary Alice Heinbach, November 29, 1913, book 80, 543; Henry T. Sykes and Mary Alice Heinbach, "Affidavit of Payment, and Loss or Destruction of Note, March 28, 1918, book 101, 352; Mary Alice Heinbach to Charles T. Grisham, April 29, 1918, book 104, 36; all in Ralls County, Office of the Circuit Clerk and Recorder, New London.
4. Mary Alice Heinbach and Euphemia B. Koller, "Affidavit," May 2, 1918, Miscellaneous Record, book 101, 370, Ralls County, Office of the Circuit Clerk and Recorder, New London.
5. *Gardener S. Brockenbrough vs. Euphemia B. Koller et al.*, March 16, 1923, case no. 12,594, Office of the Clerk, Hannibal Court of Common Pleas, Hannibal.
6. *Ralls County Record*, July 19, 1918; *Euphemia B. Koller vs. Mary Alice Heinbach and her Guardian John E. Megown et al.*, January 24, 1923, case no. 11606, Ralls County, Office of the Circuit Clerk and Recorder, New London. On the meeting between Mollie and True in Quincy, see *Brockenbrough vs. Koller et al.*, March 16, 1923, Office of the Clerk, Hannibal Court of Common Pleas, Hannibal.
7. "Affidavit for Continuance by Defendant Euphemia B. Koller," 1–2, and "Statement and Brief on behalf of Defendant Euphemia B. Koller, 8; both in *Heinbach et al. vs. Koller et al.*, October term, 1919, film no. 72, box 222, no. 21, Pike County, Office of the Circuit Clerk, Bowling Green.
8. Ibid., 2–3.
9. "Injunction Restraining the Renting of the Heinbach Orchard Tract for the Purpose of Pasturing Stock and the Damaging Thereby of Fruit-bearing

Trees," in *Euphemia Belle Koller vs. John Lendak*, May 9, 1919, case no. 11255, Ralls County, Office of the Circuit Clerk and Recorder, New London. By threatening Feemy's chickens, Lendak specifically targeted an enterprise that was widely associated with rural women. For example, in an editorial blasting chicken theft on March 25, 1910, the *Ralls County Times* insisted that "of all thieves, the stealer of chickens is the most despicable, for chickens are usually the product of a woman's care and worry, and it is stealing from the women to take them."

10. "Injunction Restraining the Renting of the Heinbach Orchard Tract for the Purpose of Pasturing Stock and the Damaging Thereby of Fruit-bearing Trees."
11. Ibid.
12. "Affidavit for Continuance by defendant Euphemia B. Koller," 2–5, in *Heinbach et al. vs. Koller al.*, October term, 1919, film no. 72, box 222, no. 21, Pike County, Office of the Circuit Clerk, Bowling Green.
13. *Mary Alice Heinbach et al. vs. Euphemia B. Koller et al.*, case no. 1219, Lewis County, Circuit Court Record, 231–32, Office of the Circuit Clerk and Recorder, Monticello.
14. "Motion to Compel Defendant to Return and File Depositions and to Strike Out Her Answer," in *Heinbach et al. vs. Koller et al.*, October term, 1919, film no. 72, box 222, no. 19; Record book 46, 218; both in Pike County, Office of the Circuit Clerk, Bowling Green. Feemy's six witnesses were James Kennedy, Effie Purcell, Mrs. Nelson [Lula] Brown, Joseph Gillum, [?] Balthrop, and Elmer Smith.
15. Ibid.
16. *Wilma Wallace vs. Euphemia Belle Koller*, February 25, 1930, case no. 13,144, Pottawatomie County, Office of the Court Clerk, Shawnee, Oklahoma; Miscellaneous Record, book 101, 546, Ralls County, Office of the Circuit Clerk and Recorder, New London.
17. Record 38, 230–31, Office of the Clerk, Hannibal Court of Common Pleas, Hannibal; Miscellaneous Deed Record, book 262, 91, Marion County, Office of the Circuit Clerk and Recorder, Palmyra.
18. "Statement and Brief on Behalf of Defendant Euphemia B. Koller," 1, *Heinbach et al. vs. Koller et al.*, October term, 1919, film no. 72, box 222, no. 21, Pike County, Office of the Circuit Clerk, Bowling Green; "Historical Notes and Comments," *Missouri Historical Review* 36 (October 1941): 111.
19. "Statement and Brief on Behalf of Defendant Euphemia B. Koller," 2, *Heinbach et al. vs. Koller et al.*, October term, 1919, film no. 72, box 222, no. 21, Pike County, Office of the Circuit Clerk, Bowling Green.
20. Ibid.
21. Quoted in ibid., 8–9.
22. Quoted in ibid., 9.
23. Ibid., 8–9.
24. Ibid., 6.
25. Ibid., 3, 6.
26. Ibid., 10.
27. Ibid., 6.
28. Ibid., 5–6.
29. Ibid., 7.

30. Ibid.
31. Ibid., 7–8.
32. Record book 46, 625–26, Pike County, Office of the Circuit Clerk, Bowling Green.
33. "Affidavits in Claim and Delivery of Personal Property," January 26, 1921, in Miscellaneous Deed Record, book 112, 396, Ralls County, Office of the Circuit Clerk and Recorder, New London.
34. Ibid.
35. "Affidavit in Claim and Delivery of Personal Property," January 28, 1921, in Miscellaneous Deed Record, book 112, 482. Copies of the contract with Hill and Mollie's notification of the probate court that she had dismissed her appeal to the high court are in *Euphemia B. Koller vs. Mary Alice Heinbach and her Guardian John E. Megown et al.*, case no. 11606, January 24, 1923; all in Ralls County, Office of the Circuit Clerk and Recorder, New London; Record book 47, 97, Pike County, Office of the Circuit Clerk, Bowling Green.
36. March, *The History of Missouri*, vol. 4, 1105. Until 1941, the Ralls County circuit court had yet to admit the first woman to practice law in its history. See "Historical Notes and Comments," *Missouri Historical Review* 35 (July 1941): 627.

Seven. A Combined and Confederated Conspiracy: Mollie's Sanity Bargained Away

1. On Haley and Hostetter, who later ran an unsuccessful gubernatorial campaign, see Schwadron, comp. and ed., *Pike County*, 57, 115, 425–27. Hostetter's obituary is in "Historical Notes and Comments," *Missouri Historical Review* 34 (January 1940): 287.
2. *Hannibal Courier-Post*, February 24, 1921. On Watson and Atlas's low tax assessments, see Andrews, *City of Dust*, 128–30.
3. Shoemaker, *Missouri and Missourians*, vol. 5, 266–68; *Portrait and Biographical Record of Marion, Ralls, Pike Counties Missouri*, 453; Goldena Howard to State Historical Society of Missouri, Manuscripts Collection, undated letter, in Ralls County, Supervisor of Registration, 1866, WHMC–Columbia.
4. *Ralls County Record*, February 25, 1921; *Hannibal Courier-Post*, February 21, 22, 1921.
5. Ibid.
6. *Ralls County Record*, February 25, 1921; *Hannibal Courier-Post*, February 22, 1921; "Suggestions in Opposition to Motion to Reinstate Appeal," March 10, 1921, 4–5, *Heinbach vs. Koller*, case no. 21498, MSCF–MSA.
7. *Ralls County Record*, March 4, 1921. On the Megowns, see Shoemaker, *Missouri and Missourians*, vol. 5, 266–68, and *Portrait and Biographical Record of Marion, Ralls, Pike Counties Missouri*, 439–40, 453–54.
8. "Affidavit of Charles E. Rendlen," March 3, 1921; "Affidavit of Mary Alice Heinbach," March 2, 1921; both in *Mary Alice Heinbach vs. Euphemia B. Koller*, case no. 21498, MSCF–MSA.
9. "Motion to Redocket Case and Set Aside Order of Dismissal of the Appeal," in ibid.
10. Ibid. Reuben F. Roy and Maggie M. Hays had married on December 19, 1882.

See Index to Ralls County Marriages, 1821–1897, MSA; Davis, comp., "From the *Ralls County Record*," 62.

11. This letter, dated March 14, 1921, is in *Heinbach vs. Koller*, case no. 21498, MSCF–MSA.
12. Ibid.
13. Ibid.
14. Ibid.
15. *Ralls County Record*, April 22, 1921.
16. *Euphemia B. Koller vs. Mary Alice Heinbach et al.*, April 4, 1921, case no. 11,418; Circuit Court Record, book S, 320; both in Ralls County, Office of the Circuit Clerk and Recorder, New London.
17. *Mary Alice Heinbach by her Guardian J. E. Megown vs. Euphemia B. Koller et al.*, May 7, 1921, case no. 11,429; "Interlocutory Decree in Partition, and Order of Sale," May 24, 1921, Circuit Clerk Record, book S, 334–35; both in Ralls County, Office of the Circuit Clerk and Recorder, New London. On Hays's career, see his obituary in "Historical Notes and Comments," *Missouri Historical Review* 43 (April 1949): 308.
18. *Gardener S. Brockenbrough vs. Euphemia B. Koller et al.*, case no. 12,594, Office of the Clerk, Hannibal Court of Common Pleas, Hannibal.
19. Circuit Court Record, book S, 343, 349, Ralls County, Office of the Circuit Clerk and Recorder, New London.
20. Circuit Clerk Record, book S, 349–50, Ralls County, Office of the Circuit Clerk and Recorder, New London; *Ralls County Record*, November 11, 1921; "Suggestions in Support of Motion," in *Mary Alice Heinbach by her Guardian J. E. Megown vs. Euphemia B. Koller*, October term, 1924, case no. 23,970, MSCF–MSA.
21. *Ralls County Record*, December 23, 1921. A copy of Sheriff Holt's report of sale is in Circuit Clerk Record, book S, 375–76, Ralls County, Office of the Circuit Clerk and Recorder, New London. See also "Suggestions in Support of Motion," in *Heinbach vs. Koller*, October term, 1924, case no. 23,970, MSCF–MSA, and *Hannibal Courier-Post*, December 23, 1921.
22. Andrews, *City of Dust*, 126–28, 221.
23. Ibid., 134–36, 212–23.
24. *Ralls County Record*, November 18, 1921.
25. "Motion for New Trial," in *Heinbach vs. Koller et al.*, May 7, 1921, case no. 11,429, and *Euphemia B. Koller vs. Mary Alice Heinbach and her Guardian, et al.*, case no. 11606, January 24, 1923; both in Ralls County, Office of the Circuit Clerk and Recorder, New London.
26. *Euphemia B. Koller vs. Mary Alice Heinbach and her Guardian, et al.*, case no. 11606, January 24, 1923; Ralls County, Office of the Circuit Clerk and Recorder, New London.
27. Ibid.; Circuit Court Record, book S, 383–86, 393, 401, 404, Ralls County, Office of the Circuit Clerk and Recorder, New London.
28. Estate of Mary Alice Heinbach, case no. 4533, February 24, 1921, Ralls County, Office of the Probate Clerk, New London; Mary Alice Heinbach to J. D. Hostetter and J. H. Haley, trust deed, February 7, 1921, Deed Trust Record, book 110, 72, Ralls County, Office of the Circuit Clerk and Recorder, New London; *Ralls County Record*, February 16, 1923.
29. *Ralls County Record*, November 12, 1920; *Koller vs. Heinbach et al.*, April 4,

1921, case no. 11,418; Circuit Clerk Record, book S, 334–35; *Heinbach by her Guardian J. E. Megown vs. Koller et al.*, May 7, 1921, case no. 11429; Miscellaneous Record, book 101, 370; all in Ralls County, Office of the Circuit Clerk and Recorder, New London.

30. For the "Interlocutory Decree in Partition, and Order of Sale," May 24, 1921, and sheriff E. S. Holt's "Report of Sale Approved and Order of Distribution Made," December 16, 1921, see Circuit Clerk Record, book S, 334–35, 375–76, Ralls County, Office of the Circuit Clerk and Recorder, New London.
31. Circuit Court Record, book T, 129, Ralls County, Office of the Circuit Clerk and Recorder, New London.
32. *Euphemia B. Koller vs. Mary Alice Heinbach and her guardian John E. Megown, et al.*, January 24, 1923, case no. 11,606, Ralls County, Office of the Circuit Clerk and Recorder, New London, Mo.
33. Ibid.
34. Ibid.
35. Ibid.
36. Ibid.
37. Ibid.
38. For newspaper coverage of Croll's hosting of Conn family reunions and other dinners that included prominent Ralls County officials, see *Ralls County Record*, September 1, 1922, and December 14, 1923; and *Hannibal Courier-Post*, August 12, 1930.
39. *Brockenbrough vs. Koller et al.*, March 16, 1923, case no. 12,594, Office of the Clerk, Hannibal Court of Common Pleas, Hannibal.
40. Ibid.; Index to Record 42, 138, 163, 188, Office of the Clerk, Hannibal Court of Common Pleas, Hannibal.
41. Index to Record 42, 138, 163, 188, 196, 218, 239, Office of the Clerk, Hannibal Court of Common Pleas, Hannibal.
42. *Koller vs. Heinbach and her guardian John E. Megown et al.*, January 24, 1923, case no. 11606, and Circuit Court Record, book S, 487, 552, 600, 618, 624; both in Ralls County, Office of the Circuit Clerk and Recorder, New London.
43. Circuit Court Record, book T, 9, 11, 70; *Koller vs. Heinbach and her guardian John E. Megown et al.*, January 24, 1923, case no. 11606; both in Ralls County, Office of the Circuit Clerk and Recorder, New London.
44. *Heinbach, by her guardian J. E. Megown, respondent, v. Kohler* [sic], *appellant*, April term, 1924, case no. 23970, MSCF–MSA.
45. On the farmers' protests against Atlas, see Andrews, *City of Dust*, 128–30.

Eight. Probate Judges and "Old Nuts": The Politics of Euphemia B. Koller's Insanity

1. E. S. Holt, informant, "In the Matter of the Alleged Insanity of Euphemia B. Koller," April 7, 1925, case no. 13,217, Office of the Clerk, Hannibal Court of Common Pleas, Hannibal.
2. Ibid.; Estate of Euphemia B. Koller, Samuel Elzea, Guardian, Appointment made January 5, 1925, case no. 4713, Ralls County, Office of the Probate Clerk, New London.

3. Ibid.; William Leonard Bradshaw, *The Missouri County Court: A Study of the Organization and Functions of the County Board of Supervisors in Missouri*, 65–68.
4. William Robert Dittmar, *Insanity Laws*, 42–43.
5. *Heinbach, respondent, vs. Kohler* [sic], *appellant*, April term, 1924, case no. 23970, MSCF–MSA.
6. Ibid.; *Heinbach, by her guardian J. E. Megown vs. Koller et al.*, May 7, 1921, case no. 11429, Ralls County, Office of the Circuit Clerk and Recorder, New London.
7. Circuit Court Record, book T, 116, Ralls County, Office of the Circuit Clerk and Recorder, New London.
8. Estate of Euphemia B. Koller, Samuel Elzea, Guardian, appointment made January 5, 1925, case no. 4713, Ralls County, Office of the Probate Clerk, New London; E. S. Holt, Informant, "In the Matter of the Alleged Insanity of Euphemia B. Koller," case no. 13,217, Office of the Clerk, Hannibal Court of Common Pleas, Hannibal; Davis, comp., "Cemetery Inscriptions from Ralls County Missouri," 10, 11, 14; *Hannibal City Directory*, 1920, 272. On the kinship ties between Judge Harry G. Weaver and the jurors, see the U.S. Federal Manuscript Censuses, 1880, 1900, 1920, Spencer township, Ralls County; Howard, *Ralls County Missouri*, 246, 314, 342, 428; and Hagood and Hagood, *The Story of Hannibal*, 134, 198.
9. "In the Matter of the Alleged Insanity of Euphemia B. Koller," April 7, 1925, case no. 13,217, Office of the Clerk, Hannibal Court of Common Pleas, Hannibal.
10. Ibid.
11. *Ralls County Record*, January 2, 1925; Estate of Euphemia B. Koller, Samuel Elzea, Guardian, appointment made January 5, 1925, case no. 4713, Ralls County, Office of the Probate Clerk, New London; George A. Smoot, *The Law of Insanity*, 148, 150–51. On Elzea's banking career, see *Ralls County Record*, July 12, 1918, January 16, 1920, September 7, 1923, and November 16, 1923.
12. Estate of Euphemia B. Koller, Samuel Elzea, Guardian, appointment made January 5, 1925, case no. 4713, Ralls County, Office of the Probate Clerk, New London.
13. Angelo Venditti, interview by author, July 9, 1993; *Ralls County Record*, January 16, 1925.
14. Circuit Court Record, book T, 165, Ralls County, Office of the Circuit Clerk and Recorder, New London; Almon H. Maus, *Missouri Practice: Probate Law and Practice*, vol. 3, 538–39; Charles U. Becker, comp., *Laws of Missouri*, 124; Estate of Euphemia B. Koller, Samuel Elzea, Guardian, Appointment made January 5, 1925, case no. 4713, Ralls County, Office of the Probate Clerk, New London.
15. Missouri Bar Association, *Report of Proceedings of the Annual Meeting*, 1924, 8. On popular attitudes toward lawyers in Ilasco, where many injured victims of job accidents at the cement plant (or their families) sued Atlas for compensation, see Andrews, *City of Dust*, 63–84, 229.
16. *E. S. Holt, Informant, vs. Euphemia B. Koller*, case no. 13,217, April 7, 1925, and Record 43, 459, 508–9, 515, 587, both in Office of the Clerk, Hannibal Court of Common Pleas, Hannibal; *Hannibal Courier-Post*, April 27, 1925;

Ralls County Record, May 1, 1925. On monomania in the nineteenth century, see, for example, Norman Dain, *Concepts of Insanity in the United States, 1789–1865,* 6–7, 72, 73, 157, 158. On its use against free thinkers and reformers, see Myra Samuels Himelhoch and Arthur H. Shaffer, "Elizabeth Packard: Nineteenth-Century Crusader for the Rights of Mental Patients," 359.

17. Smoot, *The Law of Insanity,* 20–21.
18. Ibid., 21–23; *Ralls County Record,* May 1, 1925.
19. Estate of Euphemia B. Koller, Samuel Elzea, Guardian, Appointment made January 5, 1925, case no. 4713, Ralls County, Office of the Probate Clerk, New London.
20. A list of witnesses at this hearing is included in ibid.
21. The *Hannibal Courier-Post,* April 27, 1925, published a list of the jurors: Roy Tuley, Roy Ellis, J. W. Fry, James Traynor, Harry E. Schneider, Lloyd Hewett, E. H. Price, W. H. Ravenscraft, Anton Stolte, Fred H. Jacobi, W. T. Greenville, and Sam P. Brammer.
22. *Hannibal Courier-Post,* April 28, 1925; Record 43, 515, 587, and *Holt vs. Koller,* April 7, 1925, case no. 13,217, Office of the Clerk, Hannibal Court of Common Pleas, Hannibal.
23. Feemy's letters to Elzea, the probate judge, and the Bank of New London are in the Estate of Euphemia B. Koller, Samuel Elzea, Guardian, Appointment made January 5, 1925, case no. 4713, Ralls County, Office of the Probate Clerk, New London. On Elzea's departure from and return to New London, see *Ralls County Record,* August 14, 1925, and April 16, 1926.
24. Numerous canceled checks and Elzea's record of transactions and final settlement are in Estate of Euphemia B. Koller, Samuel Elzea, Guardian, Appointment made January 5, 1925, case no. 4713, Ralls County, Office of the Probate Clerk, New London. Guardianship arrangements have received very little scholarly attention. For a recent attempt to remedy this, see Lawrence M. Friedman, Joanna L. Grossman, and Chris Guthrie, "Guardians: A Research Note."
25. Estate of Euphemia B. Koller, Samuel Elzea, Guardian, Appointment made January 5, 1925, case no. 4713, Ralls County, Office of the Probate Clerk, New London.
26. Melvin Sanders, interview by author, July 17, 1993; Angelo Venditti, interview by author, July 9, 1993; Anna Venditti, interview by author, July 27, 1993; and Fay Scheiner, interview by author, July 13, 1996.
27. "First Biennial Report of the Board of Managers of the State Eleemosynary Institutions of the State of Missouri, 1921–1922," 6–8; Malcolm A. Bliss, M.D., "What the Mental Hygiene Movement Has Meant in Missouri," 625–29. The creation of this board was part of a wider national trend toward a more uniform, centralized authority over mental institutions. See Gerald N. Grob, *Mental Illness and American Society, 1875–1940,* 209. On Elliott, see his obituary in the *Hannibal Courier-Post,* October 15, 1935; Howard, *Ralls County,* 201; *Ralls County Record,* August 16, 1912, and January 19, May 1, 1917.
28. *Ralls County Record,* May 4, 1923, June 20, 1924, January 2, 1925; John Starrett Hughes, *Alabama's Families and Involuntary Commitment of the Insane, 1861–1900: New Solutions to Old Problems,* 19–20. On the occupation

of Brown, see U.S. Federal Manuscript Census, 1920, Fulton township, Callaway County, Mo.

29. *Ralls County Record,* April 24, 1925, January 15, 1926; Missouri Secretary of State, *Official Manual, 1923–1924,* 649; *Hannibal Courier-Post,* May 8, 1925. Dr. Malcolm Bliss, of St. Louis, also publicly criticized Governor Baker for playing politics with the state board. See Bliss, "What the Mental Hygiene Movement Has Meant in Missouri," 625–29.
30. Circuit Court Record, book T, 265, Ralls County, Office of the Circuit Clerk and Recorder, New London.
31. Andrews, *City of Dust,* 134–35, 140, 143.
32. Bradshaw, *The Missouri County Court,* 187.
33. Hughes, "Alabama's Families and Involuntary Commitment of the Insane, 1861–1900," 19–20. For a penetrating study of the civil commitment process in California during this period, see Richard W. Fox, *So Far Disordered in Mind: Insanity in California, 1870–1930.* For a brief discussion of the nation's commitment laws at that time, see Albert Deutsch, *The Mentally Ill in America: A History of Their Care and Treatment from Colonial Times,* 417–39.
34. Charles U. Becker, comp., *Laws of Missouri Passed at the Session of the Fifty-fourth General Assembly,* 98.
35. Estate of Euphemia B. Koller, Samuel Elzea, Guardian, Appointment made August 22, 1927, case no. 4858, and Estate of Euphemia B. Koller, Deceased, Henry T. Sykes, Administrator, Appointment made March 10, 1930, case no. 4998; both in Ralls County, Office of the Probate Clerk, New London. On the friendship of Newlon and Croll, see *Ralls County Record,* November 7, 1919.
36. Estate of Euphemia B. Koller, Samuel Elzea, Guardian, Appointment made August 22, 1927, case no. 4858, Ralls County, Office of the Probate Clerk, New London. On criticism of jury trials to determine insanity, see Deutsch, *The Mentally Ill in America,* 437–38. For years many medical authorities, in order to undercut popular stereotypes of the insane as criminals, had been pushing to eliminate the role of the sheriff's office in transporting such patients in restraints to state hospitals. See Fox, *So Far Disordered in Mind,* 182–83.
37. Estate of Euphemia B. Koller, Samuel Elzea, Guardian, Appointment made August 22, 1927, case no. 4858, Ralls County, Office of the Probate Clerk, New London; Maus, *Missouri Practice: Probate Law and Practice,* vol. 5, 245. On James Allison and Harry Wood's connections with the Bank of New London, see *Ralls County Record,* November 3, 1916, and January 15, 1926. On their role in the county Democratic Party, see *Ralls County Record,* April 16, 1920.
38. Hughes, "Alabama's Families and Involuntary Commitment of the Insane, 1861–1900," 8–9. Peter McCandless, *Moonlight, Magnolias, and Madness: Insanity in South Carolina from the Colonial Period to the Progressive Era,* 265–69, points out that certifying doctors in South Carolina in the late nineteenth century were often very vague in their diagnosis of insanity patients, sometimes even relying on hearsay information. In some cases, they even questioned the ethics of the proceedings but agreed to cooperate with county commissioners and probate judges and to sign the appropriate commitment papers. This at times frustrated state hospital officials because they were

then required to house patients who were unlikely to benefit from institutionalized care. After South Carolina officials gained the legal right to refuse patients, they at times urged probate judges not to send them the patient in question but rarely turned patients away.

39. Elaine Showalter, "Victorian Women and Insanity," in Andrew Scull, ed., *Madhouses, Mad-Doctors, and Madmen: The Social History of Psychiatry in the Victorian Era*, 324; Smith-Rosenberg, *Disorderly Conduct*, 261.
40. Edwin M. Lemert, "Legal Commitment and Social Control," 373; Melvin Sanders, interview by author, July 17, 1993. On the culture of Ilasco, see Andrews, *City of Dust*, 228–54.
41. Lemert, "Legal Commitment and Social Control," 371.
42. James Green, "Democracy Comes to 'Little Siberia': Steel Workers Organize in Aliquippa, Pennsylvania, 1933–1937," 11–12.
43. See especially Erving Goffman, *Asylums: Essays on the Social Situation of Mental Patients and Other Inmates*; David J. Rothman, *The Discovery of the Asylum: Social Order and Disorder in the New Republic*; and Rothman, *Conscience and Convenience: The Asylum and Its Alternatives in Progressive America*. For a sample of the literature that vigorously opposes the "social-control" interpretation of mental health care, see especially Gerald Grob, *The State and the Mentally Ill: A History of the Worcester State Hospital in Massachusetts, 1830–1920*; and Edward Shorter, *A History of Psychiatry: From the Era of the Asylum to the Age of Prozac*. For fuller discussions of this debate and the literature on asylums and the mentally ill, see John Starrett Hughes, ed., *The Letters of a Victorian Madwoman*, 1–12; McCandless, *Moonlight, Magnolias, and Madness*, 1–11; and Andrew Scull, "Humanitarianism or Control: Observations on the Historiography of Anglo-American Psychiatry," *Rice University Studies* 67 (1981): 21–41.
44. Hughes, "Alabama's Families and Involuntary Commitment of the Insane," 38–39, 53; Hughes, "Commitment Law, Family Stress, and Legal Culture: The Case of Victorian Alabama." For other works by Hughes that incorporate gender into the analysis of insanity, see his essay, "The Madness of Separate Spheres: Insanity and Masculinity in Victorian Alabama"; and *The Letters of a Victorian Madwoman*. In an excellent article, "Labeling and Treating Black Mental Illness in Alabama, 1861–1910," he also explores the connections between racial control and the classification and treatment of Alabama's black mental patients around the turn of the century.

    In some ways, Sheffield's case is similar to the well-known nineteenth-century case of Elizabeth Packard, whose rebellious spirit and attraction to spiritualism and other unorthodox beliefs prompted her husband, a Congregational minister, to have her committed to the Illinois State Hospital in 1860. In both cases, family members sought their confinement to control them. For a discussion of Packard and her role as an asylum reformer, see Deutsch, The Mentally Ill in America, 306–7, 423–26; Himelhoch and Shaffer, "Elizabeth Packard: Nineteenth-Century Crusader for the Rights of Mental Patients"; and Hughes, ed., The Letters of a Victorian Madwoman, 11–12, 237–39. Mary Elene Wood, The Writing on the Wall: Women's Autobiography and the Asylum, analyzes the autobiographies of Packard and several women who endured the ordeal of asylum confinement.

Epilogue. An Unmarked Grave and a Buried Community: Insanity's Outcomes and Legacies

1. "38th Biennial Report of State Hospital No. 1, Fulton, Mo.," 50; "Biennial Report of the Board of Charities and Corrections of Missouri, for the Biennial Period Ending December 31, 1928," 25. The former report is included in "Fourth Biennial Report of the Board of Managers of the State Eleemosynary Institutions to the Fifty-fifth General Assembly of the State of Missouri for the Two Fiscal Years Beginning January 1, 1927, and Ending December 31, 1928." For comparative rates of first admissions among male and female patients nationwide in the early twentieth century, see Grob, *Mental Illness and American Society*, 191–92.
2. *Ralls County Record*, September 21, 1923; "First Biennial Report of the Board of Managers of the State Eleemosynary Institutions of the State of Missouri, 1921–1922," 18.
3. *Ralls County Record*, September 21, 1923; *Mental Patients in State Hospitals, 1926 and 1927* (Washington, D.C.: Government Printing Office, 1930), 115; "Fifth Biennial Report of the Board of Managers of the State Eleemosynary Institutions to the Fifty sixth General Assembly of the State of Missouri for the Two Fiscal Years Beginning January 1, 1929, and Ending December 31, 1930," 11, 23. McCandless, *Moonlight, Magnolias, and Madness*, 297–317, points to the limited impact of similar Progressive reforms upon asylum care in South Carolina, where overcrowding remained a serious problem in the state hospital in the 1920s. Similar problems in other mental hospitals at that time called into question claims by hospital authorities that their mission was primarily therapeutic rather than custodial. See, for example, John Maurice Grimes, M.D., *Institutional Care of Mental Patients in the United States*.
4. *Hannibal Courier-Post*, March 13, 1930; *Missouri Telegraph*, May 22, July 24, 1930.
5. *Hannibal Courier-Post*, May 29, 1930; "Fifth Biennial Report of the Board of Managers of the State Eleemosynary Institutions to the Fifth-sixth General Assembly of the State of Missouri for the Two Fiscal Years Beginning January 1, 1929, and Ending December 31, 1930," 11. Such reports challenge the glowing view of institutionalized care often expressed by asylum officials around the nation in the early 1900s. See, for example, Friedman, et al., "Guardians," 159–60. On daily life and conditions inside South Carolina's asylum around the turn of the century, see McCandless, *Moonlight, Magnolias, and Madness*, 270–96. Hughes, ed., *The Letters of a Victorian Madwoman*, provides important insights into daily life in Alabama's Bryce Hospital. Calvin Bulkley, at Feemy's behest, had testified on Mollie's behalf during the second trial of the Heinbach will in 1916.
6. *Ralls County Record*, February 28, 1930; Missouri State Board of Health, Bureau of Vital Statistics, certificate of death, Euphemia B. Koller, February 24, 1930. Hospital authorities refused to grant me access to her records without an expensive court order. To explore the possibility of getting a court order, I contacted an attorney who told me that in a conversation with hospital authorities he learned that Euphemia B. Koller's medical file allegedly contains

only a single page of information—date of birth, death, and admission, as well as a diagnosis code. I then dropped the matter.

7. *Ralls County Record*, February 28, 1930.
8. Estate of Mary Alice Heinbach, case no. 4877, January 25, 1928, Ralls County, Office of the Probate Clerk, New London.
9. Ibid.
10. Estate of Euphemia B. Koller, Samuel Elzea, Guardian, August 22, 1927, case no. 4858, Ralls County, Office of the Probate Clerk, New London.
11. Estate of Euphemia B. Koller, Henry T. Sykes, administrator, March 10, 1930, case no. 4998; Estate of Henry T. Sykes, Margaret Sykes, administrator, October 27, 1930, case no. 5024; both in Ralls County, Office of the Probate Clerk, New London.
12. *Wilma Wallace vs. Euphemia Belle Koller, an Incompetent, Samuel D. Elzea, Guardian*, February 25, 1930, case no. 13144, Pottawatomie County, Office of the County Clerk, Shawnee, Oklahoma.
13. Ibid.
14. For Sykes's obituary, see the *Ralls County Record*, October 24, 1930, and *Hannibal Courier-Post*, October 20, 1930.
15. Maxine Harris to Gregg Andrews, February 23, 1998.
16. For biographical sketches of the Rendlen family, see David March, *The History of Missouri*, vol. 4, 1104–6. On Albert L. Rendlen's tenure on the state supreme court, see Gerald T. Dunne, *The Missouri Supreme Court: From Dred Scott to Nancy Cruzan*, 211.
17. On Allison's election as permanent county chair of the Democratic Party, see *Ralls County Record*, April 16, 1920. His obituary is in the *Missouri Historical Review* 24 (October 1929–July 1930): 463.
18. Shoemaker, *Missouri and Missourians*, vol. 5, 266–68; *Missouri Historical Review* 36 (October 1941): 113; *Ralls County Record*, August 1, 1924.
19. *Hot Springs Sentinel-Record*, March 19, 20, 1925; *Ralls County Record*, March 28, 1925; *Hannibal Courier-Post*, March 20, 21, 1925.
20. Dunne, *The Missouri Supreme Court*, 211–12. For Hays's obituary, see "Historical Notes and Comments," *Missouri Historical Review* 43 (April 1949): 308. On Hays's role in damages suits by injured Atlas workers and their families, see Andrews, *City of Dust*, 81. The Hannibal area was well represented on the Missouri Supreme Court during this period. Berryman Henwood, a Hannibal Republican, served as a court commissioner between 1927 and 1930 and then as a justice until 1932. New London's Reuben Roy was a commissioner between 1911 and 1919.
21. Andrews, *City of Dust*, 257, 305–22.

Bibliography

Archives

Maryland State Archives, Annapolis, Md.

Equity Papers A, Miscellaneous, Baltimore City Circuit Court
Marriage Index, Male, Baltimore City Court, 1851–1885

Missouri State Archives, Jefferson City, Mo.

County Records, Pike and Ralls
Missouri State Penitentiary, Register of Inmates
Missouri Supreme Court Files

Western Historical Manuscripts Collection, University of Missouri, Columbia

Richard Dalton Papers, 1859–1922
Guy D. Helmick Manuscript, collection no. 995
Ralls County Supervisor of Registration Ledger, 1866
U.S. Work Projects Administration, Historical Records Survey, Missouri, 1935–1942

New York State Library, Albany

New York Supreme Court, Appellate Division, Cases and Briefs, 1896–1911

National Archives, Washington, D.C.

Record group 28, Records of the U.S. Postal Service

Missouri State Board of Health, Bureau of Vital Statistics, Jefferson City

Certificates of Death

Cemetery Records

Barkley Cemetery, New London, Mo.
Mt. Olivet Cemetery, Hannibal, Mo.
Riverside Cemetery, Hannibal, Mo.

Published and Unpublished Censuses

United States Bureau of the Census. Federal Manuscript Censuses, 1820–1920. Rock Island County, Ill.; City of Baltimore, Baltimore County, Md.; Marion County, Pike County, Ralls County, Mo.; Carter County, Grant County, Pottawatomie County, Tulsa County, Okla.; Delaware County, York County, Pa.

United States Census. *Census Reports.* Ninth Census—Volume I: The Statistics of the Population of the United States, 1870. Washington, D.C.: Government Printing Office, 1872.

———. *Census Reports.* Ninth Census—Volume III: The Statistics of the Wealth and Industry of the United States, 1870. Washington, D.C.: Government Printing Office, 1872.

———. *Census Reports.* Twelfth Census of the United States Taken in the Year 1900. Vol. 1: Population, pt. 1. Washington, D.C.: United States Census Office, 1901.

———. *Census Reports.* Thirteenth Census of the United States Taken in the Year 1910. Vol. 2: Population. Washington, D.C.: Government Printing Office, 1911.

———. *Census Reports.* Thirteenth Census of the United States Taken in the Year 1910. Vol. 6: Agriculture 1909 and 1910. Washington, D.C.: Government Printing Office, 1913.

———. *Census Reports.* Fourteenth Census of the United States Taken in the Year 1920. Vol. 1: Population. Washington, D.C.: Government Printing Office, 1921.

"Persons Who Served in the Army, Navy, and Marine Corp. of the United States During the War of the Rebellion," Special U.S. Census Schedule, June, 1890.

1860 Census Population Schedules, Missouri: Slave Schedules, Pike, Ralls Counties, Missouri, microfilm roll 146.

City Directories

Baltimore City Directory, 1866, 1873–1877, 1880, 1884, 1887, 1897, 1900, 1902, 1905

Hannibal City Directory, 1871, 1892–1920

Local Court Records

Hannibal Court of Common Pleas, Office of the Clerk, Hannibal, Mo.

Lewis County, Office of the Circuit Clerk and Recorder, Monticello, Mo.

Marion County, Office of the Circuit Clerk and Recorder, Palmyra, Mo.

Pike County, Office of the Circuit Clerk, Bowling Green, Mo.

Pike County, Recorder's Office, Bowling Green, Mo.

Pottawatomie County, Office of the Court Clerk, Shawnee, Okla.

Ralls County, Office of the Circuit Clerk and Recorder, New London, Mo.

Ralls County, Office of the County Clerk, New London, Mo.

Ralls County, Office of the Probate Clerk, New London, Mo.

Published Court Proceedings

American School of Magnetic Healing and J. H. Kelly, Appts., vs. J. M. McAnnulty. United States Supreme Court Reports: Cases Argued and Decided in the Supreme Court of the United States, October term, 1902. Rochester, N.Y.: The Lawyers' Co-operative Publishing Company, 1903. Lawyers' Edition. Book 47, 90–97.

Mary Alice Heinbach, Appellant, vs. Jesse Heinbach et al., November 24, 1914. *Missouri Reports: Reports of Cases Determined by the Supreme Court of the State of Missouri.* Columbia: E. W. Stephens Publishing Company, 1915. Vol. 262, 69–91.

Mary Alice Heinbach vs. Jesse Heinbach et al., April 26, 1918. *Missouri Reports: Reports of Cases Determined by the Supreme Court of the State of Missouri.* Columbia: E. W. Stephens Publishing Company, 1919. Vol. 274, 301–26.

Euphemia B. Koller, Respondent, vs. John H. Woodbury Dermatological Institute and Fred S. Kolle, Appellants, First Department, April 1907. *Reports of Cases Heard and Determined in the Appellate Division of the Supreme Court of the State of New York.* Albany: J. B. Lyon Company, 1907. Vol. 119, 865.

Bulletins, Reports, Proceedings, and Statutes

The Atlas Circle (Atlas Portland Cement Company).

Becker, Charles U., comp. *Laws of Missouri.* Jefferson City, Mo.: Hugh Stephens Press, 1921.

———. *Laws of Missouri Passed at the Session of the Fifty-fourth General Assembly.* Jefferson City, Mo.: Hugh Stephens Press, 1927.

"Biennial Report of the Board of Managers of the State Eleemosynary Institutions, State of Missouri," 1921–1930.

Burchard, Ernest F. *The Cement Industry in the United States in 1909, 1910, 1911, 1914.* Washington, D.C.: Department of the Interior, U.S. Geological Survey.

Grimes, John Maurice, M.D. *Institutional Care of Mental Patients in the United States.* Chicago: n.p., 1934.

Koren, John, comp. *Summaries of Laws Relating to the Commitment and Care of the Insane in the United States.* New York: The National Committee for Mental Hygiene, 1912.

Maus, Almon H. *Missouri Practice: Probate Law and Practice.* 5 vols. Kansas City: Vernon Law Book Company, 1960.

Mental Patients in State Hospitals, 1926/27–1931/32. Washington, D.C.: Government Printing Office, 1930–1934.

Missouri, *Journal of the House of Representatives.*

Missouri, *Journal of the Senate.*

Missouri Bar Association, *Report of the Proceedings of the Annual Meeting,* 1880–1930.

Missouri Bar Journal.

Missouri Secretary of State. *Official Manual, 1923–1924.* Jefferson City, Mo.: Hugh Stephens Press, 1923.

Missouri State Hospital, Fulton. *Biennial Report,* 1911–1920.

Silvers, E. B. *Missouri Titles.* Kansas City: Vernon Law Book Company, 2d ed., Revised and Fully Annotated, 1923.

Southwestern Reporter.

Woerner, J. G. *A Treatise on the American Law of Guardianship of Minors and Persons of Unsound Mind.* Boston: Little, Brown, and Company, 1897.

Missouri Newspapers

Bowling Green Times.
Hannibal Courier-Post.
Hannibal Daily Courier.
Hannibal Labor Press.
Hannibal Morning Journal.
Louisiana Journal.
Missouri Telegraph (Fulton).
Perry Enterprise.
Ralls County Record.
Ralls County Times.

Other Newspapers

Baltimore Sun.
Hot Springs Sentinel-Record (Arkansas).

Interviews by Author

Hemeyer, Jane, July 11, 1996, Jefferson City, Mo.
Sanders, Melvin, July 17, 1993, Hannibal, Mo.
Scheiner, Fay, July 13, 1996, Hannibal, Mo.
Venditti, Angelo, July 9, 1993, Hannibal, Mo.
Venditti, Anna, July 27, 1993, Ilasco, Mo.

Telephone Conversations with Author

Hemeyer, Jane, October 30, 1994
Sudholt, Virginia, February 15, 1993

Correspondence and Other Family Materials

J. Allen Eichenberger Papers
Maxine Harris to Gregg Andrews, January 11, February 23, 26, 1998.
Jane Hemeyer to Gregg Andrews, October 29, 1994; February 10, October 24, 1995; September 30, 1996; February 26, March 9, 10, 1998.
Pickett, Ruth. "Abstract of Title to the Following Described Real Estate Situated in the County of Ralls and the State of Missouri towit:—The South Half of the South West Quarter of Section Twenty Five (25) Township Fifty Six (56) Range Four (4)."

Sarah J. Sykes Family Bible. Presented by her Mother Mary Ann Webb, December 25, 1870.

Books

Andrews, Gregg. *City of Dust: A Cement Company Town in the Land of Tom Sawyer.* Columbia: University of Missouri Press, 1996.

Bacon, Thomas H. *A Mirror of Hannibal.* Hannibal, Mo.: C. P. Greene, 1905.

Baker, Jean H. *Mary Todd Lincoln: A Biography.* New York and London: W. W. Norton and Company, 1987.

Banner, Lois W. *Women in Modern America: A Brief History.* 3d ed. Fort Worth: Harcourt Brace College Publishers, 1995.

Bardaglio, Peter W. *Reconstructing the Household: Families, Sex, and the Law in the Nineteenth-Century South.* Chapel Hill: University of North Carolina Press, 1995.

Basch, Norma. *In the Eyes of the Law: Women, Marriage, and Property in Nineteenth-Century New York.* Ithaca, N.Y.: Cornell University Press, 1982.

Beard, George M. *American Nervousness: Its Causes and Consequences.* New York: Putnam's, 1881.

———. *Sexual Neurasthenia: Its Hygiene, Causes, Symptoms and Treatment, with a Chapter on Diet for the Nervous.* New York: Arno Press, 1972. Originally published in 1898.

Beik, Mildred Allen. *The Miners of Windber: The Struggles of New Immigrants for Unionization, 1890s–1930s.* University Park: Pennsylvania State University Press, 1996.

Berkin, Carol. "Private Woman, Public Woman: The Contradictions of Charlotte Perkins Gilman." In *Women of America: A History,* edited by Carol Ruth Berkin and Mary Beth Norton, 150–76. Boston: Houghton Mifflin Company, 1979.

Bernhard, Virginia, Betty Brandon, Elizabeth Fox–Genovese, Theda Perdue, and Elizabeth H. Turner, eds. *Southern Women: Hidden Histories of Women in the New South.* Columbia: University of Missouri Press, 1994.

Blair, Karen J. *The Clubwoman as Feminist: True Womanhood Redefined, 1868–1914.* New York: Holmes and Meier, 1980.

Blunt, Roy D., Secretary of State, comp. *Historical Listing of the Missouri Legislature.* Jefferson City, Mo., 1988.

Bolton, Charles C., and Scott P. Culclasure, eds. *The Confessions of Edward Isham: A Poor White Life of the Old South.* Athens: University of Georgia Press, 1998.

Bradshaw, William Leonard. *The Missouri County Court: A Study of the Organization and Functions of the County Board of Supervisors in Missouri.* Columbia: University of Missouri Studies: A Quarterly of Research, 1931.

Braude, Ann. *Radical Spirits: Spiritualism and Women's Rights in Nineteenth-Century America.* Boston: Beacon Press, 1989.

Brophy, Patrick. "The Weltmer Institute and Magnetic Healing in Nevada, Missouri." In *Mystic Healers and Medicine Shows: Blazing Trails to Wellness in the Old West and Beyond,* edited by Gene Fowler, 111–26. Santa Fe: Ancient City Press, 1997.

Brumberg, Joan Jacobs. *The Body Project: An Intimate History of American Girls.* New York: Random House, 1997.

Bynum, Victoria E. *Unruly Women: The Politics of Social and Sexual Control in the Old South.* Chapel Hill: University of North Carolina Press, 1992.

Carlton, David L. *Mill and Town in South Carolina, 1880–1920.* Baton Rouge: Louisiana State University Press, 1982.

Carroll, S. S., et al. *Atlas of Ralls County Missouri.* Des Moines: Kenyon Printing and Manufacturing, 1904.

Cayleff, Susan E. *Wash and Be Healed: The Water-Cure Movement and Women's Health.* Philadelphia: Temple University Press, 1987.

Chesler, Phyllis. *Women and Madness.* New York: Doubleday, 1972.

Christensen, Lawrence O., and Kremer, Gary R. *A History of Missouri: Volume IV, 1875 to 1919.* Columbia: University of Missouri Press, 1997.

Cott, Nancy F. *The Bonds of Womanhood: "Woman's Sphere" in New England, 1780–1835.* New Haven: Yale University Press, 1977.

Crone, J. O. *The Magnetic Healer's Guide or Personal Experiences in Magnetic and Suggestive Healing.* N.p., 1903.

Dain, Norman. *Concepts of Insanity in the United States, 1789–1865.* New Brunswick, N.J.: Rutgers University Press, 1964.

Deutsch, Albert. *The Mentally Ill in America: A History of Their Care and Treatment from Colonial Times.* Garden City, N.Y.: Doubleday, Doran, 1937.

Dittmar, William Robert. *Insanity Laws.* New York: Oceana Publications, 1952.

Donegan, Jane B. *Hydropathic Highway to Health: Women and Water-Cure in Antebellum America.* New York: Greenwood Press, 1986.

Dowdall, George W. *The Eclipse of the State Mental Hospital: Policy, Stigma, and Organization.* New York: State University of New York Press, 1996.

Dunne, Gerald T. *The Missouri Supreme Court: From Dred Scott to Nancy Cruzan.* Columbia: University of Missouri Press, 1993.

Eakin, Joanne Chiles, and Donald R. Hale, comps. *Branded as Rebels: A List of Bushwhackers, Guerrillas, Partisan Rangers, Confederates and Southern Sympathizers from Missouri during the War Years.* Lee's Summit, Mo.: J. C. Eakin and D. R. Hale, 1993.

Eby, Ezra E. *A Biographical History of the Eby Family, Being a History of Their Movements in Europe during the Reformation and of Their Early Settlement in America.* Berlin, Ontario, Canada: Hett and Eby, Printers, 1889.

Edwards, Laura F. *Gendered Strife and Confusion: The Political Culture of Reconstruction.* Urbana: University of Illinois Press, 1997.

Engle, David M. "Law in the Domain of Everyday Life: The Construction of Community and Difference." In *Law in Everyday Life,* edited by Austin Sarat and Thomas Kearns, 123–70. Ann Arbor: University of Michigan Press, 1993.

Faragher, John Mack. *Women and Men on the Overland Trail.* New Haven: Yale University Press, 1979.

Farber, Bernard. *Kinship and Class: A Midwestern Study.* New York: Basic Books, Inc., 1971.

Faulkner, Howard J., and Virginia D. Pruitt, eds. *Dear Dr. Menninger: Women's Voices from the Thirties.* Columbia: University of Missouri Press, 1997.

Fellman, Michael. *Inside War: The Guerrilla Conflict in Missouri during the American Civil War.* New York: Oxford University Press, 1989.

Fergusson, Erna. *Our Southwest.* New York: Alfred A. Knopf, 1940.

Foner, Eric. *Reconstruction: America's Unfinished Revolution, 1863–1877.* New York: Harper and Row, 1988.

Foucault, Michel. *Madness and Civilization: A History of Insanity in the Age of Reason.* New York: Pantheon, 1965.

Fowler, Gene. *Crazy Water: The Story of Mineral Wells and Other Texas Health Resorts.* Fort Worth: Texas Christian University Press, 1991.

Fowler, Gene, ed. *Mystic Healers and Medicine Shows: Blazing Trails to Wellness in the Old West and Beyond.* Santa Fe: Ancient City Press, 1997.

Fox, Richard W. *So Far Disordered in Mind: Insanity in California, 1870–1930.* Berkeley: University of California Press, 1978.

Frankel, Noralee, and Nancy S. Dye, eds. *Gender, Class, Race, and Reform in the Progressive Era.* Lexington: University Press of Kentucky, 1991.

Fraser, Walter J., Jr., and Winfred B. Moore, Jr., eds. *From the Old South to the New: Essays on the Transitional South.* Westport, Conn.: Greenwood Press, 1981.

Friedman, Lawrence M. *A History of American Law.* New York: Touchstone, 1973.

Fulton, Eleanore Jane, and Barbara Kendig Mylin, comps. *An Index to the Will Books and Intestate Records of Lancaster County, Pennsylvania, 1729–1850: With an Historical Sketch and Classified Biography.* Baltimore: Genealogical Publishing Co., Inc., 1973.

Gabriel, Mary. *Notorious Victoria: The Life of Victoria Woodhull, Uncensored.* Chapel Hill: Algonquin Books of Chapel Hill, 1998.

Gamwell, Lynn, and Tomes, Nancy. *Madness in America: Cul-*

tural and Medical Perceptions of Mental Illness before 1914. Ithaca, N.Y.: Cornell University Press, 1995.

Gawalt, Gerald W., ed. *The New High Priests: Lawyers in Post–Civil War America.* Westport, Conn.: Greenwood Press, 1984.

Gibson, John. *History of York County Pennsylvania.* Chicago: F. A. Battey Publishing Co., 1886.

Gilman, Charlotte Perkins. *Women and Economics.* New York: Harper Torchbooks, 1966.

———. *The Yellow Wallpaper.* Old Westbury, N.Y.: Feminist Press, 1973.

Goffman, Erving. *Asylums: Essays on the Social Situation of Mental Patients and Other Inmates.* Garden City, N.Y.: Doubleday, 1961.

Goldsmith, Barbara. *Other Powers: The Age of Suffrage, Spiritualism, and the Scandalous Victoria Woodhull.* New York: Alfred A. Knopf, 1998.

Grob, Gerald N. *The Mad Among Us: A History of the Care of America's Mentally Ill.* Cambridge, Mass.: Harvard University Press, 1994.

———. *Mental Illness and American Society, 1875–1940.* Princeton, N.J., 1983.

———. *Mental Institutions in America: Social Policy to 1875.* New York: The Free Press, 1973.

———. *The State and the Mentally Ill: A History of the Worcester State Hospital in Massachusetts, 1830–1920.* Chapel Hill: University of North Carolina Press, 1966.

Grossberg, Michael. *Governing the Hearth: Law and the Family in Nineteenth Century America.* Chapel Hill: University of North Carolina Press, 1985.

———. "Institutionalizing Masculinity: The Law as a Masculine Profession." In *Meanings for Manhood: Constructions of Masculinity in Victorian America,* edited by Mark C. Carnes and Clyde Griffen, 133–51. Chicago: University of Chicago Press, 1990.

Hadley, Earl J. *The Magic Powder: History of the Universal Atlas Cement Company and the Cement Industry.* New York: G. P. Putnam's Sons, 1945.

Hagood, Roberta, and J. Hurley Hagood. *Hannibal Yesterdays: Historic Stories of Events, People, Landmarks and Happenings In and Near Hannibal.* Marceline, Mo.: Jostens, 1987.

———. "History of the Hannibal National Bank, 1888–1988." Hannibal, Mo.: n.p., 1988.

———. *The Story of Hannibal.* Hannibal, Mo.: Standard Printing, 1976.

———, comps. "A List of Deaths in Hannibal, Missouri, 1880–1910." Hannibal: n.p., rev. ed., 1990.

Haller, John S., Jr. *American Medicine in Transition, 1840–1910.* Urbana: University of Illinois Press, 1981.

Haller, John S., Jr., and Robin M. Haller. *The Physician and Sexuality in Victorian America.* Urbana: University of Illinois Press, 1974.

Hammond, W. A. *Spiritualism and Allied Causes and Conditions of Nervous Derangement.* New York: G. P. Putnam's Sons, 1876.

Harris, Alex H. *A Biographical History of Lancaster County: Being a History of Early Settlers and Eminent Men of the County.* Baltimore: Genealogical Publishing Co., Inc., 1977.

Hart, Bernard. *The Psychology of Insanity.* Cambridge: Cambridge University Press, 1925.

Hartman, Mary S. *Victorian Murderesses: A True History of Thirteen Respectable French and English Women Accused of Unspeakable Crimes.* New York: Schocken Books, 1976.

History of Marion County, Missouri. St. Louis: E. F. Perkins, 1884.

Hoff, Joan. *Law, Gender, and Injustice: A Legal History of U.S. Women.* New York: New York University Press, 1991.

Holcomb, Marjoriebell Stakley. *Deaf Women: A Parade through the Decades.* Berkeley: Dawn Sign Press, 1989.

Holstein, James A. *Court-Ordered Insanity: Interpretive Practice and Involuntary Commitment.* New York: Aldine de Gruyter, 1993.

Howard, Goldena. *Ralls County Missouri.* Marceline, Mo.: Walsworth, 1980.

Hughes, John Starrett. *Alabama's Families and Involuntary Commitment of the Insane, 1861–1900: New Solutions to*

Old Problems. Madison, Wis.: Institute of Legal Studies, University of Wisconsin Law School, 1987.

———. "Commitment Law, Family Stress, and Legal Culture: The Case of Victorian Alabama." In *The Constitution, Law, and American Life: Critical Aspects of the Nineteenth-Century Experience,* edited by Donald G. Nieman, 133–61. Athens: University of Georgia Press, 1992.

———. "The Madness of Separate Spheres: Insanity and Masculinity in Victorian Alabama." In *Meanings for Manhood: Constructions of Masculinity in Victorian America,* edited by Mark C. Carnes and Clyde Griffen, 51–63. Chicago: University of Chicago Press, 1990.

———, ed. *The Letters of a Victorian Madwoman.* Columbia: University of South Carolina Press, 1993.

Hurt, R. Douglas. *Agriculture and Slavery in Missouri's Little Dixie.* Columbia: University of Missouri Press, 1992.

Johnston, Carolyn. *Sexual Power: Feminism and the Family in America.* Tuscaloosa: University of Alabama Press, 1992.

Jones, Billy M. *Health-Seekers in the Southwest, 1817–1900.* Norman: University of Oklahoma Press, 1967.

Kairys, David, ed. *The Politics of Law: A Progressive Critique.* New York, 1982.

Kenzer, Robert C. *Kinship and Neighborhood in a Southern Community: Orange County, North Carolina, 1849–1881.* Knoxville: University of Tennessee Press, 1987.

Kirkendall, Richard S. *A History of Missouri, Volume V: 1919 to 1953.* Columbia: University of Missouri Press, 1986.

Larson, Edward J. *Sex, Race, and Science: Eugenics in the Deep South.* Baltimore: Johns Hopkins University Press, 1995.

Lerner, Gerda. *The Majority Finds Its Past: Placing Women in History.* Oxford: Oxford University Press, 1979.

Leslie, Robert W., John B. Lober, and George S. Bartlett. *History of the Portland Cement Industry in the United States.* New York: Arno Press, 1972. Originally published in 1924.

Loam, Jayson. *Hot Springs and Hot Pools of the Southwest.* Santa Cruz, Calif.: Aqua Thermal Access, rev. ed., 1995.

Lutz, Tom. *American Nervousness.* Ithaca, N.Y.: Cornell University Press, 1991.

McArthur, Judith N. *Creating the New Woman: The Rise of Southern Women's Progressive Culture in Texas, 1893–1918.* Urbana: University of Illinois Press, 1998.

McCandless, Perry. *A History of Missouri: Volume II, 1820 to 1860.* Columbia: University of Missouri Press, 1972.

McCandless, Peter. *Moonlight, Magnolias, and Madness: Insanity in South Carolina from the Colonial Period to the Progressive Era.* Chapel Hill: University of North Carolina Press, 1996.

Mackay, Richard V. *Guardianship Law.* New York: Oceana Publications, 1948.

March, David D. *The History of Missouri.* 4 vols. New York and West Palm Beach: Lewis Historical Publishing, 1967.

Merry, Sally E. *Getting Justice and Getting Even: Legal Consciousness among Working-Class Americans.* Chicago: University of Chicago Press, 1990.

Mintz, Steven. *A Prison of Expectations: The Family in Victorian Culture.* New York: New York University Press, 1983.

Missouri: The Center State, 1821–1915. Chicago–St. Louis: S. J. Clarke Publishing Company, 1915.

Mitchell, Franklin D. *Embattled Democracy: Missouri Democratic Politics, 1919–1932.* Columbia: University of Missouri Press, 1968.

Moore, R. Laurence. *In Search of White Crows: Spiritualism, Parapsychology, and American Culture.* New York: Oxford University Press, 1977.

Morello, Karen Berger. *The Invisible Bar: The Woman Lawyer in America, 1638 to the Present.* New York: Random House, 1986.

Murr, Erika L. "Exploring the Myths of the Southern Lady through the Writings of Elizabeth Scott Neblett." Master's thesis, Southwest Texas State University, 1995.

Neely, Mark E., Jr., and R. Gerald McMurtry. *The Insanity File: The Case of Mary Todd Lincoln.* Carbondale, Ill.: Southern Illinois University Press, 1986.

Neider, Charles, ed. *The Autobiography of Mark Twain.* New York: Harper and Row, first Perennial Library Edition, 1975.

O'Brien, Gail Williams. *The Legal Fraternity and the Making of a*

New South Community, 1848–1882. Athens: University of Georgia Press, 1986.

O'Neill, William L. *Divorce in the Progressive Era.* New Haven: Yale University Press, 1967.

Parrish, William E. *A History of Missouri: Volume III, 1860 to 1875.* Columbia: University of Missouri Press, 1973.

———. *Missouri under Radical Rule, 1865–1870.* Columbia: University of Missouri Press, 1965.

Parrish, William E., Charles T. Jones, Jr., and Lawrence O. Christensen. *Missouri: The Heart of the Nation.* 2d ed. Arlington Heights, Ill.: Harlan Davidson, Inc., 1992.

Peiss, Kathy Lee. *Hope in a Jar: The Making of America's Beauty Culture.* New York: Metropolitan Books, 1998.

Portrait and Biographical Record of Marion, Ralls, Pike Counties Missouri, 1895. New London, Mo.: Ralls County Book Co., rev. ed., 1982.

Prowell, George R. *History of York County Pennsylvania.* 2 vols. Chicago: J. H. Beers and Co., 1907.

Rafter, Nichole Hahn, ed. *White Trash: The Eugenic Family Studies, 1877–1919.* Boston: Northeastern University Press, 1988.

Reppy, Alison, and Leslie J. Tompkins. *Historical and Statutory Background of the Law of Wills, Descent and Distribution, Probate and Administration.* Chicago: Callaghan and Company, 1928.

Riley, Glenda. *Divorce: An American Tradition.* Lincoln: University of Nebraska Press, 1997. Originally published in 1991.

———. *Inventing the American Woman: A Perspective on Women's History.* Arlington Heights, Ill.: Harlan Davidson, Inc., 1986.

Ring, Lucile Wiley. *Breaking the Barriers: The St. Louis Legacy of Women in Law, 1869–1969.* Manchester, Mo.: Independent Publishing Corporation, 1996.

Rothman, David J. *Conscience and Convenience: The Asylum and Its Alternatives in Progressive America.* Boston: Little, Brown, 1980.

———. *The Discovery of the Asylum: Social Order and Disorder in the New Republic.* Boston: Little, Brown, 1971.

Ruth, Kent, et al., comps. *Oklahoma: A Guide to the Sooner State.* Norman: University of Oklahoma Press, rev. ed., 1957.

Salmon, Marylynn. *Women and the Law of Property in Early America.* Chapel Hill: University of North Carolina Press, 1986.

Scharf, J. Thomas. *History of Delaware, 1609–1888.* 2 vols. Port Washington, N.Y.: Kennikat Press, 1972. Originally published in 1888.

Scheff, Thomas J. *Being Mentally Ill: A Sociological Theory.* 2d ed. New York: Aldine Publishing Co., 1984.

Schur, Edwin M. *Labeling Women Deviant: Gender, Stigma, and Social Control.* New York: Random House, 1984.

Schwadron, Karen, comp. and ed. *Pike County, Missouri: People, Places and Pikers.* Marceline, Mo.: Walsworth Publishing Company, 1981.

Scott, Anne Firor. *The Southern Lady: From Pedestal to Politics, 1830–1930.* Chicago: University of Chicago Press, 1970.

Scull, Andrew, ed. *Madhouses, Mad-Doctors, and Madmen: The Social History of Psychiatry in the Victorian Era.* Philadelphia: University of Pennsylvania Press, 1981.

Shoemaker, Floyd. *Missouri and Missourians: Land of Contrasts and People of Achievements.* 5 vols. Chicago: Lewis, 1943.

Shorter, Edward. *A History of Psychiatry: From the Era of the Asylum to the Age of Prozac.* New York: John Wiley and Sons, Inc., 1997.

Sicherman, Barbara. *The Quest for Mental Health in America, 1880–1917.* New York: Arno Press, 1980.

Sklar, Kathryn Kish. *Catharine Beecher: A Study in American Domesticity.* New York: W. W. Norton and Company, Inc., 1973.

Smith-Rosenberg, Carroll. *Disorderly Conduct: Visions of Gender in Victorian America.* New York: Alfred A. Knopf, 1985.

Smoot, George A. *The Law of Insanity.* Kansas City: Vernon Law Book Company, 1929.

Spring, Raymond L., Roy B. Lacoursiere, and Glen Weissenberger, *Patients, Psychiatrists and Lawyers: Law and the Mental Health System.* 2d ed. Cincinnati: Anderson Publishing Co., 1997.

Stow, Mrs. J. W. *Probate Confiscation: Unjust Laws which Govern Woman.* New York: Arno Press, 1974. Originally published in 1876.

Szasz, Thomas. *Ideology and Insanity.* Garden City, N.Y.: Doubleday, 1970.

Thelen, David. *Paths of Resistance: Tradition and Democracy in Industrializing Missouri.* Columbia: University of Missouri Press, paperback ed., 1991.

Thomas, Alan J. *Acquired Hearing Loss: Psychological and Physiological Implications.* Orlando, Fla.: Academic Press, 1984.

Turner, Elizabeth Hayes. *Women, Culture, and Community: Religion and Reform in Galveston, 1880–1920.* New York: Oxford University Press, 1997.

Twain, Mark. *A Connecticut Yankee in King Arthur's Court.* New York: Signet, n.d. Originally published in 1889.

———. *Letters from the Earth.* Edited by Bernard DeVoto with a Preface by Henry Nash Smith. New York: Harper and Row, Perennial Library Edition, 1974.

Vernon, McCay. *The Psychology of Deafness: Understanding Deaf and Hard-of-Hearing People.* New York: Longman, 1990.

Warbasse, Elizabeth Bowles. *The Changing Legal Rights of Married Women, 1800–1861.* New York: Garland Publishing, Inc., 1987.

Weiss, Harry B., and Howard R. Kemble. *The Great American Water-Cure Craze.* Trenton: Past Times Press, 1967.

Wentz, Abdel Ross. *The Beginnings of the German Element in York County, Pennsylvania.* Lancaster, Pa.: Press of the New Era Printing Company, 1916.

Wheeler, Marjorie Spruill. *New Women of the New South: The Leaders of the Woman Suffrage Movement in the Southern States.* New York: Oxford University Press, 1993.

Whites, LeeAnn. *The Civil War as a Crisis in Gender: Augusta, Georgia, 1860–1890.* Athens: University of Georgia Press, 1995.

Williams, Walter, ed. *A History of Northeast Missouri.* 3 vols. Chicago: Lewis Publishing Company, 1913.

———, ed. *The State of Missouri: An Autobiography.* Columbia: E. W. Stephens, 1904.

Wood, Mary Elene. *The Writing on the Wall: Women's Autobiography and the Asylum.* Urbana: University of Illinois Press, 1994.

Woods, Betty. "Medicine Water." In *This Is New Mexico,* edited by George Fitzpatrick, 198–200. Santa Fe: Rydel Press, 1948.

Articles

Allen, C. N. "Psychological Factors in Continuous Bath Hydrotherapy for Psychotic Patients." *Journal of Abnormal and Social Psychology* 31 (1936–1937): 418–22.

Anderson, Nancy Fix. "Cousin Marriage in Victorian England." *Journal of Family History* 11, no. 3 (1986): 285–301.

Andrews, Gregg. "From Robber Caves to Robber Barons: New South Missouri and the Social Construction of Mark Twain, 1910–1935." *Gateway Heritage* 15 (fall 1994): 4–15.

———. "Ilasco Cement Workers and the War on Booze in Ralls County, Missouri, 1903–1914." *Gateway Heritage* 16 (spring 1996): 2–13.

———. "Immigrant Cement Workers: The Strike of 1910 in Ilasco, Missouri." *Missouri Historical Review* 89 (January 1995): 162–83.

Barnes, Janette. "Women and Entrance to the Legal Profession." *Journal of Legal Education* 23, no. 2 (1970): 276–308.

Basch, Norma. "The Emerging Legal History of Women in the United States: Property, Divorce, and the Constitution." *Signs* 12 (autumn 1986): 97–117.

———. " 'Invisible Women': The Legal Fiction of Marital Unity in Nineteenth-Century America." *Feminist Studies* 5 (summer 1979): 346–66.

Bliss, Malcolm A., M.D. "What the Mental Hygiene Movement Has Meant in Missouri." *American Journal of Psychiatry* 5 (April 1926): 625–29.

Brandimarte, Cynthia A. "Darling Dabblers." *American Ceramic Circle Journal* 6 (1988): 6–27.

———. "Somebody's Aunt and Nobody's Mother: The American China Painter and Her Work, 1870–1920." *Winterthur Portfolio* 23 (winter 1988): 203–24.

Chused, Richard H. "Late Nineteenth Century Married Women's

Property Law: Reception of the Early Married Women's Property Acts by Courts and Legislatures." *American Journal of Legal History* 29 (January 1985): 3–35.

———. "Married Women's Property Laws: 1800–1850." *Georgetown Law Journal* 71 (June 1983): 1359–1425.

Crisler, Robert M. "Missouri's 'Little Dixie.'" *Missouri Historical Review* 42 (October 1947–July 1948): 130–39.

Friedman, Lawrence M., Joanna L. Grossman, and Chris Guthrie. "Guardians: A Research Note." *American Journal of Legal History* 40 (April 1996): 146–66.

Gilliam, Nancy T. "A Professional Pioneer: Myra Bradwell's Fight to Practice Law." *Law and History Review* 5 (spring 1987): 105–33.

Gorn, Elliott J. "'Gouge and Bite, Pull Hair and Scratch': The Social Significance of Fighting in the Southern Backcountry." *American Historical Review* 90 (February 1985): 18–43.

Grawley, Ernestine. "Fifty Years Ago in Shawnee and Pottawatomie County." *The Chronicles of Oklahoma* 31 (winter 1953–1954): 381–91.

Green, James. "Democracy Comes to 'Little Siberia': Steel Workers Organize in Aliquippa, Pennsylvania, 1933–1937." *Labor's Heritage* 6 (summer 1993): 4–27.

Green, Milton D. "Fraud, Undue Influence and Mental Incompetence: A Study in Related Concepts." *Columbia Law Review* 43 (January 1943): 176–205.

———. "Judicial Tests of Mental Incompetency." *Missouri Law Review* 6 (April 1941): 141–65.

———. "Proof of Mental Incompetency and the Unexpressed Major Premise." *Yale Law Journal* 53 (1943–1944): 271–311.

Hall, Jacquelyn Dowd. "'The Mind That Burns in Each Body': Women, Rape, and Racial Violence." *Southern Exposure* 12 (November/December 1984): 61–71.

Himelhoch, Myra Samuels, and Arthur H. Shaffer. "Elizabeth Packard: Nineteenth-Century Crusader for the Rights of Mental Patients." *Journal of American Studies* 13 (December 1979): 343–75.

Hudson, Manley O. "The Transfer and Partition of Remainders in

Missouri: Notes on Recent Cases." *University of Missouri Bulletin* 18, no. 2 (1917): 1–31.

Hughes, John S. "Labeling and Treating Black Mental Illness in Alabama, 1861–1910." *Journal of Southern History* 58 (August 1992): 435–60.

Jordan, Kathryn, and Mary Hellen Emery. "Records of Fawn Grove Quakers (York County, PA)." *Maryland Genealogical Society Bulletin* 36 (spring 1995): 197–256.

Kagan, Robert A., Bliss Cartwright, Lawrence M. Friedman, and Stanton M. Wheeler. "The Business of State Supreme Courts, 1870–1970." *Stanford Law Review* 30 (November 1977): 121–56.

Kohl, Martha. "Enforcing a Vision of Community: The 'Test Oath' and Missouri's Reconstruction." *Civil War History* 40 (December 1994): 292–307.

———. "From Freedom to Franchise: The Debate over African American Enfranchisement, 1865–1870." *Gateway Heritage* 16 (spring 1996): 22–35.

Lasser, Carol. "'Let Us Be Sisters Forever': The Sororal Model of Nineteenth-Century Female Friendship." *Signs: Journal of Women in Culture and Society* 14 (autumn 1988): 158–81.

Lemert, Edwin M. "Legal Commitment and Social Control." *Sociology and Social Research* 30 (May–June 1946): 370–78.

McCandless, Peter. "Liberty and Lunacy: The Victorians and Wrongful Confinement." *Journal of Social History* 11 (spring 1978): 366–86.

———. "Mesmerism and Phrenology in Antebellum Charleston: 'Enough of the Marvellous.'" *Journal of Southern History* 58 (May 1992): 199–230.

Mead, E. Genevieve. "Social Control of Insanity." *Journal of Abnormal and Social Psychology* 31 (1936–1937): 430–34.

Murphy, Lucy Eldersveld. "Business Ladies: Midwestern Women and Enterprise, 1850–1880." *Journal of Women's History* 3 (spring 1991): 65–89.

Obiora, L. Amede. "Neither Here Nor There: Of the Female in American Legal Education." *Law and Social Inquiry* 21 (spring 1996): 355–432.

Rothman, David J. "Social Control: The Uses and Abuses of the Concept in the History of Incarceration." *Rice University Studies* 67 (winter 1981): 9–20.

Salmon, Marylynn. "The Legal Status of Women in Early America: A Reappraisal." *Law and History Review* 1 (spring 1983): 129–51.

Scull, Andrew. "Humanitarianism or Control: Observations on the Historiography of Anglo-American Psychiatry." *Rice University Studies* 67 (1981): 21–41.

Shammas, Carole. "Re-Assessing the Married Women's Property Acts." *Journal of Women's History* 6 (spring 1994): 9–30.

Sicherman, Barbara. "The Paradox of Prudence: Mental Health in the Gilded Age." *Journal of American History* 62 (March 1976): 890–912.

Smith, Reverend Franklin C. "Pioneer Beginnings at Emmanuel, Shawnee." *Chronicles of Oklahoma* 24 (spring 1946): 2–14.

Smith-Rosenberg, Carroll, and Charles Rosenberg. "The Female Animal: Medical and Biological Views of Woman and Her Role in Nineteenth-Century America." *Journal of American History* 60 (September 1973): 332–56.

"Water to Quench the Fires of Mania." *Literary Digest* (December 6, 1913): 1109–10.

Weisberg, D. Kelly. "Barred from the Bar: Women and Legal Education in the United States, 1870–1890." *Journal of Legal Education* 28, no. 4 (1977): 485–507.

Welter, Barbara. "The Cult of True Womanhood: 1820–1860." *American Quarterly* 18 (summer 1966): 151–74.

Wood, Ann Douglas. "'The Fashionable Diseases': Women's Complaints and Their Treatment in Nineteenth-Century America." *Journal of Interdisciplinary History* 4 (summer 1973): 25–52.

Young, John L. "Court-Ordered Insanity: Interpretive Practice and Involuntary Commitment." *Journal of Psychiatry and Law* 22 (summer 1994): 293–96.

Index